Protective Discrimination

Other Backward Classes in India

Protective Discrimination
Other Backward Classes in India

Dr. Shish Ram Sharma

Raj Publications
Delhi-110 009 (INDIA)

First Published in 2002

ISBN 81-86208-23-2

Published by : Mrs. Poonam Goel
Raj Publications
R-115/2, Model Town - III,
Delhi - 110009
Tel. : 011- 7466486
E Mail:- rajpub@now-india.net.in.

Laser Typesetting by : Aarati Computers, Delhi-110 009

Printed at : Chawla Offset Printers, Delhi-110 052

PRINTED IN INDIA

Contents

Preface ix
List of Tables xi
Introduction xiv

1. Identification of Other Backward Classes 1
2. Composition of Other Backward Classes 36
3. Classification: The Caste Factors 64
4. Anthropological Perspective on Other Backward Classes 78
5. Divisions by Occupations 107
6. Emerging Trends 166
7. Protective Discrimination: An Overview 172
8. A Postscript: Towards a Class Cohesion 196

Bibliography 203
Appendices 211
Index 411

Dedicated To
Brigadier Chandan Singh
AVSM, M-IN-D
of My Village Panhera Khurd

Preface

This book deals with the reservation policy of the government. The book highlights the issues have direct bearing on the reservation for Other Backward Classes such as the mode process and concepts of identification and listing of OBCs. In this book an attempt has been made to bring out the efforts of the government and judiciary in implementation of the reservation policy. An effort has also been made to focuss the dimensions of the politics of reservation and existing reservation policy. The book also discuss the emerging patterns, occupational mobility and social mobilization of caste/ communities.

The book is divided into seven chapters. The first chapter gives a picture of identification of OBCs. Mode of identification and concepts has been discussed in detail. The second chapter deals with composition of listing of OBCs and analysis. Chapter three deals with classification of OBCs. Caste/ Communities falling in various categories and sub-categories are discussed with their tradition and present occupation, etc. A brief description of the certain ex-criminal tribes, nomadic and semi-nomadic tribes in anthropological prespective in chapter four. Chapter five give us a vivid picture of the divisions of the caste/communities by their occupations. The six chapter discusses the emerging trends in identification and classification of OBCs. Chapter seven gives an overview on protective discrimination policy in its historical background. Chapter eight, the last chapter of the book is conclusion.

The book has two appendices. Appendix I consist of the state list of OBCs and appendix II, the central list of OBCs. These lists of caste/communities are given upto date in alphabetical order.

My thanks goes to Prof. Hennry Lamin, Head of the Department of Anthopology, North-Eastern Hill University, Shillong to provide me an opportunity to present a paper on identification and listing of OBCs and have discussion with prominant social scientist and the participants of the National Seminar on Protective Discrimination in September, 2000.

I am thankful to Shri K.S. Singh, former Director General of Anthropological Survey of India for encouragement and cooperation on many occassions. My thanks goes to Dr. M.M. Rehman for his personal interest in bringing out this book.

I remain grateful to Sh. P.D. Seth (Joint Secretary to Government of India), for his encouragement. I extends my special thanks to my colleague Shri C.M. Bhatt for helping me in updating the lists. I am grateful to my friends Tarun Bose, Shekhar Nambiar and Sh. A.B. Bhardwaj, my colleagues Sh. M.L. Mathur, Smt. P. Rajwanshi, Sh. V. Chandrashekhar, Sh. H.P. Joshi, Ms. S. Bodra and Sh. M.K. Shaji.

To Veena, my wife, I am especially indebted for her help and cooperation in completing this book. I am grateful to my children Neha and Devakshu who have had to bear my pre-occupation with this book.

Finally, I thank to Smt. Poonam Goel of Raj Publications for taking keen interest in the publication of the book.

14th November, 2001 **Shish Ram Sharma**

New Delhi

List of Tables

2.1	Year-wise and state-wise number of caste/communities found place in the central common list of OBCs.	37
2.2	State-wise number of caste/communities apear in the Mandal list, State list and Central list.	40
2.3	State-wise number of caste/communities of Mandal list and State list not included in the Central common list.	42
2.4	Year-wise and State-wise number of new caste/ communities included in the central list of OBCs on the recommendation of the NCBC.	44
2.5	State-wise total number of caste/communities appear in the central list of OBCs.	45
2.6	Caste/communities found place in the Mandal list but not in the State list.	47
2.7	Caste/communities found place in the state list but not in the Mandal list.	47
2.8	Caste/communities found place in the state list but not in the Central list.	50
2.9	Caste/communities found place in the Central list but not in the State list.	51

2.10	State-wise distribution of sub-caste/synonyms of certain caste/communities in the central list of OBCs.	53
2.11	State-wise number of main caste and sub-caste/ synonyms in the Central list of OBCs.	56
2.12	Distribution of caste/communities with area restiction.	57
2.13	OBCs partly appear in SC/ST list.	62
3.1	State-wise distribution of number of caste/ communities of different categories.	66
3.2	Percentage of reservation to OBCs in the state services.	73
4.1	State-wise distribution of De-notified, Nomadic and Semi-Nomadic caste/communities.	78
5.1	State-wise distribution of weaving caste/ communities in the Central list of OBCs.	113
5.2	State-wise distribution of caste/communities working on metal.	120
5.3	State-wise distribution of caste/communities engaged in Tailoring.	126
5.4	State-wise distribution of artisan/artisanal caste/ communities of clear occupation.	127
5.5	State-wise distribution of caste/communities of Artists and Magicians.	135
5.6	State-wise distribution of OBCs traditionally engaged in fishing and related occupations.	136
5.7	State-wise distribution of castes/communities of the central list of OBCs traditionally engaged in Toddy Tapping/Distilling.	140
5.8	State-wise distribution of caste/communities of Earth workers, Stone, Salt and Lime workers in the Central list of OBCs.	141
5.9	Distribution of untouchable caste/communities in the central list of OBCs.	143

5.10 Peasantry as an occupational class. 145

5.11 State-wise distribution of Peasant caste/ communities in the central list of OBCs. 146

5.12 State-wise distribution of Cattle rearing and Pastoral caste/communities. 152

5.13 State-wise distribution of caste/communities associated with gardening, growing and selling of vegetable, fruit, flowers and betal leaves. 154

5.14 State-wise distribution of Priestly caste in the central list of OBCs. 159

6.1 Occupation-wise distribution of number of caste/ communities included in the central list of OBCs during 1999 to 2001 (till 6th September). 167

Introduction

Once again the issue of reservation for Backward Classes (B.C.) (other than Scheduled Castes (S.C.) and Scheduled Tribes (S.Ts.)) is being highlighted by the media. This time it is not forward *versus* backward but in real sense, backward *versus* backward. The categorization of OBCs is neccessitated with a view to providing equal opportunities to one and all and ensuring that the lion's share is not taken away by advanced category among them. In fact, it is rather aimed at percolating the benefits of reservation to the lower categories of backward classes. *'The Pioneer'* (June 29, 2001) reported that adopting the social engineering formula, the Chief Minister of Uttar Pradesh set up a Cabinet Sub-Committee for Social Justice to fix a quota for the Most Backward Classes (MBC) within the 27 percent reservation for the OBCs and to review the quota for the dalits in order to ensure that its benefits reach them. The five point terms of reference of the Committee include review of all the programmes, facilities and welfare schemes for the SCs, STs and OBCs; review the study of the ST population and changes therein following the creation of Uttaranchal; the situation of employment among the SCs, STs and OBCs as per the norms; and recommendations for possible improvements keeping an eye on social justice and the quota. Meanwhile, the

Samajwadi Party and the Bahujan Samaj Party have described the Chief Minister's announcement as nothing more than an election stunt; and the move is aimed at dividing the backward communities. "*Dainik Jagaran*" (Ist August, 2001) reported that the Rajasthan Government has rejected the recommendations of the Backward Classes Commission of Rajasthan pertaining to the apportionment of reservation quota into three categories on the following grounds:

i) Distribution of 21 percent reservation available for OBCs into three parts i.e. 6 percent, 7 percent and 8 percent respectively, has no scientific base.

ii) Categorization of OBCs without detailed survey of the castes/communities and their population and their representation in Government services cannot be done.

iii) Apart from this, categorization of OBCs in Northern India is not relevant.

This may be a burning issue in the coming Assembly elections in U.P. but categorization of backward classes is not new. It already existed in some of the States i.e. Andhra Pradesh, Bihar, Karnataka, Kerala, Haryana, Maharashtra, etc.

Presently, the Backward Classes in India broadly carry four types of identities. First, one of them is political identity which defines the backward classes as vote bank, not only regional but even national level political parties are identified with particular castes/sub-castes/ communities and vice versa.

Second, purity and pollution determine the social status of castes/communities. Thousands of castes and sub-castes that comprise the Hindu society even today try to establish their origin from one or the other of the four varnas because varna concept played and important role in the evoluation and development of Hindu social organisation. With the passage of time the original concept might have degenerated into the practical form of the castes and sub-castes that we see with all their glaring absurdities even in the present day Hindu society. History shows that *varna* is changeable but not caste. The caste is by birth and cannot be changed till death.

Third, identification can be made for the purpose of demanding reservation benefits.The Caste/communities identified as socially and educationally backward. Fourth, identification reflects the existing structural and functional relationship of OBCs with the advanced castes/communities (Brahmins, Kshatriyas, Vaishyas); and SCs & STs to whom they consider lowly or inferior; and among the OBCs in the context of commensal hierarchy, marriage alliances and occupational relationship.

It seems that political identity is dominating and therefore it is necessary to understand the role of the political parties to project the state-society relationship and the dynamics of functioning of the state to have a proper understanding on mode of identification of the backward classes.

India's backward classe population is estimated to be 52 percent of the total population and there is enormous diversity among OBCs in terms of occupation, customs and level of development.

The purpose of including creamy layer in the reservation for BCs was that genuine BCs (most backward) will get the benefit and raise their status, thus reservation will not be required after some time. But it did not happen due to many reasons. As a result a debate on the issue of creamy layer started and many alternatives are suggested as to raise the limit of creamy layer from annual income of rupees one lakh to 5 lakh, to remove the creamy layer from reservation of OBCs as it is not applicable in case of SCs & STs to implement is strictly.

Inclusion of castes/communities in the different lists of BCs is mainly based on caste which poses many complications. Other criterian suggested by different commissions/committees appointed by the government for identification of socially and educationally backward castes/communities from time to time but were not accepted by the concerned state government. As a result many forward castes/communities included in one list but not in other list. Some of the genuinely backward castes/ communites could not found place in these lists.

It is also widely noticed that whenever a member of a caste moves socially upward there is generally a total or partial abandonement of his traditional occupation. There can be occasional upward or downward movement of the caste/ community, depending in the change of vocation. Many denotified, ex-criminal, nomadic and semi-nomadic castes/ communities who are outside the reckoning of caste hierarchy rank lower that other castes, found place in the OBC list alongwith numerous other small castes of artisans/artisanal, priestly, peasantary, etc. Thus the classification of OBCs need to be dealt carefully, particularly in the context of revision of the lists. Classification in haphazard way will certainly pose many problems for OBCs in future.

Though the caste is ascribed by birth in India but there are instances of occupational mobility in the past. Planned development and private enterprise created employment opportunities. Thus political, economic and cultural changes gave a big boost to occupational and vertical upward mobility. The constitution of India made certain provisions for the welfare and upliftment of OBCs. Article 16 contained the rule of equality of opportunity in matters of public employment.

Supreme Court of India in its historical judgement (Indira Sawhney v/s Union of India, 1992 (Sup) 3 SCC 217 at 714) defines caste in the following terms: "a caste is nothing but a social class - a socially homogeneous class. It is also an occupational grouping, with this difference that its membership is hereditary. One is born into it. Its membership is involuntary. Even if one ceases to follow that occupation. Still he remains and continues a member of that group."

For the last 50 years, starting with the Assembly debate in 1950, a debate is still going on about the criteria for identification of socially and educationally backward castes/

communities for purposes of Article 16 (4). It is argued that caste is a reality in our society. Caste system here is age old and every person is born into a particular caste and some of these sections of society suffer from social disabilities of various kinds and are so weakened that they are not in a position to take equal advantage of equal opportunities compared to socially and educationally stronger castes. Caste is a clearly recognizable social entity which can be used a device to identify a backward class. There is yet another opinion that caste should neither be sole criterian not it should be equated with class. It is thus obvious that the caste system has the sanction from the constitution, judiciary, legislature and it has been glorified by the political parties. Some castes have indeed fared better than the others. Therefore, it would be interesting to explore as to what accounts for such differences. Structural and functional features of castes/communities have to be found before doing its classification, apportionment of reservation and revision of the OBC lists.

Many scholars have written on different aspects of reservation policy and its implementation but role of caste organizations in the implementation of reservation for backward classes remains untouched. Thus, it is appropriate to highlight this issue alongwith identification of OBCs, MBCs by the government as this has bearing on the very purpose of reservation and its implementation.

1

Identification of Other Backward Classes

The term 'Backward' is contextual which implies the presence of a forward or advanced. It may also mean the presence of disadvantaged and advantaged sections in mutual interaction. It implies presence of inequality. Whether there are some social, educational and economic inequality which can be tied up with practically all types of disadvantages in a society and whether there are some inequalities which imply no disadvantage for the concerned section of the population. The term 'backward class' was used as far back as 1880 to describe a list of groups also called illiterate or indigent classes, entitled to allowances for study in elementary schools. The Fort St. George Gazette No. 40 of November 5, 1895 mentions grant-in-aid to schools for a list of 'Backward Classes' which includes most of 'untouchable' castes of Madras Presidency. The first Govt. circular reserving certain posts in favour of backward castes was made on June 19-21, 1895 by the Mysore Govt. In 1925 a Government resolution proclaimed in the then Bombay, defined Backward Classes "as all except Brahmins, Prabhus, Marwaris, Parsis, Banias and Christians". The Justice party had laid down caste-wise reservation in public appointment in 1926. In 1928 Hartog Committee defined Backward Classes in their glossary as castes or classes which are educationally backward, it includes depressed classes, aboriginals, hill tribes and criminal tribes. In 1929 the United Provinces Hindu Backward Classes League prepared a list of 115 castes (non Dwijas or degenerated or Sudra classes of Hindus). The Objective Resolution of the Constituent Assembly moved by Nehru on December 13, 1946 required adequate safeguards to be made for 'other backward classes' along with several other categories of population.[1]

Identification of castes/communities and their listing have had a long history which started from the early period of our history with Manu. Medieval chronicles contained a description of communities located in various parts of the country. Listings in the colonial period were undertaken on an extensive scale, after 1806. The process gathered momentum in course of the censuses from 1881 to 1941. The Constituent Assembly Debates indicates that the draftsmen themselves were not sure as to the criteria to be adopted in determining "backwardness." They wanted to maintain a flexibility in the matter and to base the matter to every State Government to determine "backwardness" with ultimate review by the court. One or two members did express view that the case of backwardness may be literacy and occupation, etc.[2] After independence Jammu and Kashmir Government restored to a large scale communal reservation policy in 1952. It had reserved 50 percent to Dogra Hindus of Jammu and 10 percent was left to the Pandits. Anthropological Survey of India has identified 4693 communities, 325 languages belonging to 12 different language families, 24 scripts and 91 cultural zones all over India under the People of India project. The project was inaugurated on 2nd October, 1985. It has probably being one of the most complete survey of Indian communities that has documented socio-economic-cultural, linguistic and ecological diversities.[3] As per the Constitution (Scheduled Castes) order, 1950 and the constitution(Scheduled Tribes) order, 1950

Government of India has issued a list of 1086 castes of SCs and 443 communities of STs. The Backward Classes Commissions/ Committees set up by various State Governments from time to time have identified socially and educationally backward classes for the purpose of State Lists.

State Governments of Andhra Pradesh, Bihar, Gujarat, Haryana, Jammu and Kashmir, Karnataka, Kerala, Madhya Pradesh, Maharashtra, Orissa, Punjab, Uttar Pradesh, West-Bengal have setup the following commissions/committees on backward classes from time to time and these commissions/ committees suggested different criterion for identification of socially and educationally backward classes and their listing.

Andhra Pradesh

1. Backward Classes Commission (1968-70)

   Chairman: Shri Mandhai Pershad

2. Committee of the Fifth Legislature Assembly to recommend further measures for the welfare of Backward Classes (1977)

   Chairman : Shri Agisam Veerappa

3. One man Commission of Inquiry for Backward Classes (1970)

   Chairman: Sh. K.M. Anantharaman

4. One man Commission of Inquiry for Backward Classes (1982) Chairman: Shri N.K. Murlidhara Rao

Bihar

Backward Classes Commission (1971-76)

Chairman: Shri Mungerilal

Delhi

Backward Classes Commission (1994)

Chairman: Shri G.C. Jain

Gujarat

1. Backward Class Investigation Committee (1953)
   Chairman: Shri P.Majumadar
2. Backward Classes Commission (1972-76)
   Chairman: A.R. Bakshi
3. Second Backward Classes Commission (1983)
   Chairman: C.V. Rane

Jammu and Kashmir

1. Backward Classes Committee (1969)
   Chairman: Sh. J.N. Wazir
2. Backward Classes Committee (1976-77)
   Chairman: Justice Adarsh S. Anand
3. Gajendra Gadkar Commission (1967-1968)
   Chairman: Gajendregadkar

Haryana

Backward Classes Commission (1990)
Chairman: Justice Gurnam Singh

Karnataka

1. Backward Classes Commitee (1960-61)
   Chairman: Dr. R. Naganna Gowda
2. Karnataka Backward Classes Commission (1971-1975)
   Chairman: L.G. Havanur
3. Karnataka Third Backward Classes Commission (1986-1990)
   Chairman: O. Chinnappa Raddy

Kerala

1. Evaluation Committee (1961-63)
   Chairman: V.K. Vishwanathan

2. Backward Classes commission (1964-65)

   Chairman: Sh. G. Kumare Pillai

3. Backward Classes Reservation Commission (1967-1970)

   Chairman: Sh. M.P. Damodaran

Madhya Pradesh

Madhya Pradesh State Commission for Backward Classes (1980-1983)

Chairman: Ramji Mahajan

Maharashtra

1. Depressed Classes and Aboriginal tribes committee Bombay Presidency (1930)

2. Committee to Report on Reservation of Backward Classes in the Services (1961-1964)

   Chairman: Sh. B.D. Deshmukh

Manipur

Expert committee on OBCs (1994)

Orissa

Commission of Enquiry reparding Mandal Commission report

Chairman: Justice N.K. Das

Punjab

1. Evaluation committee (1965-66)

   Chairman: Shri Brish Bhan

2. Vidhan Sabha committee on welfare of SC, ST & OBC (1975-76)

Rajasthan

1. Rajasthan State Backward Classes Commission (1993-1998)

   Chairman: Justice Indrasen Israni

Tamil Nadu

1. Backward Classes Commission (1969-70)

   Chairman: Sh. A.N. Sattanathan

2. Tamil Nadu Second Backward Classes Commission (1982-85)

   Chairman: Shri J.A. Ambasankar

Uttar Pradesh

Uttar Pradesh State Sarvadhik Pichhada Varg Ayog (1975-77)

Chairman: Sh. Chhedi Lal Sathi

West Bengal

Committee on Backward Classes (1980)

Government of India setup following two Backward classes commission for determining the criteria for identification of socially & educationally backward classses for the purpose of central list :

i) Backward classes commission 1953-1955

   Chairman : Sh. Kakasaheb Kalelkar.

ii) Backward classes commission, 1979-1980.

   Chairman: Sh. B.P. Bandal.

II

State Governments of Andhra Pradesh, Bihar, Delhi, Gujarat, Haryana, Jammu and Kashmir, Karnataka, Kerala,

Madhya Pradesh, Maharashtra, Manipur, Orissa, Rajasthan, Tamil Nadu and Uttar Pradesh set up Commissions/Committees for defining criteria for backwardness and recommending measures for its removal. These Commissions/Committees in their Reports have attempted to define and identify social and educational backwardness, suggested different criteria and listed the OBCs for the purpose of State List.

Chinnappa Reddy Commission in its report (1990) suggestes that social and economic criteria be paramount factor to identify Socially and Educationally Backward Classes (SEBCs). Caste alone can not be criteria for deciding backwardness, but it should be based on income and occupation. Social and educational backwardness is the outcome of economic underdevelopment, educational unawareness and caste degradation yet in identifying backwardness 'caste' was projected as the primary key because India's despairingly vast socio-economic inequalities, with the superior priestly, landlord, merchant and such other castes at one end of the spectrum, the SCs/STs 'outcastes at the other end and the numerous other castes in between, who because of the low gradation of caste to which they belong in the rural social hierarchy, because of a humble occupation which they pursue or because of their poverty and ignorance are also condemned to backwardness, social and educational. It explains that the social gradation of the caste in India appears to be based broadly on the traditional occupational pursuits of the castes, castes whose traditional occupations necessarily involve learning appear to take precedence over the castes who are primarly land owners, the land owning castes take precedence over the trading castes, the trading castes over castes engaged in manual labour over those engaged in noxious labour, etc. There are also many regional/local variations and sometimes trading castes supersede the landowning castes and artisans precede the petty traders. There are also numerous other small castes. Generally nomadic or semi-nomadic who are outside the reckoning of caste hierarchy rank lower than other castes.

It further clarifies that whenever a member of a caste moves socially upward there is generally a total or partial abandonment of his traditional occupation. A land owner who acquires learning move up in the social scale, a trader who acquires land similarly moves up, as also the craftsman who becomes a trader, the manual worker who becomes a craftsman and a person engaged in noxious work who becomes a manual worker. As such, there can be occasional upward or downward movement of the caste/community, depending in the change of vocation.[4]

Mungeri Lal Commission (1976) for Bihar adopted the following criteria in its report :

(i) Low social status in the traditional caste hierarchy of Hindu society.

(ii) Lack of general education in greater number of people in any caste or community.

(iii) Inadequate representation or absence of representation in Govt. services.

(iv) Inadequate representation in the area of trade, commerce and industries.

It is made clear that reservations are not permanent and with the upward mobility of the backward classes the facility would be gradually abolished and reservation would apply only in direct recruitment and not for promotion.

The peculiarity of Karpoori formula is that even though caste continue to be basis of reservation, an economic element to the reservation criteria was also introduced by making only those BC families with an family income below the income tax limit eligible for reservation. This limit is a means of ensuring that the benefits of reservations go to the really needy such as Lohar, Badhai, Kumbhar, Nai, Bari, etc.

Gajendragadkar Commission for Jammu and Kashmir in its report in 1968 recommended that economic backwardness, occupation, habitation, literacy and caste (in respect of Hindus) may be made criteria for determining backwardness.

Shri G. Kumara Pillai Commission for Reservation of Seats in Educational Institutions for Kerala recommended in its report (1965) that families belonging to those 95 castes and whose aggregate income (i.e. income of all members in the family from all sources taken together) is less than 4,200/- per annum constitute SEBCs. Reservation of seats in Post Graduate Courses in Arts and Science colleges and in professional colleges (other than law and Ayurveda colleges).

N.P. Damodaran Commission adopted the following criteria for identification of OBCs in Kerala:

i) The test of education; (ii) The test of appropriation of appointments; (iii) The test of social backwardness due to historical reasons; and (iv) The economic test.

Gurnam Singh Commission (1990) for Haryana adopted the following criteria:

A. Social

(i) Castes/Classes considered as socially backward by others and by themselves.

(ii) Castes/Classes which mainly depend on manual labour for their livelihood particularly of female in work and its quantum is more than 15% of the State everage.

(iii) Castes/Classes where percentage of persons employed in unorganised sector is more than that of the State average by 15 percent.

(iv) Castes/Classes where participation of children in unskilled manual labour in the unorganised sector is 15% above the State average.

(v) Castes/Classes where child marriages are common.

(vi) Castes/Classes where widow remariages like Karewa/ Chaddarandazi/Reet are common.

(vii) Castes/Classes labouring for their livelihood under the sun and in open air.

(viii) Castes/Classes where in a female child is considered as inferior to that of the male child and there is a lot of discrimination between the two in terms of necessary investment like food, clothing, education etc.

(ix) Castes/Classes held as backward by the Government or by the courts of law.

(x) Castes/Classes lacking basic civic amenities like latrines, toilet facilities etc. and who are residing under unhygenic and insanitary conditions in villages and towns.

B. Educational

(i) Castes/Classes where the rate of student drop out in the age group of 6-14 years is 15 percent above the State average.

(ii) Castes/Classes where female literacy rate is 15 percent below the State average.

(iii) Castes/Classes wherein the percentage of population who have passed matriculation or its equivalent is 15 percent above the State average.

(iv) Castes/Classes in which the percentage of students studying in ordinary Government School is 15 percent above the State average;

OR

Castes/Classes in which the percentage of students studying in Public/Convent Schools (English Schools) is 15 percent lower than that of the State average.

(v) Castes/Classes in which the percentage of students getting a Ist division in the matricultion examination is 15 percent below the State average.

(vi) Castes/Classes in which the percentage of illiterate parents-mother and father of the children in a household is 15 percent above he State average.

(vii) Castes/Classes in which the pass percentage of students in the matriculation examination is 15 percent below the State average.

(viii) Castes/Classes in which the percentage of people educated upto graduation level is 15 percent below the State average.

(ix) Castes/Classes in which the percentages of people educated jupto Posgraduate level or degree level in professional courses like MBBS, BE etc. is 15 percent below the State average.

(x) Castes/Classes in which the percentage of students studying in vocational courses like ITI's is 15 percent below the state average.

It suggested that the basis of identification of backward classes should not be 'caste'.

Mahajan Commission (1990) for Himachal Pradesh adopted the following criteria.

1. Agricultural labourers holding not more than five bighas of landin the State and wholly dependent for their livelihood upon agricultural operations on their own land or as agricultural labourers on the land of others;

2. Persons who have been working as manual workers for a continuous period of not less than one year in hotels, restaurants or other private commercial establishments in the State and who have no other means of livelihocd.

3. Persons who have been working as licensed coolies at railway stations or bus-stands in the state for a continuous period of not less than one year and who have no other means of livelihood.

A.R. Bakshi Commission (1972-76) for Gujarat has adopted the following criteria for identification of OBCs in Gujarat.

(i) Social backwardness in general

(ii) Poverty and economic backwardness

(iii) Illiteracy and educational backwardness

(iv) Occupational and environmental factors

(v) Poor representationin public services

(vi) Social status in general

(vii) Mode of living, customs and beliefs

(viii) Caste only as one of the relevant factors

(ix) Nomadic way of life and criminal tendencies

(x) Backwardness in other ways

L.G. Havanor State Backward Classes Commission, Karnataka has in indicated reasons of social backwardness as:

(i) Residence in rural, isolated and segregated areas.

(ii) Their economic condition is so poor that the majority are incapable of owning land, house or other property.

(iii) They are engaged in very unremunerative occupations are considered unclan or inferior and therefore low,

(iv) People of the advanced castes and communities entertain prejudice against them,

(v) Low status or inferiority associated with their castes make it difficult, to have access to places of cultural training or to have religious and secular education.

(vi) Many have been segregated from the advanced communities due to social taboos against inter-dining and inter-marriage and against similar opportunities of association.

(vii) They are prevented from enjoying status in society due to the age-old social customs.

(viii) Consequent apathy for education.

T. Vankatswami Commission for Karnataka has adopted the following criteria for identification of OBCs in Karnataka:

(i) Social: Houseless and siteless

(ii) Economic: Landless, incomeless than Rs. 5000/- per year, agricultural labours.

(iii) Educational: Illiteracy, drop-outrate below 7th standard.

(iv) Employment: No. of class iv employees are more.

G.C. Jain Commission (1994) for Delhi has adopted the following criteria for identification of OBCs:

A. Social

i) Caste/Classes considered as socially backward by others.

ii) Caste/Classes by their main livelihood.

iii) Caste/Classes by female age at marriage.

B. Educational

iv) Caste/Classes where number of children in the age group of 5-15 years never attended school.

v) Caste/Classes by students drop out rate from the class they dropped.

vi) Caste/Classes by educational level of males.

vii) Caste/Classes by educational level of females.

C. Economic

viii) Caste/Classes by possession of :

Household goods and material objects.

Assets of Trade & Commerce.

Ownership of cultivable land.

Professional related tools/machinery etc.

ix) Caste/Classes by type of house in which they are living.

x) Caste/Classes by distance of source of drinking water.

xi) Caste/Classes by indetedness status of households.

Shri Chhedi Lal Sathi, Chairman, Sarvadhik Pichhada Varg Ayog (1977) for the State of Uttar Pradesh recommended 15 castes for specific benefits in government jobs and 59 castes only for educational facilities:

> The Government of West Bengal set up a Committee in 1980 for the identification but this Committee was not in favour of reservation in government jobs and was of the opinion that poverty and low levels of living standards rather than caste should be the important criteria for identifying backwardness and this report has been excepted by the State Government in toto.

On the basis of the recommendations of the Commissions/Committees, the State Govts. have adopted different criteria for identification of OBCs. For example, Assam, Andhra Pradesh, Bihar, Gujarat, Haryana, Kerala, Maharashtra, Punjab, Rajasthan and Uttar Pradesh had recognized caste as one of the criteria for identifying backwardness. Delhi, Dadra and Nagar Haveli, Haryana, Himachal Pradesh had state caste should not be made a criterion for BCs. Bihar, Gujarat, Himachal Pradesh, Kerala, Punjab, Rajasthan and Uttar Pradesh have suggested low econimic status as one of the significant tests. Delhi, Haryana and Dadra and Nagar Haveli have desired the economic factor to be the sole determinant of backwardness.

State Government of Assam stated that there are classes of socially discriminated people among non-Hindus also. State Governments of Gujarat, Maharashtra, Madhya Pradesh expressed similar views and preferred literacy test for non-Hindus while State Governments of Haryana was in favour of economic criterion. Kerala State Governments considered traditional occupations, economic backwardness and low social status of converts to be criteria for this purpose. Punjab and Orissa State Governments put forward the same tests for both non-Hindus and Hindus.

These reports of State Commission have not faired better. In most of the cases the courts have decided against them on the basis of facts placed before them and have laid down certain broad guidelines for the determination of social backwardness. As regards educational backwardness, even though the court has laid down guidelines, not much seems to be done in this direction. Successive recommendations of these Backward Classes Commissions have been reported for one reason or the other by courts and unassailable criteria is not available.

III

The first All India Backward Classes Commission was appointed by the Governments of India to satisfy the Articles 15 (4) and 340 (1) of the Indian Constitution in 1953 with Kaka Kalelkar as its Chairman. The Commission formulated the following criteria for identifying socially and educationally backward classes:

i) Low social position in the traditional caste hierarchy of Hindu society.

ii) Lack of general educational advancement among the major section of a caste or community.

iii) Inadequate or not represented in government service.

iv) Inadequate representation in the field of trade, commerce and industry.

Kaka Kalelkar Commission prepared a list of 2399 backward castes/communities for the entire country and 837 of these were classified as 'most backward', but it is not made clear as to how the lists of backward classes were derived by the application of the criteria.

This Commission submitted its report on March 30, 1955. According to it, the relevant factors to be considered while classifying backward classes should be based on their traditional occupation and profession, the percentage of literacy or the general advancement made by them, estimated population of the community and their distribution throughout the State or their concentration in certain areas.[5]

Some of the members of the Commission opposed the view of linking caste with backwardness while one member of the Commission was in favour of acceptance of caste as the criterian for identification on socially and educationally backward class. The Chariman of the Commission opposed the acceptance of caste as the basis of backwardness in his forwarding note by mentioning that families whose income is less than Rs. 800 a year do need special help irrespective of the community to which they belong. Such poor and deserving may even belong to the upper communities or the educationally backward but otherwise prosperous people of the dominant communities among the backward classes. The extreme poor can't be denied special help simply because they happen to belong to a particular community. The Memorandum of action appended to the report of the Commission pointed out that the caste system is the greatest hindrance in the way of our progress to egalitarian society and that in such a situation recognition of certain specified castes as backward may serve to maintain and perpetuate the existing distinctions on the basis of caste. The memorandum also found fault with certain tests adopted by the Commission for identifying the backward classes the report was considered by the Central Governments which apparently was not found satisfied with the approach adopted by the Commission in determining the criteria for identifying the backward classes under Article 15(4), as the criteria lacked its objectivity. Finally the Government of India rejected the report in 1961. This led individual State Governments to appoint their own Backward Classes Commissions under the Commission of Inquiry Act and have drawn out lists of BCs for reservation in educational institutions and public appointments. The Central Governments on 14th August, 1961 wrote to all the State Govts. stating inter alia that while the State Govts. have the discretion to choose their own criteria for defining backwardness, it would be better to apply economic tests than to go by the caste. The State Governments were also requested to undertake the adhoc surveys to determine the numbers of BCs and in the meantime to give all reasonabel facilities to the BCs in accordance with their existing lists and also such others who in their opinion deserved to be considered as SEBC.

It is worth mentioning that no meaningful action was taken till 1979 when the Mandal Commission was constituted for evolving a complete and scientific criteria for defining the socially and educationally backward classes.

IV

The second All India Backward Classes Commission, popularly known as Mandal Commission was appointed by the Governments of India in 1979 under Article 340 of the Constitution to investigate the conditions of socially and educationally backward classes; to determine the criteria for defining the socially and educationally backward classes; to recommend steps to be taken for the advancement of the socially and educationally backward classes of citizens so identified; to examine the desirability or otherwise of making provision for the reservation of appointments or posts in favour of such backward classes of citizens which are not adequately represented in public services and posts in connection with the affairs of the Union or of any State. The Commission submitted its report in 1980.

The commission evolved eleven 'Indicators' or 'Criteria' for determing social and educational backwardness. These 11 'Indicators' were grouped under three broad heads, i.e., Social, Educational and Economic.

The commission evolved eleven 'Indicators' or 'Criteria' for determing social and educational backwardness.

These 11 'Indicators' were grouped under three broad heads, i.e., Social, Educational and Economic.

A. Social

(i) Caste/Classes considered as socially backward by others.

(ii) Caste/Classes which mainly depend on manual labour for their livelihood.

(iii) Caste/Classes where at least 25% females and 10% males above the State average get married at an age below 17 years in rural areas and at least 10% females and 5% males do so in urban areas.

(iv) Caste/Classes where participation of females in work is atleast 25% above the state average.

B. Educational

(v) Caste/Classes where the number of children in the age group of 5-15 years who never attended school is at least 25% above the state average.

(vi) Caste/Classes where the rate of student drop out in the age group of 5-15 years is at least 25% above the state average.

(vii) Caste/Classes amongst whom the proportion of matriculates is at least 25% below the state average.

C. Economic

(viii) Caste/Classesd where the average value of family assets is at least 25% below the stage average.

(ix) Caste/Classes where the number of families living in kuccha house is at least 25% above the state average.

(x) Caste/Classes where the source of drinking water is beyond half a kilometer for more than 50% of the households.

(xi) Caste/Classes where the number of housenhold having taken consumption loan is at least 25% above the state average.

One of the Members of the Commission, Shri L.R. Naik dissended the findings on the ground that the castes/communities listed as socially and educationally backward classes by the Mandal Commission are not at the same degree or level of social and educational backwardness. Some of the communities (intermediate backward classes) on the lines delineated from the report have made their presence felt in the caste hierarchical society either on their numerical strength or their age old co-existence along with other advanced communities and they would integrate with the general populace sooner than later. But the castes and classes (depressed backward classes) who are incapable of making such dent, in the near future being extermely backward. Their economic backwardness is evidently the consequence of their age old social and educational backwardness. So there is a need to shift them from the main common list and create a separate entity of equals or near equals to bring about a healthy competition among them. The rest of the communities in the common list should then found a distinct category for the same reason of creating an atmosphere for competition among equals.[6]

The first and foremost criticism leveled against the approach and the procedure adopted by the Mandal Commission is that it has adopted caste alone as the basis of its approach through out. Justice Thommen in para 284 of the judgement in the case of Indira Sawhney and Other. v/s Government of India and Others has also observed:

> "The indicators or criteria adopted in the Mandal Report are broadly grouped as social, educational and economic on the basis of castes/classes. The Commission has identified classes with castes and backwardness with particular castes. Castes which are socially, educationally and economically backward are

characterized as backward classes entitled to the benefit of reservation. Persons are grouped on the basis of caste either because they are members of it by reason of their being Hindu or because they are member of it in the past prior to their conversion to other religions. Identification of backwardness is thus made with reference to the present of past caste affiliations of the people."

Among the 11 criteria formulated by the Mandal Commission four relate to social backwardness, three to educational and four to economic backwardness. The first criterion namely, castes or classes considered as socially backward by others itself depends on certain objective criteria. As the second criterion relating to castes/classes mainly depending on manual labour for their livelihood, this itself needs elaboration. Should castes or hereditary groups of small farmers mainly depend on their own family labour be regarded as socially groups of small farmers mainly depend on their own family labour be regarded as socially backward? A distinction may have to be made between manual labour or self-employed and the manual work of those who offer their labour for wages. Regarding the practice of early marriage it seems not relevant because some backward sections may be practicing early marriage but some of the forward sections also practise child marriages. Regarding the fourth criterion requiring participation of women in work we should consider whether it should include any kind of work or only manual work and again whether it includes even selfemployed sector or only wage labour.

The Mandal Commission stops at the consideration of the proportion of matriculates. Perhaps the proportions of all the three categories - the matriculates, the graduates and the post-graduates cum professionals need to be considered besides the overall literacy among those aged above 15 years.

The criteria suggested by the Mandal Commission relating to the distance of the source of drinking water may not be relevant because in many areas drinking water provided at the very doorstep even in remote villages and where the source of drinking water is at some distance, the disadvantage is experienced by all caste and classes alike.

The Mandal Commission has adopted a cut off point in respect of each criteria in such a way that it amounts to dual opinion of yes or no type. Each of the criteria requires castes to be 25 percent more or less than state average. In each of the cases castes with criteria which are just less than 25 percent become backward whereas those with criteria just more than 25 percent become forward.

Mandal Commission's assumption of homogeneity within the backward classes in the absence of any economic criteria as the cut off point is bound to be a disadvantage to the majority of the backward castes. In that event the prosperous and powerful sections of OBCs would certainly grab the major chunk of the reservation benefits.

As a matter of fact the criteria neither evolved properly nor implemented scientifically. As a result many genuine backward castes/communities were not included in the list of SEBCs by the Commission. On the other hand many advanced castes/communities were also included in the list of SEBCs.

V

The NCBC, after studying the criteria/indicators framed by the Mandal Commission and the Commissions set up in the past by different State Governments and other relevant meterials, formulated the following guidelines for considering requests for inclusion in the list of Other Backward Classes:-

A. Social

1. Castes and communities, generally considered as socially backward.

2.(a) Castes and Communities, which mainly depend on agricultural and / or other manual labour for their livelihood and are lacking any significant resource base.

(b) Castes and Communities,which, for their livelihood, mainly depend on agricultural and/or other manual labour for wage and are lacking any significant resource base.

(c) Castes and Communities, the women of which, as a general practice, are for their/family's livelihood, engaged in agricultural and/or other manual labour, for wage.

(d) Castes and communities, the children of which, as a general practice, are, for family's livelihood or for supplementing family's low income, mainly engaged in agricultural and/or manual labour.

(e) Castes and Communities, which in terms of the caste systems, are identified with traditional crafts or traditional or hreditary cuupations considered to be lowly or undignified.

(f) Castes and Communities, which in terms of the caste system, are identified with traditional or hereditary occupations considered to be 'unclean' or stigmatised.

(g) Nomadic and semi-nomadic castes and communities.

(h) Denotified or Vimukta Jati castes and communities.

Explanation: This terms refers to castes/communities which had been categorised as Criminal Tribes under the Criminal Tribes Act, 1924, Act No. VI or 1924, passed by the Indian Legislature and repealed by the Criminal Tribes (Repeal) Act, 1952, Act No. XXIV of 1952 and subsequently referred to as Denotified or Vimukta Jatis.

3. Castes and communities, having no representation or poor representation in the State Legislative Assembly and/or district-level Panchayati Raj institutions during the ten years preceding the date of the application.

Explanation: This is only intended to measure, as an indicator, the presence of a caste or community in these bodies.

The term poor representation may be taken to refer to a caste or community whose presence in the body is less than 25% of its proportion in the population.

B. Educational

1. Castes and Communities, whose literacy rate is at least 8% less than the State or district average.
2. Castes and Communities which the proportion of matriculates is at least 20% less than the State or district average.
3. Castes and communities, or which the proportion of graduates is at least 20% less than the State or district average.

C. Economic

1. Castes and Communities, a significant proportion of whose members reside only in Kaccha houses.
2. Castes and Communities, the share of whose members in number of cases and in extent of agricultural lands surrendered under the Agricultural Land Ceiling Act of the State, is nil or significantly low.
3. Castes and Communities,the share of whose members in State Government posts and services of Groups A and B Classes 1 and 2, is not equal to the population-equivalent proportion of the caste/community.[7]

VI

Article 14 of the Constitution requires the State not to deny any person equality before the law or the equal protection of the laws within the territory of India. Articles 15 contains the rule of equal protection of the law in positive and affirmative terms. Clasue (1) of Article 15 provides that the state shall not discriminate against any citizen on grounds only of religion, race, caste, sex, place of birth or any of them. Clause (2) of Article 15 declares that no citizen shall on grounds only of religion, race, caste, sex, place of birth or any of them be subject to any disability, liability, restriction or condition with regard to (a) the access to shops. public restaurants, hotels and place of public entertainment (b) the use of wells, tanks, bathing ghats, roads and place of public resort maintained wholly or partly out of the State funds or dedicated to the ise of general public. However, to ameliorate the condition of women and children a provision was made in clause (3) that nothintg in this Article shall prevent the state from making any special provision for women and children. Clause (4) of Article 15. which, was inserted by the Constitution (First Amendment) Act. 1951, provides that nothing in this Article or clause (2) of Article 29 shall prevent the State from making any special provision for the advancement of any socially or educationally backwards classes of citizens or for the Scheduled Castes and Scheduled Tribes.

Article 16 contained the rule of equality of opportunity in matters of public employment. It reads as under:

16 (1) There shall be equality of opportunity for all citizens in matters relating to employment or appointment to any office under the state.

(2) No citizen shall, on grounds only of religion, race, caste, sex descent. place of birth residence or any of them be ineligible for or discriminated against in respect of, any employment or office under the state.

(3) Nothing in this article shall prevent Parliament from making any law prescribing, in regard to a class or classes of employment of appointment to an office under the government of or any local or other authority within a State or Union Territory, any requirement as to residence within that State or Union Territory, prior to such employment or appointment.

(4) Nothing in this article shall prevent the State from making any provision for the reservation of appointments or posts in favour of any backward class of citizens which, in the opinion of the State, is not adequate represented in the services under the State.

(5) Nothing in this article shall affect the operation of any law which provides that the incumbent of an office in connection with the affairs of any religious or denomicational institutions or any member of the governing body there of shall be a person professing a partcular religion or belonging to a particulat denomination.

Clause (1) of this Article guarantees equality of opportunity to all citizens in the matter of appointment to any office under the State. Clause (2) prohibits discrimination on grounds of religion, race, caste, sex, descent, place of birth, residence or any of them. Clause (3), however, makes an exception. It enables the Parliament to make a law prescribing any requirement as to residence within a State or Union Territory prior to appointment, as a condition of employment in that State or Union Territory.

Clause (4) of Article 16 permits the State to make any provision of the reservation of appointments or posts in favour of any backward class of citizens, which is its opinion is not adequately represented in the services of the state. The main objective for providing reservations to OBCs in civil posts and services of the government is not just to give jobs to some persons belonging to these communities and thereby increase their representations in the services but to uplift these people socially and educationally and make some place for them in the Society.

"The employment - whether private or public - this, is a means of social levelling and when it is public, is also a means of directly participating in the running of the affairs of the society. A deliberate attempt to secure it to those who were designedly denied the same in the past is an attempt to do social and economic justice to them as crdained by the Preamble of the Constitution." (Justice Sawant in Indira Sawhney V/s Government of India; Supreme Court Judgement para 384)

Two conditions are necessary to attract clause (4) of Article 16: (i) a class of citizens who are backward: and (ii) the said class is not adequately represented in the services under the State. The words "backward class of citizen" occuring in Article 16(4) are neither defined nor explained in the Constitution the word "backward class" occuring in Article 15(4) is qualified by the words "socially and educationally" preceding the words "backward class of citizens"- No qualifying words, however have been used in Article 16(4). The expression "Backward Class of Citizens" used in Article 16(4) - therefore is not the same as the expression "socially and educationally backward classes" used in Article 15(4). The word "Backward Class" in clause (4) of Article 16 are very wide and take in its fold social backwardness economic backwardness, policial backwardness and even physical backwardness. The class of citizens which do not qualify for being called backward in Article 15(4) may fall within the meaning of backward used in clause (4) of Article 16.

To fall within the definition of the term "backwardness" used in Article 16(4), the class/community/caste must be a socially backward class. Educational backwardness however cannot be althogether ignored.

Education is the key to socio-economic advancement so all sections of society must participate in the process of educating themselves for getting government services in proportion to their population.

The sicio-economic upliftment of the educational backwardness can be achieved only through the State Policy of positive discrimination by providing them reservations in educational institutions and government services in proportion to their population. The country cannot be allowed to be the exclusive club of the elitest along. As far as the efficient working of the system is concerned, the special educational and training inputs can be injected into it to make the candidates of the reserved categories proficient.

Now, it has been settle in Indira Sawhney case that backwardness contemplated by Article 16(4) is mainly social

It is well-known fact that till independence, the administrative apparatus was manned almost exclusively by members of the "upper" caste. The Shudras, the Scheduled Castes and Scheduled Tribes and other similar backward social groups among Muslims and Christians had practically no entry into the administrative apparatus. It was this imbalance which was sought to be redressed while providing for reservation in favour of such backward classes........... We are, according, of the opinion that the backwardness contemplated by Article 16(4) is mainly social backwardness."

(Indira SawhneyV/s Government of India; Supreme Court Judgement para 85)

Thus, backwardness under Article 16(4) is social backwardness which leads to educational and economic backwardness.

Article 46 of the Constitution contains a very significant directive to the State. It says promotion of educational and economic interests of SCs, STs and other weaker sections - the State shall promote with special care the educational and economic interests of weaker sections of the people and in particular of SCs and STs and shall protect them from social injustice and all forms of exploitation. It is evident that 'the weaker sections of the people' do include the 'backward class of citizens' contemplated by Article 16(4). Article 15(4) of the Constitution does not speak of 'castes' but speaks of 'classes'. Article 16(4) speaks of inadequate representation in services. Article 340 provided for the appointment of a commission to investigate the conditions of the backward classes and empowers the State to investigate the conditions of the BCs and to help them by grants etc.

The indications given by the above mentioned Articles give some idea of the nature of the backwardness and the categories of classes, whose welfare, the constitution seek to protect and promote.

The contradiction came out just after the commencement of the Constitution in April 1951. In the case of State of

Madras V/s Champakam Dorairajan the Supreme Court Struck down reservations in educational institutions in Madras and by implications barred all preferential treatment outside the areas of government employment, for all groups other than the SCs and backward Hindus confining potential recipients to those who would qualify as the 'backward classes' mentioned in Article 16(4).

Then promptly addition of Clause 4 to Article 15 of the Constitution was made. It reads "Nothing in this Article or in Clause (2) of Article 29 shall prevent the State from making any special provision for the advancement of any socially and educationally backward classes of citizens or for the SCs and STs." Pradhan, H. Prasad (Rise of Kulak Power and Class Struggle in North India, EPW, 17.8.91) is of the view that the purpose of insertion of Clause (4) of Article 15 was not so much based on legal necessity as on political expediency. It was according to Prasad, the starting point of a misguided journey.

Artical 15(4) does not speak of 'castes', but only speaks of 'classes'. If the makers of the constitution intended to take 'castes' also as units of social and educational backwardness, they would have said so as they have said in the case of the SCs and STs. The widest expression 'classes' is used in Clause (4) of Article 15 as there are communities without castes, if the intention was to equate classes with castes nothing prevented the makers of the constitution to use the expression 'Backward Classes or Castes'. The juxtaposition of the expression 'Backward Classes' and 'Scheduled Castes' in Article 15 (4) also leads to a reasonable inference that the expression 'Classes' is not synonymous with 'Castes'.

Justice Havanur argues that Articles 15(4) and 16(4) did not permit new classifications, they only permit specification of the already existing and recognized social classes. Justice Hedge observed class in Article 15(4) as well as in Article 340 denotes a well knit organized section of the society based on status of rank and not any classification made by the State on diverse considerations. Justice Subba Rao - "The expression 'backward class' is an elastic and changing concept. It takes in not only the classes existing before the constitution but also those formed after the Constitution (Report of Jurists' Seminar on Backward Classes, Bangalore, September 1973).

Apart from these extra judicially statements of the member of the judiciary there are also judicial pronouncements. Mysore High Court accepted 'mechanic' as (AIR 1973 Sc 930) the Supreme Court Struck down occupations like agricultural labour, load carrier, old garment seller from the list of SEBC issued by the State Government on the ground that these are not traditional occupations. Accordingly to this judicial pronouncement "a traditional occupation means an occupation followed a the family in which it is handed down by an ancestor to his posterity. Such occupations are generally occupations in which some special skills are necessary like those of an artisan or craftsman." (In case of Sayeed Ahmed V/s State of Mysore, 1969).

While going through these conflicting judicial pronouncement it is difficult to say that in a rapidly changing society with shifting balance of political and ideological considerations the last word has been said in this regard.

In pursuance of the directions of Supreme Court in the Mandal Case, Government of India vide O.M. dated 13.8.1990 introduced reservation of 27% for OBCs. in the civil posts and services under Central Government and public sector undertakings and financial institutions for SEBCs to be filled by direct recruitment w.e.f. 7.8.90. The said O.M. laid down that the SEBCs would comprise in the first phase the castes and communities which are common to both the lists of the report of Mandal Commission and the States Governments' Lists. The Govt. of India subsequently, on its own, also issued Central List for 14 States/UTs. namely, Andhra Pradesh, Assam, Bihar, Goa, Gujarat, Haryana, Himachal Pradesh, Karnataka, Kerala, Madhya Pradesh, Maharashtra, Punjab, Tamil Nadu and Uttar Pradesh which came out with their respective State lists after the Mandal judgement. As a result only 2052 castes/ communities could be included in the Central List of OBCs.

The Supreme Court of India in its landmark judgement dated 16.11.1992. (Judgement Writ Petition (Civil) No. 930 of 1990 - Indira Sawhney and Others V/s Union of India and Others) has directed the Government of India, State Governments and Administration of UTs to constitute a permanent body in the nature of Commission or Tribunal for entertaining, examining and recommending upon requests for inclusion and complaints of over-inclusion and underinclusion in the list of OBCs. Accordingly National Commission for Backward Classes was constituted in 1993. Government of India was also directed to specify the basis applying the relevant and requisite socio-economic criteria to exclude socially advanced persons/sections (creamy layer) from other backward classes so that this become a means of ensuring flow of the benefits of reservation to the really needy people of other backward classes.

The issues of 'criteria for identification of social and educational backwardness, role of caste in determining such backwardness and categorisation of backward classes' has been dealt with by the Supreme Court in the case of Balaji V/s State of Mysore (1963) which states that a class, according to the dictionary meaning shows division of society according to status, rank or caste. In the Hindu social structure, caste unfortunately plays an important part in determining the status of the citizens. Therefore, it may not be irrelevant to consider the caste. It further held that caste, poverty, occupation, place of habitation are some relevant factors for determining backwardness. Sub-classification of backward classes into backward classes and more backward classes is not constitutionally permissible.

In case of Chitralekha V/s State of Mysore (1964) it is stated that classification of backward classes based on economic condition and occupation is permissible; caste cannot be the sole or dominant test; and class cannot be equated to a caste.

In Triloki Nath V/s State of Jammu and Kashmir (1967) the criteria for social and educational backwardness was adopted by the Supreme Court as - BCs is not synonymous with backward castes. Entire caste or community may, however, in the socio-economic and educational spheres and at a given time, be backward and may on that account, be stated as a backward class. This is not because they form a class. For purpose of Article 16(4) in determining whether a section of the class in backward, a test solely based on caste, community, race, religion, sex, descent place of birth or residence, cannot be adopted as it would be unconstitutional.

VII

In pursuance of the direction of the Supreme Court, the Government of India enacted the National Commission for Backward Classes Act, 1993 (Act No. 27 of 1993) and set up a National Commission for Backward Classes at the Centre. Section 9(1) of the Act provides that it shall "examine the Requests for Inclusion of any class of citizens as a backward class in the lists and hear Complaints of Over-Inclusion or Under-Inclusion of any backward class in such lists and tender such advice to the Central Government as it deems appropriate. Under Section 9(2) of the Act, the advice of the Commission shall ordinarily be binding upon the Central Government Section 11 provides for periodic revision of lists by the Central Government as under:-

(1) The Central Government may at any time, and shall, at the expiration of ten years from the coming into force of this Act and every succeeding period of ten years thereafter, undertake revision of the lists with a view to excluding from such lists those classes who have ceased to be backward classes or for including in such lists new backward classes.

(2) The Central Government shall, while undertaking any revision referred to in subsection (1), consult the Commission.

The Commission has evolved a procedure for examination of requests and complaints of under-inclusion and over-inclusion. For this purpose, the Commission devised a set of questionnaire to call for the relevant information from the request-makers as also from the concerned State Government. The questionnaire was divided into two parts containing information in Part-I and Part-II pertaining to general descriptive data about the caste and data on social, educational, economic, representation in services of Central Government, etc. of the caste.

In order to dispose of the genuine cases expeditiously, the Commission has devised a method to divide the castes into "Fast-Track" category. It covers the castes/communities which, in terms of the caste system, identified with traditional crafts or traditional or hereditary occupations considered to be lowly or undignified or unclean or stigmatized. These occupational categories also cover traditional artisanal craftes; fishing; hunting; bird-snaring; agricultural labour on the lands of others; earth work; stone-breaking; salt manufacturing; lime-burning; toddy-tapping; animal rearing; butchery; hair-cutting; washing of clothes; ferrying by boat; scavenging; knife grinding; grain roasting; entertaining through song and dance; acrobatics jugglery; snake-charming; acting; begging or mendicancy. The cases of castes/communities engaged in such occupations were taken on priority basis and the Commission tendered its Advice in respect of these cases as quickly as possible.

The Commission has also laid down guidelines for "Consideration of Requests for Inclusion and Complaints of Under-Inclusion in the Central Lists of OBCs" and "Procedural Clarification on Guidelines". The "Procedural Clarification on Guidelines" comprises list of traditional artisanal crafts which in the opinion of the Commission were to be taken into account while determining the social backwardness of a caste/community on priority basis. Its also states about the speedy disposal of cases of spelling errors in such lists and inclusion of synonyms/sub-castes/different names on priority basis.[8]

VIII

The identification of OBCs in not an easy task as the concept of untouchability was not practiced in the same way in different parts of the country. Thus while the practice of segregation and untouchability was very marked in the peninsula India, it was more diffused in the North. There are certain castes which are considered as untouchables in one province but not in the other. For example, Dhobis are untouchables in Uttar Pradesh but not in Bombay, Dusadh caste is not untouchable in Madhya Pradesh but untouchable in Bihar.

The Hindu society has been broadly classified on varna model or caste stratification into four fold classification of Brahmin, Kshatriya and Sudra. Among Muslims they have grouped them into two — Ajlaf and Altaf, though in strict sense, caste system do not exist among Muslims. There are Christians castes which find place in both religious groups i.e. Hindu and Muslim because certain people profess that particular religion (e.g. Gujjar, Nai, etc.). Similarly for other non-Hindu castes like Sikhs and Christian converts (not included in the category of Scheduled Castes).

The basis of Identification of caste in 'traditional' form which means hierarchical system governed by rules of purity that was elaborated fully during the British period and consolidated under colonialism. It was this 'traditional' castes/ communities identified in India by ethnographers after independence which totally missed or ignored the substantialisation in respect of modern change in the caste system and intentions beliefs about caste system and its understanding in real sense. Though in many parts of rural India process of social change remained very slow during the colonial period and even after independence while in many other parts of India considerable change has occurred and caste in particular has become increasingly unlike the institution described in earlier ethnography. But unfortunately these earlier ethnographic work have become only basis for the identification of castes/communities even today after passing over of almost 100 years. The descriptions of castes given in the earlier ethnographic literature and even by the modern sociologist seem quite different from the existing one. Their objective existence is given by a mass of concrete data that don't depend on the informants.

Almost all the South Indian States had made reservations for the backward classes before independence and these were never identified as poor people or the workers or peasants. They were all classified on the basis of the social caste strata. *Andre Beteille* (1972) describes that the identity was not derived solely or even primarily from common economic experience but from their very nature of the traditional system of stratification to which economic political and ritual factors have contributed in various ways. Caste was considered an autonomous with monolithic institution with either uniformly determinant role or a consistent set of meanings attached to it. He further explains the inequality in the Indian rural context by saying that it cannot be denied that in the traditional system these inequalities were closely related to the inequalities of castes. The caste system contributes to the persistence of these inequalities by providing by values and norms which were appropriate to the agrarian hierarchy. In reality, the backward classes are not classes at all, but aggregates of closed status factor in one's membership of the backward class; rather membership is determined generally by birth.[9]

References

1. Report of the Tamil Nadu Second Backward Classes Commission, 1985, Vol. 1, p.13.
2. Report of the Second Backward Classes Commission, 1980 Part II, p. 67.

3. People of India National series: India's Communities, 1998 Anthropological Survey of India, Oxford University Press, Delhi.

4. Report of the Karnataka Third Backward Classes Commission, 1980, Vol.1.

5. First Backward Classes Commission Report, 1955, Vol. I and II.

6. Report of the Second Backward Classes Commission, 1980, Part-Second, pp. 229-31.

7. Annual Report, 1993-94 and 1994-95, National Commission for Backward Classes, New Delhi.

8. Ibid.

9. Beteille, Andre, 1972. Inequality and Social Change, Oxford, New Delhi.

2

Composition of Other Backward Classes

The first all India effort to recommend reservation for Other Backward Classes (other than Scheduled Castes and Scheduled Tribes) was attempted by Kaka Kalelkar Commission in its report in 1955. A State-wise list of 2399 backward castes/communities for the entire country was prepared and 837 of them were classified as Most Backward. But it was not made clear by the Commission as to how the lists of backward classes were derived by the application of the criteria. Therefore, the Government of India had not accepted the list. Later, a list of 3743 backward castes/communities were prepared by the Mandal Commission in 1980. The list recommended by the Mandal Commission was also not accepted by the Government of India in toto. About 53 percent caste communities i.e. 1990 had been accepted out of 3743 caste/communities recommended by the Mandal Commission on the basis of principal of Commonality. The Government of India evolved a method to make the Central list of OBCs by adopting a principle of Commonality in 1993 as per the direction of the Supreme Court contained in the Mandal case judgement delivered on 16th November, 1992. According to this principle of Commonality, the castes/communities which were commonly found included both in the list recommended by the Mandal Commission for a State as well in the respective State Government's list were included in the Central list for that State. Since at the time of the Supreme Court judgement only 14 States, namely, Andhra Pradesh, Assam, Bihar, Goa, Gujarat, Haryana, Himachal Pradesh, Karnataka, Kerala, Madhya Pradesh, Maharashtra, Punjab, Tamil Nadu and Uttar Pradesh, had their own list of OBCs, the Government of India could prepare the Central lists in respect of only these 14 States in the first-phase, i.e., in 1993. Later on, after other States/Union Territories, namely, Orissa, Rajasthan, West Bengal, Tripura, Pondicherry, Delhi, Jammu and Kashmir, Manipur, Sikkim, Dadra and Nagar Haveli and Daman and Diu, came up with thier own State lists of backward classes, the Government of India issued the Central list of backward classes in respect of four states namely Orissa, Rajasthan, Tripura and West Bengal and 3 UTs i.e. Dadra and Nagar Haveli, Daman and Din and Pondicherry in the second phase in 1994 and in respect of 4 states (Delhi, Jammu and Kashmir, Manipur and Sikkim) in the third phase in 1995. The yearwise and state-wise number of castes/communities included in the Central lists of backward classes is given in Table 2.1.

Table 2.1

Year-wise and state-wise number of castes/ communities found place in the central common list of OBCs.

S.No.	State/Union Territory	1993	1994	1995
1.	Andhra Pradesh	93	-	-
2.	Arunachal Pradesh	-	-	-
3.	Assam	123	-	-
4.	Bihar	122	-	-
5.	Delhi	-	-	51
6.	Goa	3	-	-
7.	Gujarat	79	-	-

8.	Haryana	60	-	-
9.	Himachal Pradesh	48	-	-
10.	Jammu and Kashmir	-	-	20
11.	Karnataka	170	-	-
12.	Kerala	73	-	-
13.	Madhya Pradesh	78	-	-
14.	Maharashtra	209	-	-
15.	Manipur	-	-	4
16.	Meghalaya	-	-	-
17.	Mizoram	-	-	-
18.	Nagaland	-	-	-
19.	Orissa	-	175	-
20.	Punjab	61	-	-
21.	Rajasthan	-	52	-
22.	Sikkim	-	-	7
23.	Tamilnadu	172	-	-
24.	Tripura	-	35	-
25.	Uttar Pradesh	53	-	-
26.	West Bengal	-	14	-
Union Territories				
1.	A. and N. Islands	-	-	-
2.	Chandigarh	-	-	-
3.	Dadra and Nr. Haveli	-	10	-
4.	Daman and Diu	-	19	-
5.	Lakshdweep	-	-	-
6.	Pondicherry	-	259	-
	Total	**1344**	**564**	**82**

As shown in the above table only 1990 caste/ communities could find place in the central common list of OBCs till 1995 that is after 48 years of independence. Central common list in respect of four North-East states namely Arunachal Pradesh, Meghalaya, Mizoram and Nagaland and three UTs i.e. Andaman and Nicobar Island, Chandigarh and Lakshadweep could not be issued because State/UT lists of these State/UTs was not available by this time and Arunachal Pradesh, Nagaland and Lakshadweep also could not find place in the Mandal list. The common list of OBCs in respect of UT Chandigarh was notified on 11th December,1997 thus could not find place in this table. On the other hand the highest number of 259 caste/communities were included in the central list for the Union Territory of Pondicherry which raises doubts whether such large number of caste/communities exist in a small place of Pondicherry. The secrutiny of the list shows that more than 75, 55 and 30 cast/communities of Tamilnadu, Kerala and Andhra Pradesh found place in the list of Pondicherry recommended by the Mandal Commission, respectively.

As could be oberved in the above table the smallest number is three for Goa State e.i. North-East Manipur and Sikkim also had the small number due to more tribal population in both these states. Some states like Uttar Pradesh and Madhya Pradesh with more population but the number of Caste/ Communities in the OBCs lists are less in comparision to Bihar and Maharashtra and States of South India. This difference is mainly due to the number of Caste/Communities was more in the state lists before the Mandal list and almost all the Caste/ Communities of the state lists found place in the Mandal list. As a result of principal of commanility the Caste/Communities found place in the central common list accordingly. It seems that Mandal Commission has recommended the list of caste/ communities for Pondicherry by including more than 150 caste/ communities of boardering states of Kerala, Andhra Pradesh and Tamilnadu. Pondicherry Government also adopted the

Mandal list as it is as a UT list and thus on the basis of commonility all the 259 caste/communities found place in the central list of OBCs for Pondicherry.

Table 2.2

State-wise number of caste/communities appear in the Mandal List, State List and Central List

S. No.	State/Union Territory	Mandal List	State List	Central Common List
1.	Andhra Pradesh	292	95	-
2.	Arunachal Pradesh	-	-	-
3.	Assam	135	126	-
4.	Bihar	168	138	-
5.	Delhi	82	54	-
6.	Goa	18*	9	3
7.	Gujarat	105	127	79
8.	Haryana	76	72	60
9.	Himachal Pradesh	57	57	48
10.	Jammu & Kashmir	63	20	20
11.	Karnataka	333	200	170
12.	Kerala	208	76	73
13.	Madhya Pradesh	279	112	78
14.	Maharashtra	272	355	209
15.	Manipur	49	4	4
16.	Meghalaya	37	-	-
17.	Mizoram	5	-	-
18.	Nagaland	-	-	-
19.	Orissa	244	202	175
20.	Punjab	83	68	61

21.	Rajasthan	140	74	52
22.	Sikkim	10	7	7
23.	Tamilnadu	288	252	172
24.	Tripura	136	42	35
25.	Uttar Pradesh	116	79	53
26.	West Bengal	177	60	14
Union Territories				
1.	A and N Islands	17	-	-
2.	Chandigarh	93	60	54**
3.	Dadra and Nr. Haveli	10	10	10
4.	Daman and Diu	-	19	19
5.	Lakshadweep	-	-	-
6.	Pondicherry	260	260	259

* Figures for Goa, Daman & Diu.

** Figures for Chandigarh added in 1997 in the common central list on the basis of principle of commonality.

As mentioned earlier many caste/communities were not found common in both the list i.e. in Mandal list and State list, therefore did not find place in the central list. One should not think that all these left out caste/communities were socially or educationally advance. As a matter of fact it is difficult to say anything about their social status. But it is clear that Mandal Commission had over included the caste/ communities. Some of these caste/communities were included later in the central list on the recommendations of the NCBC after 1995 and many of them remains only in the Mandal list/ state list. The number of caste/communities which could not find place in the central common list are shown in table 2.3.

Table 2.3

Statewise number of castes/communities of Mandal list and state list not included in the central common list

S.No.	State/Union Territory	Mandal List	State List
1.	Andhra Pradesh	199	2
2.	Arunachal Pradesh	-	-
3.	Assam	12	3
4.	Bihar	46	16
5.	Delhi	31	3
6.	Goa	15	6
7.	Gujarat	26	48
8.	Haryana	16	12
9.	Himachal Pradesh	9	9
10.	Jammu and Kashmir	43	-
11.	Karnataka	163	30
12.	Kerala	132	3
13.	Madhya Pradesh	201	34
14.	Maharashtra	63	146
15.	Manipur	44	-
16.	Meghalaya	37	-
17.	Mizoram	5	-
18.	Nagaland	-	-
19.	Orissa	43	27

20.	Punjab	19	7
21.	Rajasthan	88	22
22.	Sikkim	3	-
23.	Tamilnadu	115	80
24.	Tripura	98	7
25.	Uttar Pradesh	54	26
26.	West Bengal	157	46
Union Territories			
1.	A and N Islands	17	-
2.	Chandigarh	39	6
3.	Dadra and Nr. Haveli	-	-
4.	Daman and Diu	-	-
5.	Lakshadweep	-	-
6.	Pondicherry	1	1

Government of India after issuance of different notifications in the three phases, total of 1990 caste/communities were included in the central list during 1993 to 1995 as shown in Table 2.1, one caste/community i.e. Koch Raj Bangshi of Assam omitted from the central list as the caste/community included in the SC/ST list in 1996. From 1996 onwards till now, Government of India has added 281 more caste/communities in the central list of OBCs. Out of these 281 caste/communities, 54 notified on 12th December, 1997 on the basis of commanility for UT Chandigarh and 235 caste/communities notified for inclusion in the central list of OBCs on the recommendations of the NCBC during 1996 to 2001. Thus with the addition of 235 new caste/communities the central list of OBCs contains 2278 caste/communities for 26 states and six Union Territories upto date complete central list in alphabatic order is at appendix-II.

Table 2.4

Yearwise and statewise number of new caste/communities included in the central list of OBCs on the recommendation of the NCBC

State/Union	1996	1997	1998	1999	2000	2001 (as on 4th Nov.)	Total
Andhra Pradesh	-	-	-	8	3	-	11
Arunachal Pradesh	-	-	-	-	-	-	-
Assam	-	-	-	-	-	-	-
Bihar	1	-	-	4	1	-	6
Delhi	-	-	-	1	1	-	2
Goa	5	-	-	6	1	-	12
Gujarat	1	-	-	12	5	-	18
Haryana	9	-	-	4	1	-	14
Himachal Pradesh	-	-	-	-	2	-	2
Jammu & Kashmir	20	-	-	-	-	1	21
Karnataka	-	-	-	10	4	-	14
Kerala	2	-	-	7	-	-	9
Madhya Pradesh	-	-	-	9	4	-	13
Maharashtra	1	-	-	-	4	1	6
Manipur	-	-	-	-	-	-	-
Meghalaya	-	-	-	-	-	-	-
Mizoram	-	-	-	-	-	-	-
Nagaland	-	-	-	-	-	-	-
Orissa	4	-	-	3	11	-	18
Punjab	-	-	-	4	-	-	4
Rajasthan	-	-	-	8	4	-	12
Sikkim	-	-	-	2	1	-	3
Tamilnadu	1	-	-	6	1	1	9

Tripura	-	-	-	8	-	-	8
Uttar Pradesh	2	3	-	9	7	-	21
West Bengal	12	-	-	17	11	-	40
Union Territories							
A and N Islands	-	-	-	-	-	-	-
Chandigarh	-	-	-	5	-	-	5
Dadra & Nr. Haveli	-	-	-	-	-	-	-
Daman and Diu	-	-	-	-	-	-	-
Lakshadweep	-	-	-	-	-	-	-
Pondicherry	-	-	-	1	1	-	2
Total	**38**	**3**	**-**	**129**	**62**	**3**	**235**

The analysis of the above table 2.4 shows that 41 new caste/communities found place in the central list of OBCs during the three years period i.e. from 1996 to 1998 while 194 caste/communities found place in the central list of OBCs during the three years period i.e. 1999 and 2001. Thus with the addition of these 235 new caste/communities, the central list of OBCs incorporates 2278 caste/communities for 22 states and four UTs as shown in table 2.5.

Table 2.5

Statewise total number of castes/communities appear in the Central List of OBCs

S.No	State/Union Territory	Common List	Included as per NCBC's Advice	Total of (Col. 3&4)
1.	Andhra Pradesh	93	11	104
2.	Arunachal Pradesh	-	-	-
3.	Assam	123*	-	122
4.	Bihar	122	6	127

5.	Delhi	51	2	53
6.	Goa	3	12	15
7.	Gujarat	79	18	97
8.	Haryana	60	14	74
9.	Himachal Pradesh	48	2	50
10.	Jammu & Kashmir	20	1	21
11.	Karnataka	170	14	184
12.	Kerala	73	9	82
13.	Madhya Pradesh	78	13	91
14.	Maharashtra	209	6	215
15.	Manipur	4	-	4
16.	Meghalaya	-	-	-
17.	Mizoram	-	-	-
18.	Nagaland	-	-	-
19.	Orissa	175	18	193
20.	Punjab	61	4	65
21.	Rajasthan	52	12	64
22.	Sikkim	7	3	10
23.	Tamilnadu	172	9	181
24.	Tripura	35	8	43
25.	Uttar Pradesh	53	21	74
26.	West Bengal	14	40	54
Union Territories				
1.	A and N Islands	-	-	-
2.	Chandigarh	54	5	59
3.	Daman and Diu	19	-	19
4.	Dadra & Nagar Haveli	10	-	10
5.	Lakshadweep	-	-	-
6.	Pondicherry	259	2	261
	Total	**2043**	**235**	**2278**

* One caste of Assam is Omitted from the list.

Table 2.6

Caste/communities found place in the Mandal list but not in the State list

Delhi	Kalwar
Goa	Mahar
Gujarat	Mali
Karnataka	Komarpaik
M.P.	Niyyar Scheduled Castes who have embraced Christianity Sodhi
Maharashtra	Kalal, Kalar
Orissa	Kalwar
Punjab	Ramgarhia, Turkhan
Rajasthan	Dhobi (other than those who are included in the SC list)
U.P.	Koshta/Koshti
W.B.	Rayeen (Kunjra) Chamling Kalwar Churihar

Table 2.7

Caste/communities found place in the state list but not in the Mandal list

A.P.	Kasi Kapadi
	Nagaralu
Bihar	Agrahari Vaishya Kamlapuri Vaishya
Goa	Vilip

Gujarat	Mali
	Kalal (Muslim)
	Mahia (Maiya)
	Nadoda Rajput
Haryana	Sain
	Khewat, Mehra, Nishad
Karnataka	Kamma
	24 Mane Telugu Chetty
	Bhandari
	Salaparu
	Siddi
	Croni Chetty, Goniga mane
	Poladavaru
	Golada Konkani
	Koyava
Kerala	Thachan
	Kamsala
	Kannan
	Vettuva Navithan
	Kongu Navithan
	Thechar
	Odde
	Boyan
	Kallan Moopan or Kallan Moopar
M.P.	Pemdi
	Ghoshi
	Nalband
	Raine
	Mirdha
	Koyari
	Nat
	Shakya
	Panika

	Pinjara (Hindu)
	Rajwar
Orissa	Bhanja Puran
	Sangatarash
	Arua
	Hatua
	Baisya-Karan
	Shudra
	Alia
	Raju
	Banka
	Khandayat
	Mahanayak Sudra
	Dalapati Dalua
	Rajasri Balasi/Balasi
Rajasthan	Kansara, Bharawa
	Wazir
	Saini, Bagwan
T.N.	Battu Turkas
	Devagudi ralayari
	Badaga thoraiyar
	Nangudi Vellalar
	Pulavar
Tripura	Kuri
	Shil
	Painak
U.P.	Ror
	RaiSikh
	Jat
W.B.	Dhimal
	Churihar
	Sampang
	Nambang

Table 2.8

Caste Communities found place in the State list but not in the central list

S.No.	State	Caste/Community
1.	Bihar	Agrahari Vaishya Kamlapuri Vaishya
2.	Delhi	Jat
3.	Gujarat	Nadoda Rajput
4.	Haryana	Sain Khewat, Mehra, Nishad
5.	Karnataka	Pole davaru Kamma
6.	M.P.	Pinjara (Hindu) - Raine Koyari/Koiri- Ghoshi
7.	Maharashtra	Billawa Poojari
8.	Orissa	Baisya-Karan Raju Banka Khandayat Mahanayak Sudra Dalapati Dalua Rajasri Balasi/Balasi
9.	Rajasthan	Bishnoi Kayamkhani Jat (other than Dhaulpur and Bharatpur Districts)
10.	U.P.	Jat

Table 2.9

Caste/Communities found place in the central list but not in the State lists

S.No.	State	Caste/Community
1.	Bihar	Bhar Nagar Sukiyar Kulahia Kalwar Dangi
2.	Chandigarh	Bhar, Rajbhar Ramgarhia Gujjar Saini Bhar
3.	Delhi	Arak, Arakvanshiya Kalwar
4.	Goa	Kalaikar Pagui Mahar Shimpi Teli Kumbhar
5.	Gujarat	Rajbhar, Bhar Chhipa
6.	Haryana	RaiSikh Bhar, Rajbhar Salmani Rangrez, Nilgar, Leelgar, Lallari Gramini Jaiswar
7.	Karnataka	Vanniya Vannia Gonnder Padayachi Kander Nairy

8.	Kerala	Makari alias Moovari Saraswat non-Brahmin
9.	M.P.	Pinika Niyargar Gaddi Scheduled castes who have embraced christianity Sodhi Meo-Mewati
10.	Maharashtra	Pahad/Pahadi Kalal, Kalar Kohli
11.	Punjab	Bhar, Rajbhar Saifi Rahbari
12.	Rajasthan	Rangrez, Nilgar Chungar Sakka-Bhishti, Saqqa-Bhishti, Bhishti-Abbasi Mochi (other than those who are included in SCs list) Mansoori Lodh
13.	U.P.	Dohar Kuthaliya Bora Koshta/Koshti Bhar Aheria Atishbaz Bhand
14.	W.B.	Rayeen Chamling Kalwar Rangwa Churihar Jogi

II

Sub-Castes/synonyms: The largest division within the caste is the sub-caste. Sub caste differentiation by occupation is very common. It place subordinate to the caste is shown in the way its name qualifies the caste name. The factors like size of the population, whether migrated or local of a sub-caste make a lot of difference in respect of endogomous and commensal relations with other sub castes of the same caste. Absolutle synonyms or synonyms which are co-terminous, i.e. names where the boundary denoted by one name is exactly the same as the boundary denoted by other names (s) and where one or more of these name (s) is/are included, in the list of OBCs. Synonyms which are used as surnames are included in many cases. In many cases the synonyms are added simply for respectable names such as salmani for Nai (Muslims) who are known as 'Hajjam'. Nai is an occupational term and in view of the stigma and disrespect associated with the term 'Nai' the educated persons of the community adopted the title/surname 'Salmani' just as Julaha, Kasai and Kumahar caste/communities adopted 'Ansari', 'Qureshi' and 'Prajapati' respectively in many states of Northern India. 'Sahu' and 'Rathore' along with Teli. There are castes which have many sub-caste/synonyms. Some of these are given in table 2.10.

Table 2.10

Statewise distribution of sub-caste/synonyms of certain caste/ communities in the central list of OBCs

S.No.	State/Union Territory	
1.	Andhra Pradesh	**Viswabrahmin or Viswakarma**, Ausula or Kamsali, Kammali Kachari, Vadla or Vadrangi and Silpi.
2.	Assam	**Yogi,** Jogi, Jugi Nath

3.	Bihar	Sudi, Halwai, Roniyar, Pansari, Modi, Kasera, Kesarwani, Thathera, Patwa, Sinduriya Baniya, Mathuri - Vaishya, Avadh-Bania, Agrahari - Vaishya.
4.	Delhi	**Badhai**, Barhai, Khati, Tarkhan, Jangra - Brahmin, Vishwa Karma, Ramgarhia, Panchal, Dheeman
5.	Goa	**Nhavi**, Nai, Nabhik, Napit, Mahalo
6.	Gujarat	**Waghari**, Dataniya, Vedu, Talpada, Gamachi, Godadia, Chibhadia, Marada, Wadwa, Vaghari Gamicho, Vedu Churalia, Jhakudia
7.	Haryana	**Chimba or Chhimba**, Chhipi, Chimpa, Darzi, Rohilla
8.	Karnataka	**Nayinda,** Lingayat Nayinda, Nayanaja Kshatriya, Nayanaja Kshatri, Hajjam, Nhavi, Nadig, Ambattan, Mangla, Kelasi, Kshowrad, Kshowrik
9.	Kerala	**Ezhava,** Izhavan, Ishavan, Ezhavan, Ezhuva, Ishuva, Thiyya.
10.	Madhya Pradesh	**Banjara,** Kachiriwala, Laman, Bamania, Mathura, Navi, Jogi, Nayak, Dhuriya
11.	Maharashtra	**Bhoi/Boi,** Zinga, Pardeshi, Raj, Kahar, Gadia, Kahare, Dhuria Kahar, Kirat, Machwa, Manzi, Jatia, Kewat, Dhiwar, Dhivar Bhoi, Dheevar

12.	Orissa	**Hansi,** Tanti, Sukuli, Vina, Tulabhina, Rangani, Dera, Dewanga, Kosta, Salia, Patsalia, Buna, Bunkar, Bangali Tanti, Matibansa Tanti, Asina Tanti
13.	Punjab	**Kachhi,** Kachhi Shakya, Kachhi Maurya, Kachhi Kushwaha
14.	Rajasthan	**Daroga,** Daroga-Rajput, Ravana-Rajput, Hazuhi, Wazir
15.	Sikkim	**Limboo** Tsong, Subba, Yakthungba
16.	Tamil Nadu	**Karuneegar Seer,** Keru-neegar, Srikaruneegar, Sarathi, Kekatti.
17.	Tripura	**Badyakar** Dhuli, Nagarchi, Sabdakar
18.	Uttar Pradesh	**Teli,** Samani, Rogangar, Teli-Malik (Muslim), Teli Sahu, Teli Rathore
19.	West Bengal	**Hela/Halia/Chasi** - Kabartta, Das Kaibartta
20.	Chandigarh	**Aheria**, Aheri, Heri, Naik, Thori or Turi
21.	Pondicherry	**Gound or Gowdi** Machhus, Pal, Paiko Patra or Patara, Sundior) Telli, Tanti, Yerana-gollas, Oriya or Veddy Samantho, Oriya Backward Classes Badhai, Bhokta, Darji, Gour.

Note:

Name of the main caste is in bold and others are sub-caste/synonyms

The scrutiny of the central list of OBCs shows that there are 1786 sub-caste/synonyms which were included time to time. The largest number of Sub-caste/synonyms is included for the State of Karnataka (338) followed by Madhya Pradesh (201). It has to be seen in comparision to the number of new caste for these states included in the central list. As shown in table 2.11.

Table 2.11

Statewise number of main Caste and sub-castes/ synonyms in the central list of OBCs

S.No.	State/Union Territory	New Caste	Sub-caste/ Synonyms
1.	Andhra Pradesh	104	153
2.	Assam	122	25
3.	Bihar	127	44
4.	Delhi	53	52
5.	Goa	15	-
6.	Gujarat	97	132
7.	Haryana	74	45
8.	Himachal Pradesh	50	20
9.	Jammu & Kashmir	21	12
10.	Karnataka	184	338
11.	Kerala	82	66
12.	Madhya Pradesh	91	201
13.	Maharashtra	215	150
14.	Manipur	4	6
15.	Orissa	193	109
16.	Punjab	65	28
17.	Rajasthan	64	46

18.	Sikkim	10	4
19.	Tamilnadu	181	90
20.	Tripura	43	18
21.	Uttar Pradesh	74	47
22.	West Bengal	54	4
Union Territories			
1.	Chandigarh	59	30
2.	Dadra & Nr. Haveli	10	3
3.	Daman & Diu	19	6
4.	Pondicherry	261	157

III

Area Restiction

Many of the caste/communities in the OBC list are resticated to a particular area of the region/state. In other words people of a particular caste/community are considered as backward in a area while the people of the same caste/ communities are not backward in the adjoining area. It can be called Geo-cultural boundaries. Some of the caste/communities which are included in the OBC list on the basis of resticted area are given in table 2.12.

Table 2.12

Distribution of Caste/communities with area restriction

S.No.	State	Caste/Community Restricated Area
1. A.P.	Atirasa	Polavaram, Gopalapuram, Koyyhelagudem, Buttayagudem, Chagallu Mandals of West Godavari Distt. and Devipattanam, Korukonda and Gokavaram

		Mandals of East Godavari District.
	Palinativalivelama	Srikakulam and Vishakhapatanam districts.
	Turupakapu	Srikakulam & Vishakhapatnam districts.
2. Bihar	Gorh	Saran and Rohtas districts
	Khadwar	Sivam and Rohtas districts
	Kurmi (Mahto)	Chhotanagpur district
	Sangatrash	Nawadah district
3. H.P.	Gaddi	in merged area only
	Gujjar or Gujar	in merged area only
4. J & K	Grati	Rural only
	Teeli, Teli	Rural only
5. Karnataka	Kotekshatriya	
	Servgara	South Kanara
	Kotekshatriya	
	Servgara	North Kanara
	Kubra	Coorg district
	Kulavadi Marati	Uttar Kannada district
	Kumbri Maratha	Uttar Kannada district
	Uppina Kolaga	
	Vokkaliga	Rural area only
6. Kerala	Ganjam Reddi	Malabar district
	Kammara	whole Kerala except Malabar district
	Malayekandi	- do -
	Marati	whole Kerala excluding Kasargod Taluk of Malabar district
	Boya	Malabar district
	Reddiar/Reddian	whole Kerala exciuding

		Malabar district
	Vishavan	Malabar district
7. M.P.	Kir	Excluding Bhopal, Raisen and Sehore districts
	Dhobi	Excluding Bhopal, Raisen and Sehore districts
	Kumbhar	Excluding Chhatarpur, Datia, Panna, Tikamgarh, Satna, Rewa, Sidhi and Shahdol districts
	Panika	Except in districts of Chhatarpur, Datia, Panna, Rewa, Satna, Shahdol, Sidhi and Tikamgarh
8. Maharashtra	Kaikadi	Bombay, Thana, Kolaba, Ratangiri, Nashik, Dhule, Jalgaon, Pune, Ahmednagar, Satara, Sangli, Kolhapur, Sholapur, Aurangabad, Nanded districts and Rajura tehsil of Chandrapur district.
	Raghavi	Vidarbha districts
	Thakkar	Ratnagiri district only
	Thelari	Dhulia, Nasik, Jalgaon & Aurangabad districts.
9. Rajasthan	Jat	Whole Rajasthan except in Bharatpur & Dhaulpur district.
10. TamilNadu	Arayar, Arayan,	
	Nulayar	in Kanniya Kumari district and Sheoncottah taluk of Tirunelveli district.
	Alwar, Azhavar	
	and Alavar	in Kanniya Kumari district

	& Sheoncottah Taluk of Tirunelveli district
Aryavathi	- do -
Attur Kilnad	
Koravar	in Saleem, South Arcot, Ramanathapuram Kamarajar and Pusumpon Muthuramadigam districts.
Attur Melnad	
Korvar	in Salem district
Chavalakarar	Kanniya Kumari district and Sheoncottah taluk of Tirunelveli district
Chettu or Chetty	- do -
C.S.I. formerly	
S.I.U.C.	- do -
Dabi Koravar	Thanjavur, Tiruchirapally, Pudkukottai and North Arcot district
Dobba Koravar	Salem district
Eravallar	Except Kanniya Kumari district and Shencottah taluk of Tirunelveli district
Ezhavathy	in Kanniya Kumari district and Sheoncottah taluk of Tirunelveli district
Ezhuthachar	- do -
Ezhuva	- do -
Gandarvakottai	
Korava	in Thanjavur, Tiruchirapally Pudukottai and South Arest district
Inji Koravar	in Thanjavur, Tiruchirapally and Padukottai districts

	Kala Koravar	- do -
	Kalari Kurup	in Kanniya Kumari district and Sheoncottah taluk of Tirunelveli district
	Kalinji Dabi	
	Koravar	in Thanjavur and Pudukottai districts.
	Kannada	
	Saineegar	Coimbatore, Periyar and Nilgiris districts
	Kepmari	in Chengalpattu, Pudukottai and Tiruchirapally districts.
	Kongu	in Coimbatore and Periyar districts.
	Koravar	in Chengalpattu, Ramanathapuram, Kamarajar, Pasumpen Mutouramalingam, Pudukottai, Thanjavur, Tiruchirapalli Tirunelveli, Madras, Madurai and Nilgiris districts.
	Krishnavaka	in Kanniya Kumari district and Sheoncottah taluk of Tirunelveli district
	Kudumbi	- do -
	Latin Catholic	- do -
	Naikkar	- do -
	Nanjil Mudali	- do -
	Odar	- do -
	Paravar	- do -
	Perum Kollar	- do -
	Ponnai Koravar	in North Arcot district
11. U.P.	Kuthaliya Bora	Almora, Pithoragarh, Bageswar and Nainital districts.

	Lakhera	Excluding Lakhera subcaste of Brahmins in Tehri-Garhwal region.
12. Pondicherry	Settibalijas	East and West Godavari district.
	Polinativalma	Srikakulam and Visakhapatnam districts.

The table shows that out of the total 2270 cates/communities of the central list of OBCs, 85 caste/communities are restricted to a particular district/taluk in different 12 States/UTs. The largest number i.e. 31 found in Tamilnadu state. Most of these caste/communities are located in Kanniyakumari, Salem districts and Sheoncottah taluk of Tirunelveli district of Tamilnadu. In Karnataka the caste/communities with resticted areas are in South Kanara and Uttar Kannada, in Kerala Malabar district, in Andhra Pradesh in Srikakulam and Visakhapatnam, East Godavari and West Godavari districts. Majority of these 85 area resticted caste/communities are in the Southern states. The remaining 2185 caste/communities other than resticted are caste/communities are distributed in 21 States and 4 UTs. About 300 caste/communities are found common in more than two states/UTs while about 1900 caste/communities are found in a particular State/UT.

There are caste/communities which are partly included in the SC/ST list and partly in the OBC list as shown in table 2.13.

Table 2.13

OBCs partly appear in SC/ST list

S. No.	State/UT	Name of the OBC	Included in the SC list or ST list
1.	A.P.	Mali	ST
2.	Bihar	Mahtar Muslim	SC
		Mukri(Mukeri)	SC

		Nalband (Muslim)	ST
		Pamaria(Muslim)	SC
3.	Delhi	Babaria	SC
		Bazigar	SC
		Dhinwar	SC
		Dhobi	SC
		Julaha	SC
		Mochi	SC
4.	Gujarat	Bharwad	ST
		Siddi	ST
5.	Haryana	Nat	SC
		Raigar	SC
6.	H.P.	Gujjar	ST
		Julaha, Ansari	SC
7.	J & K	Bhangi (Sweeper)	SC
		Doom	SC
		Shupriwattal	SC
8.	Karnataka	Koteyar	SC
9.	M.P.	Dhobi	SC
		Mirdha	SC
		Nat	SC
		Panika	ST
10.	Punjab	Mochi	SC
		Jullaha	SC
11.	Rajasthan	Dhobi	SC
		Mochi	SC
12.	Tamil Nadu	Eravallar	ST
		Kurumba	ST
13.	U.P.	Dhobi	SC
		Hela, Lalbegi, Nut	SC
14.	West Bengal	Dhobi	SC
		Nat	SC
		Panika	ST

3

Classification: The Caste Factors

It is observed that OBCs included in either state lists or in the central lists are far from uniform in their cultural and social standard. Some of the state governments have classified their respective state lists in different groups on the recommendations of different commissions/committees for Backward Classes appointed for this purpose from time to time. Central lists of OBCs do not have any such classification so far. This issue of classification ot OBCs have become a burning one after formation of a social justice committee under the chairmanship of Sh. Hukum Singh on 28 June, 2001 by the Uttar Pradesh Government. The purpose of classification of OBCs in the state list of Uttar Pradesh is to categorise the Most Backward Classes (MBCs) from the caste/communities listed in the state list of OBCs and apportionment of reservation.[1]

Need for classification of OBCs arises for apportionment of reservation. There may be different opinion on the purpose of classification but it is requird if the genuine OBCs have to get the benefit of the reservation. If the classification is made on a scientific and practical basis which have reference to the prevailing socital conditions and circumstances, it will definitely be favourable to certain sections of the OBCs.

Generally we find different types of classifications of OBCs in the existing state lists but without any scientific basis. One of these can be pointed out that the OBCs divided into three categories as Most Backward, more backward and generally backward. Thus a suitable criteria for classification has to be evolved keeping in view that generally the OBCs are traditionally associated with one or the other occupation which determined their social status. In other words occupation is the determining factor of social status in the Indian society and most of the caste/communities found place in the OBC lists on the basis of their traditional occupation. It is also observed that majority of the castes/communities in the OBC lists are occupational castes and their social position depends on their caste calling. In economic and occupational terms the backward classes by and large, comprise of peasant and artisanal communities and those who provide various traditional services.

It may be pointed out that certain caste/communities are dominating in terms of their share of population. Their consentration and size in a particular region make a lot of difference in determination of their social position.

The factor of commensality also play an important role in determining the social status of caste/communities and also their social relationships.

Certain castes and classes have co-relationship in terms of their socio-economic background, control of resources, political power, etc. can also be taken into consideration while classifying the OBCs.

Several State Government had merged the caste/ communities of a special category that is Ex-criminals, Nomadic and Semi-nomadic Tribes in the list of backward classes and many of the caste/communities also found place in the central list of OBCs.

Before going into the detail of the above mentioned dimensions of classification of OBCs, it is relevant to discuss the classification which is already existed in the state lists. It may help in suggesting a suitable and scientific basis of classification of the OBCs.

1) Classification exist in the state lists

State lists of backward classes on the recommendations of different commissions/committees have been categorised the castes/communities into the different groups. Some of the state governments has done it as in Bihar, Tamilnadu, Andhra Pradesh, Karnataka, Maharashtra and Haryana. State list of Andhra Pradesh is divided in four groups A, B, C, and D. Karnataka state list is divided into five categories as category I, category II (a), category II (b), category III (a) and category III (b). Maharashtra state list is divided in four categories i.e. Denotified, Nomadic, Backward Classes and a category of special castes. caste/communities in Haryana state list are distributed as block A and block B.

Another division we find in the state lists of Assam and Madhya Pradesh. In Assam state list 94 caste/communities of tea garden laboures separated from other 27 caste/communities while Teli caste is found common in both the sub categories. Twenty six muslim communities are kept under Islamic group and 86 caste/communities who profess Hindu religion are kept in other group in the state list of Madhya Pradesh.

Table 3.1

Statewise distribuion of number of caste/communities of different categories

S.No.	State/UT	Category	No. of caste/ communities covered
1.	Andhra Pradesh	Group A (Aboriginal tribes, Vimukta Jatis Nomadic and Semi-nomadic tribes)	40
		Group B (Vocational)	21
		Grouop C (Harijan converts)	1
		Group D (Other classes)	33

2.	Assam	I (OBC)	119
		II (More OBC)	7
3.	Bihar	I Most Backward	105
		II Backward	33
4.	Haryana	Block A	67
		Block B	5
5.	Karnataka	Category I	89
		Category II (a)	101
		Category II (b)	1
		Category III (a)	3
		Category III (b)	6
6.	Maharashtra	BCs	307
		Special BCs	5
		Nomadic	13
		Semi-Nomadic	30
7.	M.P.	Islamic Group	26
		Other BCs	86
8.	Tamil Nadu	BCs	143
		MBCs	41
		Denotified tribes	68
9.	U.P.	I Specific benefits in govt. jobs	15
		II Only for educational facilities	59

Categorisation of OBCs and apportionment of reservation

Some of the commissions/committees appointed by the different state Governments have reccomended to make categories of OBCs and also suggested percentage of reservation for them.

Sh. Manohar Pershad Commission (1970) for Andhra Pradesh identified four categories of OBCs and recommended 30% reservation for them in education institutions and Government services as under:

(i)	Aboriginal Tribes - Vimukta Jatis, Nomadic and Semi-Nomadic tribes	7%
(ii)	Vocational groups	13%
(iii)	Harijan convents	1%
(iv)	Other classes	9%

L.G. Havanur Commission (1975) for Karnataka recommended 32% reservation (Backward Communities- 16%, Backward Castes-10% and Backward Tribes-6%) of vacancies in government services and reservation of seats in educational institutions for OBCs Government of Karnataka has accepted the recommendations of the commission and added a new category of backward classes i.e. 'Special group' and made a reservation of 15% for this category. The commission had recommended 16% reservation in government services, the State Government enhanced it to 18%.[2]

Mungeri Lal Commission (1976) for Bihar recommended 23% of jobs including 3% for women. It also recommended 24% seats to be reserved in engineering, medical and other professional institutions for the OBC candidates.[3]

On the basis of these recommendations Karpoori Thakur Government introduced a revised reservation formula in 1978 which is known as Karpoori formula or Bihar formula. As per this formula, instead of providing 26% reservations to all BCs taken together, as initially envisaged, it was decided to provide 12% reservaiton to exceptionally backward classes, 8% to the other backward castes, 3% for women and another 3% for economically weaker sections of the upper castes.[4]

A.R. Bakshi Commission (1976) for Gujarat recommended (i) 10% seats for the category in medical, engineering and other professional institutions (ii) 10% vacancies in all class III and class IV Government services (iii) 5% of vacancies in class I and class II services in all Govt. services, local bodies, state public undertakings, etc. (iv) 10% seats in training cum production centres, and (v) scholarship and other educational facilities to OBCs students provided their family income did not exceed Rs. 4800/- per year, this limit revised to Rs. 7200 for nomadic tribes.[5]

Justice G. Kumara Pillai Commission (1965) for Kerala recommended the distribution of 25% reservation percentage among five categories as 9% to Ezhavas, 8% to Muslims, 2% to Latin Catholics, 1% to other backward Christians, 5% to Hindus.[6]

Ramji Mahajan Commission (1983) for Madhya Pradesh recommended (i) twenty five muslim communities under Muslim religious group as OBCs (ii) 35% reservation in state services and services under the state run and in the institutions getting grant in aid from the state government (iii) concessions available to SCs and STs for admission in universities for OBCs to the same extent.[7]

Gurnam Singh Commission (1990) for Haryana suggested reservation of 26% in class I and II and 14% in class III and IV job for BCs. Besides 5% of all classes of jobs reserved for economically BCs among forward classes. In addition, recommended 2% in class I and II and 1% in class III and IV jobs for Meos, treating it as a special group of its own kind.[8]

A.N. Sattanathan Commission (1970) for Tamil Nadu recommended 33% reservation in state government service for OBC candidates.[9]

B.D. Deshmukh Commission (1964) for Maharashtra recommended 34% reservation in Government jobs and educational institutions and distributed it into four categories:

(i) 13% for SCs and SCs converted to Buddhism,(ii) 7% to STs, (iii) 4% to Denotified and Nomadic tribes and (iv) 10% to Other Backward Classes.[10]

Justice Indra Sen Israni Commission (1993-98) recommended 21% reservation in service for Rajasthan.[11]

Dr. Adarsh S. Anand Committee for Jammu and Kashmir (1977) recommended 42% reservation in Government jobs, technical and professional institutions for OBCs.[12]

Sh. Chhedi Lal Sathi Commission (1977) for Uttar Pradesh recommended 15 castes for specific benefits in Government jobs and 59 castes only for educational facilities.

The commission has classified the Backward Classes into three groups and recommended 29.5% reservation in government services as under:

A. (Landless labourers, unskilled workers, non-artisans and domestic servants) 17%

B. (Marginal and small cultivators)

C. Muslim Backward Classes.[13]

Recommendations of the State Commission of OBCs for Rajasthan

State Commission of Backward Classes, under the Chairmanship of Shri R.N. Verma (2001) Rajasthan has recommended that all the 74 caste/communities appear in state list of OBCs for Rajasthan should be divided into 3 categories i.e. category A, B and C.

The following 27 peasant caste/communities are kept in category A and reservation percentage is suggested 6% out of total reservation of OBCs 21% for this category:

Jat, Ahir (Yadav), Charan, Dhakad, Gujar (Gurjar), Kalal (Tak) Kajvi, Patel, Kalvi, Patidar, Anjana, Dangi Patel, Kulmi, Mali, Saini, Bagwan, Bishnoi, Meo, Kyamkhani, Swarnkar Sunar, Soni, Janva, Khegardia, Sirvi, Sondhia and Gaddi.

Category B (Artisanal castes) 7% reservation– Badwa, Jachak, Bhat, Jaga, Rao, Badhai, Khati, Jangid, Tarkhan, Suthar, Darji, Ghanchi, Teli, Kumhar (Parjapati), Snara, Kumavat, Bhavsar, Chippa (Chippi), Khatti Chhipa, Rangrej, Nama, Neelgar, Dhiwar, Kahar, Sagarvanshi, Mali, Keet, Mehra, Mallaha (Nishad) Odu, Patwa, Raika, Rewari, Devasi, Thathera, Rawat, Satia, Sindhi, Gadit, Nagauri, Silawat, Cheyjara, Lodhy, Tanwar, Tamoli, Dhangi, Raisikh, Bari, Bhisti, Machnera, Lakhera (Lakhera), Kachera, Manihar, Lodhi (Lodha), Luhar Panchal, Mer, Mehrat, Cheeta, Kathat and Nai.

Category C (Most Backward) 8% reservation :- Banjara, Bhadbhuja, Dakaut, Nagarchi, Bagaria, Daroga, Rawana Rajput, Gadia Luhar, Giri, Gusai, Hela, Lulaha, Jogi, Nath, Sidh, Kachhi, Kandera, Pinjara, Mogira, Mirashi, Swami, Bairagi, Sadh, Sikligar, Usta, Halali, Kasai, Dhobi (Muslim), *Sapera, Bajigar, Nat, Mochi* (non Hindu), Multani and Sindhi (Muslim). Orphan children are also kept in this category.[14]

Recommendation of the committee on Social Justice in Uttar Pradesh

The Social Justice Committee was formed on 28th June, 2001 under the Chairmanship of Sh. Hukum Singh and given its report in two months with the objective of regrouping the caste/communities within the reservation category in Uttar Pradesh.

The report has suggested regrouping of 79 caste/communities found place in the state list of OBCs for Uttar Pradesh.

Some of the other findings of the Social Justice Committee's are:

(i) OBCs form 54.05 percent of the total population of Uttar Pradesh.

(ii) Share in reservation of 'Yadav'; 'Kurmi' and 'Jat' caste/communities have 19.40%, 7.46% and 3.60% population among the OBCs respectively.

(iii) There are two prominant caste/communities i.e. 'Yadav' and 'Kurmi' have grabbed nearly 44 percent seats in higher education, 39 percent in technical education and 43 percent in medical education.

(iv) Reservation quota for OBCs in government jobs and admission in educational institutions should be increased from 27% to 28%. Regrouping of 79 caste/ communities of the OBC state list and distribution of reservation percentage to them according to their population is recommended as under:

Category	No. of Caste	% of Population	% of Reservation
A. (Backward Caste	1	19.40	5
B. More Backward Caste	8	18.91	9
C. The Most Backward Caste	70	61.69	14
(Including 22 Muslim communities)			

(v) Categorywise distribution of castes as recommended by the committee is given below:

Group A (backward caste):	Ahir/Yadav
Group B (more backward castes):	Gosai, Gujar, Jat, Lodhi, Kurmi, Kamboj, Giri and Mallaha
Group C (the most backward):	All 70 in the exitised state list of OBC for U.P. other than those 9 mention above.[15]

State list of OBCs is at appendix-I.

Table 3.2

Percentage of reservation to OBCs in the state services

Sl. No.	State/UTs	Percentage of Reservation: As suggested by the respective commissions	Presently Applicable
1.	Andhra Pradesh	30	25
2.	Assam	–	–
3.	Arunachal Pradesh	–	–
4.	Bihar	23	26
5.	Delhi	27	27
6.	Goa	–	–
7.	Gujarat	–	–
8.	Haryana	–	–
9.	Himachal Pradesh	–	–
10.	Jammu and Kashmir	–	–
11.	Karnataka	32	48
12.	Kerala	25	40
13.	Madhya Pradesh	35	14
14.	Maharashtra	34	32
15.	Manipur	–	–
16.	Meghalaya	–	–
17.	Mizoram	–	–
18.	Nagaland	–	–
19.	Orissa	12	12
20.	Punjab	–	–
21.	Rajasthan	21	21
22.	Sikkim	–	–
23.	Tamilnadu	33	50
24.	Tripura	–	–
25.	Uttar Pradesh	27	27
26.	West Bengal	–	–
II) U.Ts			
1.	Andaman and Nicobar	–	–
2.	Chandigarh	–	–
3.	Dadar and Nagar Haveli	–	–
4.	Daman and Diu	–	–
5.	Lakshwadeep	–	–
6.	Pondicherry	–	–

State Governments are providing facilities to OBCs on the recommendations of it respective commissions such as reservation of jobs in state services, seats in educational institutions, financial assistance, coaching facilities, stipened to student of OBCs. The percentage of reservation for OBCs in the state services vary from state to state while it is 27% percent in the central government services. The reservation provided to SC (15%) ST (7.5%) and OBCs (27%) put together shall not exceed 50% as per the directions of the supreme court.

But, it can be seen in the above table that Karnataka, Kerala, Maharashtra, Tamilnadu have reserved more than 27%. In Tamilnadu, it is 50% for OBCs and 18% for SCs and STs. Karnataka has reserved 48% in addition to 18% for SCs and STs.

Categorization of OBCs for central list

A. **Kaka Kalelkar Commission (1955)** had recommended following nine categories of communities included under the OBCs:

i. Nomadic Communities

ii. Agricultural and landless labourers

iii. Insecure tenants

iv. Small landowness with uneconomic holdings

v. Cattle and sheep breeders and small scale fishing communities.

vi. Artisan and occupational classes without security of employment.

vii. Communities, where the majority of people did not have sufficie education and were, therefore, unable to secure adequate representation in government services.

viii. Social groups from among the Muslims, Christians and Sikhs who are still backward socially and educationally; and

ix. Communities occupying low position in social hierarchy.[16]

B. Mandal Commission has not made any category of OBCs but we find mention of two categories i.e. intermediate backward classes and depressed backward classes in the descent note of Sh. L.R. Naik, one of the members of the Mandal Commission. According to Shri. Naik the intermediate Backward Classes are those whose traditional occupation had been agriculture, market gardening, beatle-leaves growers, pastoral activities, village industries like artisans, tailors, dyers and weavers, petty business cum agricultural activities, heralding, temple service, toddy selling, oil mongering, combating, astrology, etc.

The depressed backward classes according to him are ex-criminal tribes, nomadic and wandering tribes, earth diggers, fishermen, boatmen and palanquin bearers, saltmakers, washermen, shepherds, barbers, scavangers, basket makers, furriers and tanners, landless agricultural labourers, watchmen, toddy tappers, camel -hardsmen, pigkeepers, packbullock carriers, collectors forest produce, hunters and fowlers, corn parchers, premitive tribes (not specified as Scheduled Tribes), exterior classes (not specified as Scheduled Castes), and begging communities, etc.[17]

No. clear cut categorisation is made by Government of India in the central list neither it is suggested by the commission. We find a categorization of caste/ communities in the central list for Assam and Madhya Pradesh. Ninety six castes/ communities are listed under the category of 'Tea garden labourers, Tea garden tribes, Ex tea garden labourers and Ex tea garden tribes' in the central list for Assam state. Twenty seven caste/communities belonging to occupational castes are listed under 'Islamic Groups in the central list for Madhya Pradesh. As the categorisation reflects in the common central list in case of Assam (Tea garden labours) and Madhya Pradesh (Islamic group) came automatically on the basis of principal of commanality.

Categorisation of caste/communities as reflected in the Ethnographic Literature

J.C. Nesfield (1916) puts farword the view that the whole basis of the caste system is the division of occupations and that the social gradation of castes corresponds precisely to the different periods of civilisation during which their traditional occupations. Thus the lowest castes are those allied to the primitive occupation of hunting. Pasi, Bhar, Bahelia because the pursuit of wild animals was the earlies stage in the development of human industry. Next above these come the fishing castes, fishing being considered somewhat superior to hunting, because water is a more sacred element among Hindus than land, and there is less apparent cruelty in the capturing of fish than the slaughtering of animals, these are the Kahars, Kewats, Dhimars and others. Above these comes the pastoral castes and above them the agricultural castes.

Similarly, the artisan castes are divided into two main groups; the lower one consists of those whose occupations preceded the age of metallurgy, as the Chamars and Mochis or Tanners, Koris or Weavers, the Telis or Oil-Pressers, Kalars or liquor-distillers, Kumhars or Potters and Lunias or salt-makers. The higher group includes those castes whose occupations were coeval with the age of metallurgy that is those who work in stone wood and metals, and who make clothing and ornaments, as the Barhai or worker in wood, the Lohar or worker in iron, the Kasera and Thathera, Brassmakers and the Sunar or worker in the precious metals ranking preciously in this order of precedence the Sunar being the highest.[18]

References

1. Yadav, Yogender, 2001, 'Prahsan Aur Trasdi Key Beech Arkshan Kee Rajneeti', *Hindustan Daily*, 6th September, 2001.

2. Report of the Karnataka Third Backward Classes Commission, 1975.

3. Report of the State Backward Classes Commission, Bihar, 1976.

4. Adhyapak, Gajey Singh, 1999 'Karpoori Formuley Ko Bhool Gayey, *Hindustan Daily*, 31st March, 1999.

5. Report of the Backward Classes Commission, for Gujarat, 1976.

6. Report of the Kerala State Backward Classes Commission, 1965.

7. Pichhda Varg Ayog Prativedan, Madhya Pradesh State, 1983.

8. Report of the Haryana State Backward Classes Commission, 1990.

9. Report of the Third Backward Classes Commission for Tamilnadu, 1970.

10. Report of the Maharashtra State Backward Classes Commission, 1964.

11. Report of the Rajasthan Backward Classes Commission, 1993-98.

12. Report of Dr. Adarsh S. Anand Committee on Backward Classes for Jammu and Kashmir, 1977.

13. Sarvadhik Pichhda Varg Ayog Kee Report, Uttar Pradesh, 1977.

14. Lakshkar Jagriti, 2001, 'Anya Pichhda Varg Ayog Kee Sifarish: Pichhda Varg Koo Teen Shrenio Mein Banta'- A Report; Ank 10, Year 22, Month August, Niwai, Tonk, Rajasthan.

15. A Messiah for the Most Backwards and Most Dalits: A Report, *The Indian Express,* New Delhi, 28th September, 2001.

16. Report of the First Backward Classes Commission (Kaka Kalelkar), 1955.

17. Minute of dissent by Sh. L.R.Naik, Member of the Second Backward Classes Commission, Report of the Mandal Commission, Part second Vol. VIII, 1980, PP. 229-231.

18. Nesfield J.C.; 1916, *Brief sketch for the caste system in the North-Western Provinces and Oudh.*Allahabad.

4

Anthropological Perspective on OBCs

Several state governments had merged the caste/communities of this special categories in the Backward Classes (SCs, STs and OBCs) mainly the untouchable caste/communities found place in the scheduled caste list and those who lived in the forest areas were included in the Scheduled Tribes list and those left over from inclusion in the SC and ST lists have been included in the state lists as well as central list of OBCs as shown in table 4.1.

Table 4.1

Statewise distribution of Denotified Nomadic and Semi-Nomadic caste/communities

State/UT	Denotified tribe	Nomadic and Semi-Nomadic
A.P.		Balasanthu Vearmushti
	Kaikadi	(Nettikotala)
	Kepmari or	Budabukkala Kasikapadi
	Reddika	Budabukkala Kasikapadi
		Dasari
	Kinthala Kalinga	Dommara
	Korcha	Gangiredlavaru

		Mondepatta	Jakkala
	Mudiraj	Jangam	
	Pardhi	Joshinandiwala	
	Rajaka	Jogi	
	Valmiki	Mandula	
	Kanjar	Mondivaru	
		Nakkala	
		Pamula	
		Peddammavandlu	
		Vamsa Raj	
		Yadava (Golla)	
Assam	Dandsi	Bhumji	
		Beldar	
Bihar		Gulgaliya	
		Kumarbhag Pahadia	
		Beldar	
		Bind	
		Dafali (Muslim)	
		Dhankar	
		Gandarbh	
		Kapadia	
		Khelta	
		Nat (Muslim)	
		Pamaria (Muslim)	
		Sayee (Muslim)	
Delhi	Bauria/Bawria	Pakhimara	
		Badi	
		Agri	

		Naqqal
		Bairagi
Goa		Dhangar
		Kalaikar
		Nath Jogi
Haryana	Kanjar or Kanchan	Bairagi
		Barwar Singhikant
		Faquir
		Jogi
		Madari
		Nat
Gujarat	Waghari	Raval-Ravalia Shrawan
	Bavrior Baori	Nat Targala
	Hingora Muslim	Shikligar Vadi
	Kathi	Pakhali Vahivancha Charan
		Dafer (Hindu & Muslim)
		Gola Rana
		Fakir/Faquir (Muslim)
		Madari
		Sarania
		Sargara
H.P.	Kanjar	Ard Pop, Gadaria
	Beda	Aheri or Ahori, Gawaria
		Bata
		Bairagi
		Changar
		Faquir
		Labana
		Madari

J&K	Sansi	Bhand
		Doom
Sikkim		Tamang
Karnataka	Chhaparband	Bairagi, Kasikapadi, Katabar
	Bedaru	Nandiwala, Nairy, Kothati Kalhatgi, Masanyogi Bajania, Nayadi, Shikkaligar, Dholi, Sarania, Vaidu Durgamurga, Takankar, Vasudev, Ghisadi, Vadi, Gondali, Knajari, Helava, Golla, Katabu, Bazigar, Kudubi, Kanisan,
		Masaniayogi, Lonari
Kerala	Moravan	Pulluvan, Jangam Veerasaiva Maruthuvar Kottar Chettier Poopandaram/ Maalapandaram
M.P.	Mankar Panika	Bairagi Banjara Garpagari Banjara (Muslim) Nat Lonia Tarha Vasudev Sikligar
Maharashtra	Berad/Bedar	Beldar, Yerukula Thakkar

	Bester	Bhand, Singiwala
	Bhamta	Nonia, Pangui
	Bharadi	Bhute, Raval
	Kaikadi	Bhuttal, Sikkalwar
	Rajput Bhamta	Chitrakathi, Thakkar
	Ramoshi	Dawari/Davari
	Vaghari	(in Ratnagiri District only)
	Chhapparband	Garudi/ Gavadi, Vaidu
	(including	Ghisadi, Lohar, Vasudeo
	Muslim)	Golla, Bajania
	Gopal	Gopal, Bajigar
		Helve, Basdeva/
		Vasudev, Jogi, Depala
		Joshi, Fakir, Bhandarwala
		Kasikapadi, Gondhali
		Katabu, Gondhali
		Kalhati, Kanghera
		Mairal, Karbi
		Nandiwale, Katabu
		Sarania, Sahis
Orissa	Kanjar	Bairagi, Nayadi
		Koravar, Kudubi
		Matangi, Toda
		Yerukula
Punjab	Kanjar	Bairagi, Barwar
		Singhikant
Rajasthan	Baladia	Banjara
	Mogia (Mogya)	Gadia-Lohar, Jogi
		Raika, Sikligar, Cdd

T.N.	Battu Turkas	Chakkala, Dommara (including Dom & Dommar)
	Devagudi Talayari	Jangam, Yerukula
	Kallar	Dasari
	Valmiki	Koravar
	Kepmari	Nari Koravar
	Korcha	Oddar
		Andi Pandaram
Tripura		Bhumji
Uttar		Bairagi, Naqqal
Pradesh		Madari, Aheria/Aheriya
		Banjara, Bhand
		Fakir
West Bengal		Goala
		Fakir, Tamang, Jogi, Yogi
Pondicherry	Kallar Kaikadi	Irulas, Maruthuvar
	Valmiki	Nakkala, Nakkala
	Korcha	Andi Pandaram, Yerukula, Helva
Chandigarh	Kanjar	Barwar, Bairagi, Fakir
		Singhikant
Daman & Diu		Dhangar

In this section we shall discuss about the caste/ communities of this category which were considered socially and educationally backward and found place in the OBCs lists.

A. De-notified or Vimukta Jati

Long before the British predatory tribes like Thugs and Pindaries were used to be active in the country. They used to commit highway robberies. The first criminal tribes act was passed in 1871 and was introduced in Sind, a part of then Bombay Presidency. The act was further amended in 1911 and was extended to the whole of Bombay Province, and finally the All India Criminal Tribes Act came into force in 1924 and was made applicable to the whole of British India. The number of these criminal tribes was reached up to 180 in 1924. After independence in 1949 Government of Bombay repealed the Criminal Tribes Act, 1924 in its application to the Bombay state with effect from 13th August, 1949 with the intension that no man should be treated as criminal by birth and also to give the Ex-criminal tribes the status and dignity of the citizens of free India. In 1952 the Criminal Tribes Act was, rescinded by the Government of India and these tribes are called Denotified Communities.

More than 50 castes/communities of this category had already been included in the central list of OBCs. A brief account of some of the castes/communities to understand the common characterstics and traits is explained as under:

Sansi

'Sansi' is included in the central list for Jammu and Kashmir. The Sansis were 59, 073 in 1961. They claim Rajput descent. According to Sher Singh Sher (1965) they were expelled from Rajasthan by Muslim invaders in the 13th century. They migrated to the Punjab and other regions for their livelihood as shepherds, field-hands and genealogists of the land-owning Jats. Parts of the caste are settled in the north and earn a living by cultivation or field labour, another part is still a wandering tribe, with no steady habitat. Socially the Sansis are organised into various endogamous sub section which in turn are split into exogamous clans and hundreds of sub-clans. The Sansis profess a religion which is basically Hindu, but it is of the most simple type. A few Sansis have been converted to Islam, more have become Sikhs, but one large section asserts its Rajput origin and keeps aloof from the rest of the tribe.[1]

Chhaparband

Caste/community is included in the central list of OBCs as 'Chhaparband, Chapparbanada (Muslim)' for Karnataka and as 'Chhapparband (including Muslim)' for Maharashtra. According to Misra (1964) the caste originally from the Punjab, but at present settled and operating in many parts of India, also known as Fakir Coiners. They are specialist in forgery. Many people of this caste have settled down in Bijapur district, but travel all over India. They are Sheikh Muslims, and ostensibly live by begging. But some have taken to cultivation and a few earn their living as village watchmen. Though traditionally manufactures of counterfeit coins, they are not great adepts in this craft and are able to pass on their crude product only to the more backward and simple villagers.[2]

Ramoshi

'Ramoshi' caste is included in the central list of OBCs for the state of Maharashtra. Ramoshis belong to the Denotified castes. They were famous for house-breaking and robbery. Their present occupation is that of village watchmen and cowherds. According to Fuchs (1981), in pre-British times they occupied the hill-forts from which they carried out their depredations. This was the manner how to recover their wages. The Ramoshis do not consider themselves as low castes. They are served by Brahmins, while many Ramoshish are untouchables. They are Hindus and bury their dead persons.[3]

Waghari

The caste is found place in the central OBCs for Gujarat state as Waghari, Dataniya Waghari, Wedu Waghari, Talpada Waghari, Gamachi Waghari, Gadadia Waghari, Chiphadia Waghari, Marada or Marwada Waghari, Wadwa Waghari, Vaghari Gamicho, Vedu Churalia, Jhakudia (where they are not STs). According to Shah (1967), the Waghris of Gujarat (109, 583 in Gujarat altogether over 200,000) obviously identical with the Baghris of or Bagdis of Central India, claim kinship with the Sansis of the Punjab. According to Fuchs (1967), this may be correct for they are very similar to the Sansis in physical appearance though their racial stock is somewhat changed by an admixture of local blood. They came to Gujarat via Rajasthan. From Gujarat they later spread over central India and northern Deccan. Though adopting everywhere the local languages, they have retained remnants of Gujarati in their present forms of speech. They are sub-divided according to their various main occupations, and where they are numerous, are also divided according to areas. These sections are endogamous. They are still keen hunters and bird - snarers. They also keep fowls and rent fruit trees and other productive trees by the year, selling the crop. Several sub-sections, like the Kankapdias and Talabdas, have taken to cultivation. Other are Cattle dealers, sellers of stick brushes for cleaning the teeth (Datania) or drummers during the wedding season. They have their own priests or clan-elders (bhuvas) who perform all ceremonies for them and regulate their social affairs.[4]

Gopal

'Gopal' caste found place in the central list for OBCs for the state of Maharashtra as 'Gopal, Gopal Bhorpi, Khelkari'. 'Gopal' is the main caste and 'Gopal Bhorpi' and Khelkari are the sub-castes. This caste is found in Southern Central India and Berar. The caste is a small vagrant caste and has a criminal reputation. The caste is also known as 'Borekar'. The Gopals claim to be the descendants of the cowherds of Vrindavan. Barekar is a mat-maker. Whatever their pretensions as to their descent, the Gopals are apparently recruited from children offered to the gods by Maratha Kunbis, Dhangars, Kasars, Sonars, Salis, Banjaras and even Mahars. Though originally consecrated to the Gods, they are now untouchables and their very touch is polluting. The reason of their social degradation is probably their caste mixture. They earn their living by acrobating feats with bamboos, by begging and as cowherds and daily labourers. They are Hindus but their priests are the caste elders, not any Brahmins.

Dandasi

'Dandasi' caste is included in the central list for OBCs for Assam under the category of 'Tea Garden Labourers, Tea Garden Tribes, Ex-Tea Garden Kabourers and Ex-Tea Garden Tribes'. The concentration of the caste is in Ganjam District of Orissa. Robbery and theft are their traditional caste occupations. They derive their livelihood from robbery and theft from the belief that they helped the Pandava brothers to escape from the lac fort in which their enemies wanted to burn them by digging an underground possage. Or they claim to be descendants of Dhuthika, the handmaid of Radha with whom Krishna had an illicit affair. Many Dandasis in Ganjam district are village watchman.

Kallar

'Kallar' is listed in the central list of OBCs for Tamilnadu state as well for UT Pondichery. Sub-castes of 'Kallar' i.e. Esanattu Kallar, Gandarvakottai Kallar, Koottappal Kallar, Pirampati Kallar and Periasooriyar Kallar are also included in the central list for OBCs for Tamilnadu.

Kallar means thieves. According to Fuchs (1981), their number surpases half a million. They live South of the Kaveri river and east of the western Ghats; their strong concentration is in Tanjore and Madurai districts. They consider themselves Shudras. It is quite possible that the Kallar are not a homogeneous caste, but more a conglomeration of individuals of different castes. They were formerly soldiers who with the cessation of the wars were disbanded and had to find other employment. At present they are farmers and lead a fairly sedentary life. Some of them act as watchmen and carry paddy from village to village for sale as secondary occupations. They are Hindus.[5]

Maravan

'Maravan' is included in the central list for OBCs for Kerala state. The Maravans found in Madurai and Tirunevelly districts of Tamilnadu, resemble the Kallar much in their habits and origin. They are now settled cultivators but in former times known for their warlike disposition. They have a long military tradition. After they lost their employment as soldiers, they took to cattle lifting, robbery and other criminal pursuits, while the majority were able to acquire land for cultivation. Some of the leaders even became feudal chiefs and small Rajas. Since, many are land owners and some even landlords such affuency assured them a fairly good social status in south Indian village life.

Panika

Panika is notified as OBC with area restriction in the central list of OBCs for Madhya Pradesh as 'Panika (except in Districts of Chhatarpur, Datia, Panna, Rewa, Satna, Shahdol, Sidhi and Tikamgarh where it is included in Scheduled Tribes list).' The caste is also included in the central list of OBCs for Assam and Karnataka states. The people of Panika community used to fetch water for the villagers, and thereby named Panika. They are traditionally engaged in weaving. The Panika are reported from Madhya Pradesh and Tripura. In Madhya Pradesh the Panika are also notified as a scheduled tribe. Their population in the areas where they are included in the list of scheduled tribes of Madhya Pradesh is 52,979 (1981 census). They are Hindu by religion. The Panika are mostly village watchman. Now a few have acquired land which they cultivate and work as agriculture labourers. The 1981 census returnes shows that only 9.59 percent of the Panika are literate.

Mankar

'Mankar' found place in the central list of OBCs for Madhya Pradesh. According to Russell and Hiralal (1916)

Mankar is the name of a superior class of village watchman in Nimar district, a sub caste of Joshi and a section of Mana and Halba. The title Mankar etymologically signifies their famous acts or fame. They are migrants from Gujarat and are concentrated in Rampura, Kalasura and Barodia villages of the Depalpur tehsil of Indore district in Madhya Pradesh. The main occupation is agriculture and agricultural wage-labour. They are Hindu by faith. They do not accept water from the Balai though the Balai accept water and cooked food from the Mankar.

Kanjar

'Kanjar' is included in the central list of OBCs for Andhra Pradesh, Orissa, Haryana, Himachal Pradesh, Punjab and Chandigarh, Karnataka. Kanjar were a nomadic criminal tribe prior to Independence. According to crook (1896), the name of the community has been derived from Sanskrit Kanana-chara, meaning a wanderer in jungles. Ibbetson (1916) describes the Kanjar of Delhi as vagrants who wander about the country catching and eating jackals, lizards and such other creatures, making rope and other articles of grass for sale. According to Russel and Hiralal (1916), they are a vagrant people living in tents and addicted to crime. Kanjar may have their origin from the great Dom caste of menials and scavengers. The Kanjar are also known as Sansi, Chhara, Bhantu, Bijawar or Nat Kanjarbhat in different states such as Uttar Pradesh, Gujarat, Rajasthan, Madhya Pradesh, Bihar, Jammu and Kashmir, Punjab and Maharashtra. In the past the Kanjar were notorious for their criminal activities. Now they are agriculturists. Some are engaged in cultivation on a share cropping and contract basis, some are engaged in preparing reed-mats, rickshaw pullers and shoe-shiners. They are Hindu by faith. Traditional economic linkages existed with the Dom and Dafali to whom they supplied hides for drums. The Kanjar are notified as a scheduled caste in Uttar Pradesh, Madhya Pradesh, Bihar and West Bengal.

Pardhi

The community found place in the central list of OBCs as Pardhi (Mirshikari Nirshikari) for Andhra Pradesh. The word Pardhi is derived from the Marathi word Paradh, meaning hunting. The Pardhi belonged to the great predatory Bewali tribe of Gujarat, scattered under different appellations all over India (Hassan, 1920). Traditional occupation of Pardhi is trapping of birds and animals but now they are mainly occupied in fruit-selling. Pardhi community is included in the ST list for Maharashtra and in SC list for Madhya Pradesh.

Valmiki

Valmiki included in the central list of backward classes for Andhra Pradesh as Valmiki, Boya (Boya Bedar, Kirataka Nishadi, Yellappi, Yellapu/Yellapondlu, Pedda Boya), Talayari, Chunduvallu. It is also included for Tamilnadu and Pondicherry in the central list of OBCs as 'Valmiki'. They claim that they are descendants of Rishi Valmiki. Traditionally some among them have been soldiers and village servants. Wage labour is the main source of income. Some own lands and are cultivators. Child labour also exists. They are included as SC for Orissa.

Bedaru

Bedaru caste/community found place in the central list of OBCs for Karnataka as 'Bedaru, Valmiki, Barki, Parivara, Bendar, Berad, Boya, Naikamakkalu, Naikwadi, Palegar, Ramoshi, Talwar, Valmikimakkalu, Vedan, Parivara Nayaka. Bedarus originally belongs to Karnataka but they are also found in Maharashtra. They were known for high way robbery. Devdasi was prevalent among them. Now a days most of them are employed as night-watchman or village servants. Some of them hold agricultural land, some work as labourers. They are Hindus. They bury their deads.

Kepmari

Kepmari is included in the central list of OBCs for Andhra Pradesh as Kepmari or Reddika for Tamilnadu as

Kepmari in Chengalpattu, Pudukootai and Tiruchirapally districts. The term Kepmari seems to be the corrupt of jepmari, means pocket changes, as they were pick pocketers. Their traditional occupation is begging. They are one of the ex-criminal communities of Tamilnadu. They are non-agriculturists while some work as agricultural labourers. They are Hindu by faith and Munish Waran is their caste deity. Their population is 1,65,200 (Andhra Pradesh Backward Classes Corporation Survey, 1986).

Bester

Bester is included in the central list of OBCs for Maharashtra state as Bester, Sanchalu-Wadder. This community is not indigenous to the state of Maharashtra and appears to have come from Andhra where it is known as 'Dong-dasar'. They are known as Bestars in Western Maharashtra and 'Sanchalu Vaddars' in Vidarbha. This is a separate community from Bhamtas. This is one of the ex-criminal tribes and its chief occupation was to commit decoity, house breaking, pick pocketing, most of the people of this caste at present have taken to massonry work, carpentary, etc. and few are labourers. They are Hindus. They bury their deads.

Rajput Bhamta

Rajput Bhamta is included in the central list of OBC for Maharashtra alongwith its sub - castes i.e. Pardeshi Bhamta, Pardeshi Bhamti. They are known as Pardeshi Bhamta in Western Maharashtra and Pardeshi Bhamti in Vidarbha. They claim that they have come from Rajasthan and Bundelkhand (Madhya Pradesh). They were pick-pockets and pileferers. Now some of them have taken to agriculture, hawkers and vegetable and fruit sellers, agriculture labour and preparing ropes mats from hemp.

Korcha

Korcha is included in the central list of OBCs for Andhra Pradesh, Tamilnadu and Pondicherry. The Korcha are concentrated in the South Arcot, North Arcot, Chengai Anna, Dharmapuri, Madras, Pudukkottai, Salem, Thanjavur, Madurai and Tiruchirapalli districts of Tamilnadu. They migrated from the erstwhile Mysore province to Andhra Pradesh some 300 years ago. In Andhra Pradesh they are concentrated in the Chittoor, Anantapur and Kurnool districts, According to Thurston (1909) they are also called Yerukulavandlu or Korachavandlu. Kuravan is used as a synonym for the Korcha. The community is called by different names in different states, such as Kakkalam in Kerala, Korama and Korcha in Karnataka and Yerukula in Andhra Pradesh. They are a nomadic people, though some of them are now settled agriculturists. Primary and traditional occupation is to make baskets out of split bamboo. Most of them have left their earlier profession of thieving, burglary, a cattle - lifting and dacoity and have now taken up various other occupations as agriculture labourers. Traditionally they accept water and cooked food from the Brahman, Jangama, Lingayats, Gowda, Kuruba, Golla, Kapu, Balija and some other castes while the Mala, Madiga, Haleya, Thoti and some others accept water and food from them. According to Andhra Pradesh Backward Classes Corporation Survey of 1986, the population is 2,313.

Bhamta

Bhamta is included in the central list of OBCs for Maharashtra as 'Bhamta, Bhamti, Girniwaddar, Kamati, Pathrut, Takari, Uchale'. Bhamta seem to have originated from Andhra. But the name Bhamta has been given to it in Maharashtra. Bhamta meaning is cheater or a thief. They use to lift articles and called uchale. Takari means livelihood of chiselling stones. Girni waddar because they work in mills. Those who have come from Coimbatore are called as Kamatis. Living in Vidarbha call themselves as Bhamti. The profession of the Bhamtas was stealing and picking pockets. They have recently taken to agriculture. Some of them have taken to carpentry and tailoring. A few are employed as mill hands and some prepare ropes or mats and repair gunny bags. Bhamtas are Hindus. They keep pigs and eat pork.

Kaikadi

Found place in the central list of OBCs for Maharashtra as Kaikadi (in Bombay, Thana, Kolaba, Ratnagiri, Nashik, Dhule, Jalgaon, Pune, Ahmednagar, Satara, Sangli, Kolhapur, Sholapur, Aurangabad, Nanded districts and Rajpura (Tehsil of Chandrapur District) Dhontle, Korva, Makalwale or Kochi Korva, Pamlor, Korvi). It is also included in the central list of OBCs for Andhra Pradesh and Pondicherry. This wandering ex-criminal tribe is found all over India and have come to Maharashtra from Tamilnadu. They are known per dacoity and burglary. The traditional occupation is basket making. They prepare basket, Kanagis and such other articles of bamboo and palm leaves. Some keep donkeys and let them on hire for earth work. They keep donkeys and pigs. They are Hindus and bury their dead.

Vaghri

Vaghri caste/community found place in the central list of OBCs for Maharashtra as 'Vaghari, Salat, Salat Vaghri'. Vaghris belong to Gujarat and it has following sub-divisions: Vedu, Datanis, Kankondia, Patani, Talabada, Chanacia and Salat. Vedu Datania and Kankodia are found in Maharashtra. Vaghri was a wandering Ex-criminal tribe and were famous for house breaking pick pocketing and cheating. At present, most of them sell ghee, vegetables, Neem and Babul sticks for cleaning teeth.

Beda

Beda is included in the central list of OBCs for Himachal Pradesh. Their habitiat was in Kanara & Andhra. They are still mainly a hunting and cultivating caste. In the past they used to infest the highlands and passes through the jungle for robbery. Today they are field labourers, tenant, village watchmen, peons in police and government offices. Beda ex-criminal tribes also found place in the central list of OBCs as 'Vaddar/Vadder, Gadi Vadher, Jati, Vaddar, Moti Vaddar, Pathrvat/Patharod' for Maharashtra; Nayadi for Orissa.

It can be concluded that there are about 6 crore peoples throughout India of this so called criminal tribes today and the Maharashtra state contains the largest number than any other state in the country. Now most of them are settled and earn their living by cultivation or field labourers. Many of them have adopted different occupation as village watchmen, cowherds, cattle dealers, basketmakers, daily wage labourers etc. Their past has much influenced their present position in the eyes of the Indian people with whom they live. There are criminal castes of a good social status those who can claim that they descended from Rajputs or even Brahmins, though a cruel fate has deprived them of their home and all their possessions. They have become criminals in defiance of a human society which stripped them bare and gave them no chance to recover their losses. Then there are castes which in the past formed the large armies or the even larger numbers of camp followers in the armies. When peace came all these people lost their livelihood and many found it difficult to change over to peaceful pursuits. These castes do not enjoy high rank, but they are not Harijans. These castes are often treated as untouchables. Caste traditions change slowly and if a caste has the stigma of a criminal reputation, individuals of such a caste find it extremely hard to lead on honest life and to dispel such a reputation.

Shri Anil Kumar Pandey in 'Jansatta' daily newspaper on 22nd August, 2001 described the same situation in a report titled 'Apradhi Janjati Koun' (who are criminal tribes). The gist of the same in given as under:

The Police and Aministration even today blame these caste/community for any incident of theft, murder, burgalry in the country. Home minister, Government of India has given a similar statement in Loksabha on 2nd August, 2001 in Murder case of Sirsavan village of Muradabad district, murder case of Meerut and Lakhimpur Kheeri in Uttar Pradesh. Another example is cited by quotting a circular of 19th July, 2001 issued by the Police Inspector of Malabar Hill, Mumbai by appealing to the Public that Nepali and Bihar servants are of criminal nature and they should not be appointed.

The death of with the people of Kabutra in Madhya Pradesh Khairya Sabar of Bengal, Pardhi of Maharashtra in the police custody when they were interogated because they belong to this category.

Since there caste/communities has been denotified 49 years back in 1952, even today they are treated as criminal, not only individual but caste as a whole.

National Human Rights Commission has appointed an Advisory Committee in the Chairmanship of Dr. Bram Dev Sharma to suggest the ways and means for improvement of socio-economic conditions of these caste/communities in 1998. The report of the committee noted that a section of the Indian society which is 6% of the total population and they are the aborigan Indians, have been forgotten and they are kept away from the mainstream and respected social life even after half a century of the independence.

The Committee has suggested alongwith other recommendation that Social Justice Ministry should create a special cell to make a new list of denotified communities.

The recommendation of the committee are not implemented while Madhya Pradesh Human Right Commission recently has published a report. 'Jatigat Vaishyavirti' (caste prostitution) in which some denotified tribes are made responsible directly for Prostitution. The report says that fifty percent women of these communities are found HIV positive.

B) Nomadic and Semi - Nomadic Tribes

The caste/communities of this category in the list of OBCs are identified with certain common aspects such as begging as their tradition or occupation by moving from door to door singing devotional songs. Traditionally they are engaged in the following occupations – earthwork, well digging, work in stone, lime and salt, fishing, boating and partage, basket and mat making haking and trading traditionally engaged in such a occupation which demand to move from one place to another for instance. Pastural caste/communities move from one place to another for grazing their cattle semi - skilled labourers and seasonal labourness move from one place to another in search of work. To this category certain occupations are confined. They are forced to change their habitats frequently. Their unsteadiness has other consequences which, in turn impair their social status considerably. A brief of some of the caste/communities of this category which are included in the list of OBCs, is given with the traditional occupation and the present occupation in which they are engaged:

Bharadi

This community is included in the central list of OBC for Maharashtra as "Bharadi, Balasantoshi, Kinggriwale, Nath Bava, Nath Jogi, Nath Pandhi, Davari Gosavi". This community is one of the famous nomadic tribes of Maharashtra and found wandering all over the state. They belong to Nath sect and known by the names such as Balesantoshi, Kinggriwale and Nath Jogi also. They are wandering beggars, who sing devotional songs. The traditional occupation of this community is begging. Now a days some of them have taken miscellaneous work like repairing of umbrellas, stoves, locks and keys, preparing funnels and small tin boxes, etc. Their women sell kum-kum, combs, tooth brushes, mirrors, etc. They are Hindus and belong to Nath sect. Their principal deity is Gorakhnath. The nomadic trait still exist in them.

Bairagi

Bairagi is included in the central list of OBCs for the Delhi, Madhya Pradesh, Orissa, Uttar Pradesh, Haryana, Himachal Pradesh, Punjab, Chandigarh and Karnataka. According to Ibbertson (1916), the people of this sect belong to an ascetic and mendicant order and are placed in the category of the Faqir. They are distributed in Bihar, Delhi, Gujarat,

Haryana, Karnataka, Madhya Pradesh, Maharashtra, Punjab, Orissa and West Bengal. According to 1931 census, the population of the Bairagi was 839,285 and was mainly returned from Bengal, Bombay, the Central Provinces and Berar, United Provinces, Baroda, Central India, Gwalior, Hyderabad, Rajputana and Western India states. In Bihar they are known as Bairagi Bostom, in West Bengal they are known as Baishnab or Bostom, in Himachal Pradesh the Bairagi or Vairagi are also known as Bhat Brahman, in Gujarat. Bawa is the generic term applied for Bairagi. The traditional occupations of the Bairagi are agriculture, domesticating of cows and seeking alms by singing religious songs and to act as temple priests. Now a days they are engaged in business, industry and other white-collar jobs. They are both landowners and landless.

Kasikapadi

Kasikapadi is included in the central list of OBCs for Maharashtra, Andhra Pradesh and Karnataka. This nomadic tribe seems to have originated from Andhra as their mother tongue is Telugu. Traditional occupation of this community was begging by giving the holy water to people. But this occupation has died longback. Now they sell household utensils in exchange of old clothes. Some women also sell sacred threads, necklace of Rudraksha and glass beads etc. This nomadic tribe has not yet settled down permanently.

Beldar

This community appeared in the central list of OBCs for Maharashtra, Assam and Bihar. This community originally belongs to Rajasthan where they are known as Ods. It seems that about 3000 years back they have migrated to Maharashtra. The traditional occupation of Beldars is to dig tanks and construct mud wells. Some of them still follow this occupation. But majority of them keep donkeys and wander in search of earth work. A few of them are engaged in agriculture and extracting stones from the quarries. They are Hindus and Kali is their principal deity. They bury their deads. The wandering trait still exist in them.

Bhute or Bhope

Bhute or Bhope is included in the central list of OBCs of Maharashtra. They are in small number in Maharashtra. The traditional occupation is begging after singing praises. Most of them still follow this occupation and wander from place to place. Some have taken to agriculture. They are Hindus and their principal deity is Bhavani-mata of Tuljapur. They beg only during the day time. They bury their deads.

Chitrakathi

Chitrakathi is included in the central list of OBCs for Maharashtra. This is a wandering nomadic tribe and found in Western Maharashtra and Vidarbha. They derive their name from thier tradition occupation of telling stories or kathas from Ramayana and Mahabharta by showing pictures. Their traditional occupation is begging. But now taken to keeping of she-buffaloes, a few are agricultural labourers. They sell oil and medicines for cattle. They are Hindus. They bury their deads.

Garudi

'Garudi/Gavadi, Ghisadi' caste/community is included in the central list of OBCs for Maharashtra alongwith its sub-castes i.e. Ghisadi Lohar, Gadi Lohar, Ghitodi Lohar, Rajput Lohar. The caste/community is also included in the central list of OBCs for Karnataka. Garudi or Snake chamber who are indigenous to the state of Maharashtra found in a small number in Western Maharashtra and Marathwada. They also known as Madasis. Most of them are Muslims and call themselves as Shaikh. Hindu Garudis come from Karnataka and Gujarat in fair season and return back to their states. The hereditary occupation of this community is snake charming and begging. They have not so far taken to any other means of livelihood. Ghisadis are wandering Black-Smith and are found all over Maharashtra. Originally they belong to Rajasthan and are migrated to Maharashtra and Karnataka region about 500 years back. Traditionally they make horse-shoes, cart-axles, wheels and the iron implements. They still profers the same occupation.

Golla

'Golla' is included with sub-caste/synonyms i.e. Gollewar, Goler and Golkar in the central list of OBCs for Maharashtra. Gola Rana for Gujarat; 'Golla, Ganli, Lingayat Gowli/Ganli/Kawadiga, Gopal, Yadav, Asthana Golla, Yadava, Adavigolla, Gopala, Gopali' for Karnataka in the central list of OBCs. They used to keep cow herds and called as Golla. This community originally belongs to Andhra. In Maharashtra the Gollas are wandering medicine sellers and are found only in the districts of Sholapur and Sangli in small number. This occupation is almost died. Now they prepare mats of Sindi leaves. Their women are generally engaged in begging. They are also distributed in Puri, Cuttack and Ganjam districts in Orissa, a Telugu - speaking shepherd community. In Orissa their traditional occupation is agriculture and business. Most of them are landowners and settle cultivators and sharecropers, A few are engaged in animal husbandary. Thurston (1909) describes the Golla of Madras Presidency as a pastoral caste. In Karnataka the Golla live in the Chitradurga, Bangalore, Hassan, Bellary, Shimoga and Thumkur districts. The traditional as well as present day occupation of the Golla is rearing sheep and goats. Largely, landless, a small number of them work in government service and as agricultural wage labourers.

Toda

Toda included in the central list of OBCs for Orissa. This is a pastoral tribe of South India, who live in the Nilgris group of hills. Their main occupation is rearing buffaloes which are well-fed. Todas observe a fraternal type of Polyandry.

Yerukula

'Yerukula' included in the central list of OBCs for Orissa, Tamilnadu, Maharashtra and Pondicherry. The

Yerukulas are a south Indian nomadic tribe of Telangana area of Andhra Pradesh. Being small traders they are constantly on the move, selling salt, pulses, Karivepa (leaf use for cooking vegetables), making and selling baskets, food grain containers, manure carriers, basket measures, winnows, screens and several other articles of day to day use by the farmers. Their name itself i.e. 'Yeruka' suggest knowlcdge in foretelling and thought-reading in which their women are adepts. They make baskets, leisurely ply their industry in the shade of trees. They are found in Maharashtra, Madras and Mysore states called by different names, as Koravas in Madras, Korachas in Mysore and Kaikadis in Maharashtra. A few Yerukalas monopolise in making brushes for handloom weavers used for sizing the warp yarn and strengthening the same with thick boiled rice water. They are also experts in tattooing. Some have taken to snake-charming and monkey pranks. People of this community were mainly traders in grain and salt, operating between the coastal areas of Madras Presidency and the interior districts. In Tamil speaking region, they were called Koravars, Inji, Kal or Dabbai Koravas also depending on the work they still did (Meena Radhakrishna, 1989). This community had amongst its members acrobats, singers dancers tight rope walkers and fortune tellers. Street entertainment was provided by them. Salt was a very important source of revenue for the British administration in the 19th century and the Yerukulas were at one time the only means of distributing it in remote areas, where only pack bullocks could reach. The British administration recognised this important aspect of their existence and their salt trading activities. They were also cattle breeders and traders, dealers in all kinds of forest and agricultural produce; casual workers, made baskets, mats, brooms and brushes. They got marginalised drastically as a result of British policies.

The Yerukulas were declared a criminal community under the Criminal Tribes Act, 1911. A section of those declared criminal could be interned into special settlements set up under one of the provisions of the Act. Stuartpuram settlement in Guntur district was one such settlement and it is here that about

6,000 Yerukulas lived for several decades from 1913 onwards. Stuartpuram settlement was meant to be an agricultural settlement. A large tract of waste land was given to the Salvation Army for cultivation by the Yerukulas. This needed some reorganising of the community's social and cultural priorities. Drastic transformation in the lives of the Yerukulas followed. Most important was the fact that the itinerant mode of existance was suddenly replaced by a forced settled life. The Salvation Army divided the community into families, which were now the new operational social and economic unit. Each family was given a small piece of land, which it was responsible for cultivating or else punishment followed. The family was further broken up by removing the children to another part of the settlement, so that rising generation could be kept away from their wicked parents and brought up in a more whole some atmosphere. Separate schools and dormitories were established for these children and they were allowed to meet their parents only on sundays during church activities. The Salvation Army concentrated on the children for moral education and on the adult men for work. They claim themselves the descendants of Ekalavya (the great archer of Mahabharata). They are distributed in 30 districts of the country. Traditionally they are fortune - tellers and basketmakers. In Mahabharata they are a community of semi - nomads who pursue occupations of basket making, fortune - telling and begging. At present, the Yerukula community is engaged in making date (rachi) baskets, weaving, rearing pigs, herding cattle and gethering forest produce. Their women seek alms and tell fortune to the clients while playing the tambura. Some of them work as agricultural labourers. Children are also engaged in rearing pigs and in making baskets.[6]

Godia Lohars

Godia Lohar caste community is included in the central list of OBCs for Rajasthan. Godia Lohars literally means cart smith. They are nomads from centuries and still keep wandering in their gaddi i.e. big sized country carts. They make agriculture implements, some make swords. They live in a large number in Rajasthan though they fan out to all adjacent states travelling upto Jammu and Kashmir as well as Delhi. They have their road side camps of 30 to 50 families doing a brisk business for railway contractors and other firms dealing in small implements.

Singiwala

Singiwala is included in the central list of OBCs for Maharashtra. They are nomadic tribes moving in small groups, primarilly beggars but also pursuing the profession of sucking human blood for giving relief to certain types of patients for certain diseases. They use a conical tube made of horn and with one end pressed against the human body, the air is sucked at the other end. Blood is drawn giving relief. They also live by snake charming and curing snake bites.

It is concluded that more than 200 such castes/ communities found place in the central list as well as state list for OBCs. For example Balasanthu, Bhataraja, Budabukkala, Dasari, Dommara, Jakkala, Jogi, Joshinandiwala, Mandula, Mondi- voru, Nakkala, Nokkar, Pamula, Peddammavandlu, Poosala, Gangiredlavaru and Yadav (Galla) caste/communities of this category are included in the central list of OBCs for Andhra Pradesh. Faquir, Jogi, Madari, etc. for Haryana, Kalaikar, and NathJogi of Goa, have also found place in central list of OBCs. Beldar, Bind, Dafali (Muslim), Dhankar, Gandarbh, Gulgaliya, Kapadia, Kheeta, Nat (Muslim), Pamaria (Muslim) comes under this category in the central list of OBCs for Bihar. Similarly, Raval-Ravalia, Jati or Raval Yogi, Raval Jati, Jagaria, Shikligar for Gujarat. Ard Pop, Bata, Changar, Faquir, Gadaria, Gawaria, Gujjar, Labana, Madari for Himachal Pradesh, Bazigar, Golla, Kanisan, Kanjari, Lonari, Katabu, Katabar, Kolhati, Kalhatigi, Masanyogi, Nandiwala, Shikkaligar, Vaidu, Vasudev for Karnataka. Kottar Chettier, Pulluvan, Veerasaiva (Yogi and Yogeeswara), Poopandaram/ Maalapandaram and Jangam for Kerala; Bairgi, Banjara,

Mukeri, Makrani, Nat, Loniye/Luniya, Tarha Vasudev/ Harvala / Kapdia / Goudhli and Sikligar, for Madhya Pradesh, Beldar/ Od, Bhand, Bharadi, Bhute, Chitrakathi, Dawari, Garudi/ Gavadi, Ghisadi Lohar, Golla, Gopal, Helve, Jogi, Joshi, Kasikapadi, Kolhati Dombari, Nandiwale, Pangul, Raval, Sikkalagar, Thakkar, Vaidu, Vasudeo, Mairal, Dangar, Vir, Masanjogi, Nandiwale, Tirmal, Pangul, Palparthi, Vaddar, Vaidu for Maharashtra. Faqir, Jogi, Sikligar for Rajasthan; Jangam, Koravar for Tamilnadu; Bairagi, Banjara, Bhand, for Uttar Pradesh, and Goala, Yogi, Nath for West Bengal.

The sub-division of the 'Nomadic and Semi-nomadic tribes' includes the wandering tribes whose origin ethnologically may not be aboriginal and who do not live in forest areas but who need special care as being very backward. They usually obtain their living in part at least by begging and in part by some minor trade such as weaving today - leaf mats, shaving buffaloes, etc.

C. Caste/communities with Tribal Derivation

Many nomadic tribes fall under this sub category. Most of them are engaged in polluting professions such as mat and broom manufacturing, play of music, singing and dancing. These caste/communities, take food water from nearly every one and from whom none will eat. Generally they have their own priests and do not invite Brahmins to perform ceremonies. A brief account of such caste/communities is given with their traditional and present occupation.

Mahli

Mahli found place in the central list of OBC for Assam and Maharashtra. This caste of tribal origin in Chhotanagpur and West Bengal is considered impure. Their clan names are identical with those of Munda tribe, Santhal and Bhumij tribes. They make baskets, grain bins and winnowing fans from bamboo for sale. People of this community also work as daily wage labourers in the fields of others. A few of them are cultivators.

Kadar

Found place in the central list of OBCs for Bihar. This is a Hinduised section of Naiya tribe of the forest of Bihar and West Bengal region. They are daily wage labourers in others field. They also do fishing and wood cutting as subsidiary occupations. They still worship tribal goods and the nature spirits. Socially they are considered very low.

Khaira

Khaira is included in the central list of OBCs for Orissa. They seem to be a branch of Kharwar tribe and found in West Bengal. Their social status in low. They are daily wage labourers, vegetable growers and some of them are cultivators.

Mal Paharia

Mal Paharia found place in the central list of OBCs for Orissa. They are from the Maler tribe living in the Rajmahal hills in Bihar. They are similar to Oraons or Savaras. Now they are completely Hinduised. They are cultivators. Some are fishermen or village watchmen or work as daily wage labourers.

Kol

Kol is considered socially and educationally backward caste/ community and found place in the central list of OBCs for Assam. This caste/community is former aborigonal origin but now Hinduised. The people of this community accept all kinds of jobs though most of them are daily wage labourers in others fields. They acted as palanguin bearers in the past.

Koraga

Koraga caste reflected in the central list of OBCs for Orissa. Socially, the Koragas rank even lower than the Holeyas, the main untouchable caste of Kanara. Even in some towns they are employed as scavengers. In the villages they remove the hides, horns and bones of cattle and sell them to the Mapilla merchants. In the past they had been enslaved and were sold with the land on which they lived and worked. By religion they are Hindus.

Kudiya

Kudiya is formally of tribal origin. It is found place in the central list of OBCs for Orissa. It is a low caste in South Kanara. Most of the people of this community have given up tribal culture and live now in the hills as agrestic labourers in the cardamom plantations, more or less bonded labour. They dwell in the jungles beneath rocks, incaves, in low huts, and they continually shift from, one place to another. At the season of the cardamom crop they come down from the hills and sell off cardamoms to the contractors.

Pentia

Pentia is included in the central list of OBCs for Pondicherry. This tribal artisan caste have no permanent home. They wonder village to village in search of work. They are regarded as out castes.

Kandra

Kandra caste found place in central list of OBCs for Andhra Pradesh and Pondicherry. This is a small caste of bamboo workers. They are offshoot of the Gonds, also found in Orissa. They have been specialists in the manufacture of arrows. It is an impure caste.

Korku

Korku caste/community found place in the central list of OBCs for Bihar. It is a tribe of central India.Most of the people of this community are cultivators and wage labourers in Bihar.

Kota

Kota is included in central list of OBCs for Orissa. This community is found in the Nilgiri hills. The people of this community are aboriginal smiths and musicians. They are treated as untouchables. They work in the fields of others as daily wage labourers.

The above account of certain caste/communities shows that many tribal groups, (originally without caste differences) are fully hinduized and adopted the caste system and untouchability. They are socially considered low and untouchables by Hindus as well as tribals. It is not only due to eating impure food or were lax in sex morality, but because they were poor, landless and dependent on others for their livelihood. This section of caste/communities have split off from the original communities and adopted the settled life as cultivators or landless labourers. Thus the same caste may have an endogamous section in are region completely settled, while in another part of the country it is stil in the foraging and nomadic stage of culture. In some states such caste/communities are included in the SC list or ST list or in OBC list. It is mainly because of their menial occupations. More than 50 such caste/communities found place in the central list of OBC alone such as 'Nakkala' for Andhra Pradesh; 'Mina/Meena' for Delhi and Haryana; 'Bhil and Gond' for Assam; 'Gondi' for Pondicherry, 'Dhimar' for Madhya Pradesh; 'Dhamin' for Bihar; 'Nairy' Kond (Kul) and Kondakapu for Orissa; 'Pahad', for Maharashtra.

References

1. Sher, Sher Singh, 1965, *Ex-criminal tribes of Northern India*.
2. Mishra, S.C., 1964, *Muslim Communities in Gujarat*, Bombay.
3. Fuchs, Stephen, 1981, At the Bottom of Indian Society, Munshiram Manoharlal Publishers (P) Ltd., Delhi.
4. Shah P.G. 1967, *Denotified Communities in Western India*, Bombay.
5. Fuchs, Stephen, 1981, op.cit.
6. Radhakrishna, Meena, 2000, 'Colonial Construction of a 'criminal' tribes': Yerukulas of Madras Presidency, EPW, Vol. XXV, Nos. 28 and 29 pp. 2553-63.

5

Divisions By Occupations

As caste is very closely linked to occupation, generally for each caste has a traditional occupation. It can be seen clearly in case of existence of occupational castes and their link with a specific occupation.

A. Artisanal castes/communities of Clean Occupation

Artisanal castes/communities practised occupational skills and engaged in various traditional crafts. Most of the Caste/Communities of this category often performs many operations to produce articles and then market them. Artisanal as fisher folk, toddy tappers, stone-cutters, earth workers etc. have lost their traditional occupations due to modernisation, free economy, and globalization. Some of these occupational castes have completly changed their traditional occupations due to rapid urbanisation and modernisation and have adopted new occupations. Statewise distribution of Caste/communities found place in the central list of OBCs of this category is as under:

Andhra Pradesh: Achukatlavandlu, Agnikula Kshatliya, Arekatika, Arykshatriya; Bandare, Chopemari, Ediga; Lodh, Lodha, Lodhi; Methar Muslim; Atagara, Chippalu (Mera), Devanga, Dudekula, Karikalabhakthulu, Karnabhakthula, Kashti, Kummara or Kulala or Salivahana,

Neelakanthi, Nessi or Kurni, Padmasali, Patkar (Khatri), Rangarez or Bhavasara Kshettiya, Sodhu Chetty, Swakulasali, Telikula, Jandre, Thogata, Thogati or Thogata Veerakshatriya, Viaswabrahmin or Viswakarma (Ausule or Kamsali, Kakken, Kanchari, Vadla or Vadra or Vadrangi and Silpi); Gandla, Kandre; Kanjara-Bhatta; Nayi-Brahmin (Mangla, Mangli, Bhajanthri) Pambala; Pariki Muggula; Surya Balija (Kalavanthnla); Ganika; Tammali, Veearmushti (NettiKotala); Yata.

Assam: Kumar, Rudra Paul of district of Cachar, Karimanj and Kailakandi; Yogi (Known as Katani); Napit.

Bihar: Abdal; Agariya; Bari, Bind; chain; Dhobi (Muslim), Gandarbh; Kaivartta, Kanss; Chik (Muslim); Churihar (Muslim) Barai (Vishwakarma); Beldar; Dhankar; Dhunia (Muslim) Gangai (Ganesh); Kagzi, Kamar (Lohar, Karmakar, Visvakarma), Kosta, Nunia; Prajapati (Kumbhar); Rangwa; Rangrej (Muslim); Sonar, Sunar; Sudi, Halwai, Runiyar, Pansari, Modi, Kasera, Kesarmani, Thethera, Patwa, Sinduriya-Bania, Mahuri-Vaishya, Avadh-Bania, Agrahari-Vaishay; Tanti (Tatwa), Tati, Tatin; Teli, Kasab Kewat, Khelta, Nalband (Muslim); Namsudra, Nat (Muslim); Nunia; Pamaria; Tikulhar; Tiyar.

Delhi: Abbasi, Bhishti, Sakka; Badi; Bharbhooja, Kann; Chak; Bhatiare; Chhipi; Afhi, Kharwal; Badhai, Barhai, Khati, Tarkhan, Jangra-Brahmin, Vishwakarma, Ramgarhia, Panchal, Dheeman; Bharbhooja, Kann, Luhar, Bhubharia, Saifi, Patwa; Rangrez; Sunar; Teli, Teli-Malik; Dhinwar (excluding those in SC list), Dhobi; Dhunia; Julaha (excluding those in SC list); Kalwar; Kasai; Kasera; Khatbune; Kumhar; Lakhera; Machi; Mochi; Nai, Nalband; Naqqal.

Goa: Dhangar; Kumbhar; Mahar (excluding those who are already included in SC list); Shimpi; Teli; Dhobi; Kalaikar; Nhavi.

Gujarat: Bhadbhunja; Chhipa; Teli, Modh Ghanchi, Teli Sahu, Teli Rathore, Teli Rathod; Koshti, Kumbhar

(Prajapati, Varia); Lakhara/Lakhwara/Laxkar; Luhar/Lohar/Panchal; Mistri (suthar/Sutar); Swakul Sali/Sali; Vanza (Darji), Darji/Sai Sutar; Bhandari; Nat; Od; Padmashali-Pastushali; Valand.

Haryana: Chimba or Chhimba, Chhipi, Chimpa, Darzi, Rohilla; Gramini; Dhimar; Thangra-Brahman or Jangra-Brahman or Jangid Brahman, Khati, Ram Garhia, Suthar, Dhiman, Tarkhan, Barha, Baddi; Lakhera, Manihar; Lohar or Luhar, Saifi; Rangraz; Nilgar, Leelgar, Lallari; Sunar, Zaegar, Soni; Teli; Thathera or Thater, Tamera; Weaver (Jullah including Kabir Panthi) Julaha (excluding those who are included in scheduled caste); Hajjam; Jaiswar; Madari; Mochi (excluding those who are included in SCs list); Nalband; Nat (other than those who are in SC list); Raisikh (Mahatam); raigar other than those who are in SC list).

Himachal Pradesh: Bharbunha, Bharbhuja or Bharbhunja, Dhosali, Dosal; Julaha, Ansari (other than those included in the SC list); Kumhar, Prajapati; Pinja or Penja, Panja; Rechband; Tarkhan; Thawin; Bahti; Bata; Bharbunha; Chirimar; Dhimer; Dhinwar; Ghosi; Hajam; Kahar; Kangehra; Labana; Mahatam; Madari; Mallah; Mehra; Nai (Kaleen Brahman); Nalband.

Jammu and Kashmir: Bangi; Barbers (Rural only); Bhand; Fishermen including Gada Hanz; Kumhar; Madari; Shoe repairs; Sikaligar; Teeli (Rural only); Village washermen.

Karnataka: Chitara, Chittari as sub-castes of Somavamsha Aryakshatriya; Darzi, Bhavasar Kshatriya, Chippi, Chippige, Simpi, Shimpi, Lingayat Simpy, Sivasimpy, Sai, Mirai, Rangari, Rangrez, Nilari, Namders Namdev Simpy, Rangare, Neelagar, Lingayat Neelagar; Devanga, Derang, Koshti, Hutgar/Hutkar, Jet, Lingayat Bilijedaru/Jeda, Winker, Juloha, Hulkar, Hatgar, Lingayat Hatgar, Kumbra, Kummara, Khummara, Kumbhar, Khnmbhar, Lingayat Kumbar/Kumbare, Kusavan, Kulala, Kulalar, Moolya; Neygi, Lingayat Neygi/Lingayat Kuruhinashetty, Lingayat Bilimagga, Lingayat Jadaru;

Viswakarka, Akkasale, Aksali, Lingayat Akkasali, Achari, Viswa Brahman, Davanga Brehman, kammar, Lingayet Kammera, ansala, Kammalan, Luhar (Kammari), Kamsal, Lingayat Kammasali, Kamasala, Panchal, Panchala, sutar, Badagi, Lingayat Badiga, Badiwadli, Soni, Sonar, Pattar, Gejjigar, Silpi; Gangakula, Galada Konkani; Goniga, Sadhu Chetty, Telugu Chetty, Telungupatti Chetty, 24 name Telugis Chetty, Salaparu, Sanaparn; ezhava, Thiyya; Kotari; Lingayat Banagar; Lonari sub-caste of Uppasa; Yakalara, Uppara; Nayinda.

Kerala: Kaikalan; Kallan Moopan or Kallan Mooppar; Kammara (excluding Malabar district); Kusivan (Kulala, Kulala Nair or andhra Nair or Anthura Nair); Kumbaran; Odan; Viswakarma including Assari, Chaptegra, Kallassari, Kammala, Karuvan, Kitaran, Kollan, Malayala Kammala, Pandikammala, Mossari, Perumi Kollan, Thattan, Pandithattan, Vikurup, Villasan, Viswabrahmanan or Viswabrahamanar and Viswakarmala, Thaehan, Kalthachen, Kamsala, Kannan, Agasa; Bandari; Billara; Chakkala; Dheevara; Ezhava, Thiyya; Ezhavathi; Kavuthiyan; Kongu Narithan; Latin Catholic; Madivala; Mukhamialias Moovari; Odan; Pullavan; Velaan; Vanian; Vettura Narithan; Veluthedathu Nair (Veluthedan and Ramnathan); Vilakkithala Nair (Vilakkithallvan).

Madhya Pradesh: Badhbhuja, Bhunjwa, Burji, Dhuri or Dhoori; Barhai, Sutar, Suthar, Kunder, Vishwakarma; Chippa, Chhipa, Bhavsar, Nilgar, Jingar, Nirali, Ramgari, Rangari, Rangrez/ Rangarej/Rangraz, Rangredh, Chippa-Sindhi-Khatri; Darji, Cheepi/Chhipi/chipi Shipi, Mavi (Namdev); Chippa/Chhipa; Pinjara, Naddaf, Fakir/ Faquir, Behne, Dhuniya, Dhunkar, Mansoori; Manihar; Luhar, Saifi, Nagori Luhar, Maltani Luhar, Teli; Kadere/Kadore, Dhunkar, Dhuniya, Dhanka Kodar; Khatiya, Khati; Koshta/Kosta, Kosti/ Koshti, Devangan, Dewang, Salwidewang, Mala, Padmhali/ Pademsali, Sali, Sut Sali, Salwar/Salewar, Jendra/Jandra, Kas Kati, Garhwal/Garhewal/Garewar/Garwal; Kumhar (Prajapati), Kumbhar (excluding Chhatarpur, Datia, Panna, Tikamgarh,

Satna, Rewa, Sidhi, and Shahdol districts); Lohar/Luhar, Lohpita, Godoley, Gadela, Lohpata/Lohpeta, vishwakarma; Loniya/Luniya/Lonia/Lunia; Odh, Odhe, Odhiya, Ode, Odiya, Naaniya, Muraha/Muraaha, Mudahe/Mudaaha, Nunia, Nonia; Sonar; Patka, Patki, Patwa; Pinjara (Hindu); Tarhe; Teli (Rathore, Sahu); Thathara, Thatera, Kasar, Kasera, Tamera, Tambatkar/Tamrakar, Tamer; Bharood; Bhatiyara; Chitari; Chunkar; Manihar; Dhimar/Dhimer; Dhobi; (excluding those in SC list) Dafaali, Gurav/Guraw; Bhishti-Abbasi; Hela; Bhatiyara; Kasai; Hajjam (Barber); Mochi; Kalaigar; Nalband; Nat; Kalar, Kalal; Loniya; Nail Sikligar; Sodhi.

Maharashtra: Kalal; Christian Koli, Chumle; Machhimar Koli, Panbhare, Son Koli, Pan Koli, Bari; Pareet; Singiwala; Julaha, Momin, Julaha-Ansari, Momin Ansari; Nonia, Lonia, Lunia, Nunia; Shilavat; Sonar; Sutar; Sutharia (from Sindh); Swakul Sali; Tambat; Teli, Teli-Lingayat, Teli Sahu, Teli Rathod; Ganiga.

Orissa: Ashtralohi/Ashtalohi Karmakar, Kamila, Sunari, Sunaree, Viswa Brahman (Sunari), Swarnekar/Swaransilpi; Hansi, Tanti, Sukuli, Vina, Tulabhina, Rangami, Dera, Dewanga, Kasta, Salia, Patsalia, Buna, Bunkar/Bunkara, Bangali Tanti/Bangiya Tanti, Matibansa Tanti, Asina Tanti/Aswire Tanti/Ashani Tanti/Aswinna Tanti; Khodra, Khudura; Kumbhar Kulal, Kumhar, Kumbharo, Kandha-Kumbhar; Patara/Patre, Gondia Patara; Kalwar; Mahla/Mahlar; Pathuria.

Punjab: Dhaula or Soni, Jhangra Brahman, Khati, Lohar, Rangarharia, Turkhan; Teli; Thathera, Tamera; Lakhera, Manihar; Weaver (Jullaha or Julaha including Kabir Panthi Julaha excluding those who are scheduled castes); Nai, Sain; Nalband; Rai Sikh; Saifi.

Rajasthan: Badhai, Jangid, Khati, Kheradi, Suther, Tarkhan; Bari, Bharbhunja; Chhippa (Chhipi), Nansc, Bhavsar; Kandera, Pinjara, Mansoori; Kumhar (Prajapati), Kumawat; Lakhera (lakhara), Manihar; Lohar, Panchal; Rangrez; Swarnkar, Sunar, Soni; Teli; Thathera, Kansara, Bharawa;

Damani, Nagarchi; Dhobi; Kasai; Mochi (other than those who are included in SC list); Nai; Sakka-Bhishti; Sikligar; Sirkiwal;

Tamilnadu: Chakkala; DudeKula; KaiKolan, KaiKolar, Sengunthar; Kallar Kula Thondaman; Kammalar or Viswakarma (including Thattar, Parkollar, Kannar, Karumar, Kollar, Thacher, Kalthacher, Kamsala and Viswa Vahmin; Katesar, PattamKatti; Khatri; Kulala including Kuyavar, Kumbarar and Velar; Kurhinichetty; Namdev Mahratta; Mahendra, Medara; Podikara Vellalar; Arayar; Changayampadi; Ezhavathy; Gownder; Idiga; Kabbera; Kammalar or Viswa Karma; Kavuthiyar; Kharvi, Kudumbi; Kuga Vellalas; Labbai; Latin Catholic; Mapila; Mgruthugar, Meenavar; Agasa, Madivala, Ekali Sub-castes of Vannar (Salavai Thozhilalari).

Tripura: Kaumbhakar, Kumar; Kuri; Napit, Shil; Nat, Natta.

Uttar Pradesh: Atisbaz, Darugar; Bhand; Bhatiara; Chikwa, Qassab, chak; Barhai, Badhai, Vishwakarma, Ramgarhia; Bari; Bind; Bhurji, Bharbhunja, Bharbhunja, Bhooj, Kandu; Darzi; Kasera, Thathera, Tamrakar, Kalaikar; Khumre, Sangtarash, Hansiri; Kuthaliya Bora (Belonging to Almora, Pithoragarh, Bagesunar and Nainital districts; Lonia, Noniya, Luniya, Gole Thakur, Nunere; Manihar, Kacher, Lakhera (excluding Lakkera sub-caste of Brahmins in Tehri Garwal region), Churihar; Momin; Julah; Nadalaf (Dhunia), Mansooli, Behna, Kandere, Pinjara; Patwa, Patna, Pathar, Tatwa; Raj (Memar); Rangrez, Rangura; Teli, Samani, Ragangar; Dhivar; Dohar; Hajjam (Nai); Halalkhor, Hela, Lalbegi (other than SCs), Halwai; Kalal; Madari; Mochi (other then SCs); Nalband, Sais; Rai Sikh (Mahatam).

West Bengal: Betkar (Bentkar); Chitrakar; Churihar; Dhunia; Jolah (Ansari Momin); Kansari; Kapali; Karani; Karmakar; Kosta/Kostha; Kumbhakar; Lakhera/Laahera; Rangwa; Sampang; Shankhakar; Sutradhar; Swarnakar; Tanti, Tantubaya; Teli; Kahar; Kalwar; Moira (Halwai), Madak (Halwai); Napit.

The distribution of Artisanal Castes/communities in the central list of OBCs shows that caste/communities engaged in weaving, working on matel, cooking, tailoring etc. found place kin thne OBC lists. Let us discuss these categories one by one.

Weaving castes includes those who are engaged in dying, printing of clothes, cotton carding, cotton cleaning etc. Approximately 100 caste/communities which are directly or indirectly traditionally associated with weaving found place in the central list of OBCs from different name in different states as shown in table 5.1.

Table 5.1

Statewise distribution of weaving Castes/Communities in the central list of OBCs

S. No.	State	Name of the Caste/ community	Traditional Occupation
1.	**A.P.**	Aryakshatriya	Printing on clothes and dollmaking
		Atagara	Weaving
		Devanga	Weaving
		Dudekula, Laddaf, Pinjari or Noorbash	Cotton ginning
		Karikalabhakthulu, Kaikolan or Kaikola	Weaving
		Karnabhakthula	Weaving
		Neelakanthi	Weaving
		Nessi or Kurni	Weaving
		Patkar (Khatri)	Silk-Weaving
		Padmasali (Sali, Saliyan, Pattusali,	Weaving

State	Caste	Occupation
	Senapathrulu, Thogatasali)	
	Rangarez or Bharasara Kshatriya	Dyeing
	Sadhuchetty	Jute weaving
	Swakulasali	Weaving
	Telikula Jandra	Silk weaving
	Thogata, Thogati or Thogate Veerakshatriya	Weaving
2. **Bihar**	Dhunia	Cotton Carding
	Kosta, Koshta	Weaving
	Rangwa	Dyeing of clothes
	Rangrez (Muslim)	Dyeing of clothes
	Tanti (Tatwa), Tati, Tatin	Weaving
3. **Delhi**	Rangrez	Dyeing of clothes
	Dhunia, Pinjara, Kandera-Karan, Dhunnewala	Cotton carding
	Julaha (excluding those in SC list	Weaving
	Patwa	Thread making, Rakhi making
4. **Gujarat**	Chhipa	Dyeing of cloths & block printing
	Koshti	Weaving
	Padmashali	Weaving
	Pattushali	Weaving
	Swakul Sali/Sali	Weaving
	Vanza (Dorji), Dorji/Saisutar	Weaving
	Padmashali-Pattushali	Handloom Weaving

5.	**Haryana**	Pinja, Penja	Cotton carding
		Rangrez	Dyeing of clothes
		Nilgar, Leelgar, Lallari (Julaha including Kabir Panthi Julaha)	Weaver Weaving
6.	**H.P.**	Julaha, Ansari (other than those in SC list)	Weaving
		Pinja or Penja	Cotton carding
		Rech band	Making thread on handloom
7.	**Karna.**	Devanga, Devang, Koshti, Hutgar/Hutkar, Lingayat Billijedaru/Jeda, Winker, Julaha, Hulkar, Hatgar, Lingayat Hutgar	Weaving
		Pinjara, Pinjari, Nadaf, Ladaf, Mansoori	Cotton carding
		Neygi, Pattasale, Lingayat Neygi/Nekar/Neygi, Lingayat Kurnthinashetty, Lingayat Bilimagga, Patra	Weaving
8.	**Kerala**	Devanga	Weaving
		Kaikolan	Weaving cotton and manufacturing of white towel
		Pattariya	Silk-Weaving
9.	**M.P.**	Chippa/chipa	Printing on clothes
		Kadera/Kadore, Dhunkar, Dhuniya, Dhanka Kodar	Cotton carding
		Koshta/Kosta,	Weaving

	Kosti/Koshti, Devaugan, Dewang, Salwidewang, Mala, Padamhali, Pademsali, Sali, Sutsali, Salwar, Salewar, Jendra/Jandra Koskati, Garhwal,	
	Garhewal, Garewar,	
	Garwal,Patka, Patki,	
	Patwa	Weaving of clothes
	Pinjara	Weaving
10. **Maha.**	Devanga	Weaving
	Julaha, Momin	Weaving
	Kaskanti Devanga Julaha-Ansari, Momin-Ansari	Weaving
	Panka	Weaving
	Rangari	
	Patkar	Silk-Weaving
	Rangrez	Dyeing on clothes
	Rangrez (Bahawsar or Rangari)	
	Naqashi/ Naqqashi	Textile Printing
	Neeli, Nilgar, Nirali	Weaving of Clothes
	Swakulsali/Sali	
11. **Orissa**	Hansi, Tanti, Sukuli, Vina, Tulabhina, Dera, Dewanga, Kosta, Salia, Patsalia, Buna, Bunkar/Bunkara, Bangali Tanti/Bangiya,Tanti,Rangani,	Weaving

	Matibansa, Tanti, Asina Tanti/Aswina Tanti/Ashani Tanti/Aswina Tanti, Patara/ Patra/Gondia Patara	Thread making and weaving of pat clothes
12. **Punjab**	Weaver (Jullaha or Julaha including kabirpanthi)	Weaving
13. **Raj.**	Kandera, Pinjara, Mansoori	Weaving
	Rangrez, Nilgar	Dyeing on clothes
14. **T.N.**	Dudekula	Cotton cleaning
	Sadhu Chetty	Gunny bags weaving
	Saliyar	Textile Printing
	Kaikolan, Karikolar Sengunnthar	Weaving
	Khatri	Silk Weaving
	Kurthini Chetty	Wool Weaving
	Namdev Mahratta	Tailoring & dyeing clothes
	Panar	Clouring of thread and processing for cloth making
15. **U.P.**	Koshta/Koshti Kuthaliya Bora (Belonging to Almora, Pithoragarh, Bagewar and Nainatal districts)	Weaving
	Monin (Ansar, Ansari),	Weaving
	Julah, Naddaf(Dhunia), Mansoori, Behna, Kandere, Kadere, Pinjara	Cotton Carding

16. **West Bengal**	Baishya Kapali	Weaving
	Dhunia	Cotton Carding
	Jolah Ansari Momin	Cotton Carding
	Kapali	Weaving
	Karani	Weaving
	Kosta/Kostha	Weaving
	Rangwa	Weaving
	Tanti, Tantubaya	Weaving
17. **Pondicherry**	Devanga	Weaving
	Kaikalan	Weaving
	Jandara	Weaving

Weaving community can further be divided in two groups i.e. and Rangrez. A brief description of these groups is given as under:

Julaha

Julaha are a community of weavers. A section among them call Kabir Panthi. They are also known as Keer in Himachal Pradesh, Bunkar, Bunia, Paoli, Koli, Kori, Patua, Ganda, Panka, Devanga, Toyata, Jugi, Julaha and Dhanak Julaha. Agriculture and the preparation and sale of liquor are the main source of income for the Keer. The Julaha are a landless community whose traditional occupation is weaving and dyeing . Business, trade and animal husbandary are their other occupation. Some of them are skilled labourers. Child labour exists and there is a rise in the number of daily wage and industrial labourers among them.

Rangrez

They are distributed in 54 districts of the country. According to 1931 census, the population of Rangrez was 58, 044. In West Bengal and Bihar, they are dyers and also known as Nilgar or Lilgar. Rose (1919) describes them under the Nilgar and says that the Nilari is hardly distinguishing from the Rangrez. They are both dyers and artisans and not menials. In Gujarat they are also called Chhipa. They embraced Islam. A good number of the Rangrez practise their traditional occupation of dyeing and printing in Gujarat. In Madhya Pradesh they are also called Nilgar. In Uttar Pradesh they are divided into three subgroups, namely Lalgarh, Nilgarh and Chhipa. The Chhipa are placed lower because they dye and print where as the Lalgarh and Nilgarh enjoy a higher status for they prepare colours. The Rangrez in Uttar Pradesh are mostly landless people settled in urban and semi-urban centres. Dyeing and printing on cotton fabric is their traditional occupation. At present, very few of them are involved in this occupation, most of them are involved in wage- labour, government service, laundry or petty business. In Bihar, Rangrez are also known as Sabbagh, Rangrez, Nilgar or Lilgar. Their traditional occupation in Bihar is dyeing and printing. They polish cloth and print artistic designs on them. In Rajasthan they are also known as Lilgar or Nilgar. Their primary occupation is dyeing of clothes. In Maharashtra Rangrez/ Rangari identified themselves as Kshatriya Bhavasar. The Rangari are traditionally dyers of cotton-thread and cloth but this art is fast fading in the face of mechanized mills. Now a days most of them are doing small business of selling cloth, grocery, metal, fancy items etc. Some of them own land and are doing cultivation. In Andhra Pradesh the name Rangariju refers to their traditional occupation of dyeing. They are variously known as Simpi, Bhavasar, Bahusar, Bahusagara, Bhavasarigi, Wannekar or Rangari. The census report of 1901 states that the Chimpiga (tailor) and Unupulavadu (dyer) are the sub castes of the Rangari. In Orissa the Rangari are distributed in Puri and Cuttuck districts. Some of them have their own land and engaged in cultivation while others depend on their traditional occupation of dyeing and weaving. A good number of them are also working as skilled or unskilled labourers in agriculture and plantations.

The Caste/community found place in the central list of OBCs as Rangrez (Muslim) for Madhya Pradesh, Bihar, Delhi and Maharashtra 'Rangrez (Bhavasar or Rangari)' and 'Rangari' for Maharashtra, Rangrez for Delhi, Rangrez, Nilgar for Rajasthan, Rangrez or Bhavasara Kshtriya for Andhra Pradesh; Rangrez, Nilgar, Lilgar, Lallari for Haryana; Rangrez, Rangwa for Uttar Pradesh; Rangwa for Bihar and West Bengal.

The caste/communities traditionally engaged in Gold smithy, brash smithy, copper smithy, tin metal etc. can be put together as a sub-category of caste/communities of working on matel. Caste/communities of this sub-category are not considered polluting while black-smithy is considered non-pulluting in many places. A few caste/community of dust collecter (dust of gold and silver) are not artisans. They are labourers thus not included. Thus such caste/community engaged in black-smithy are not included in this sub-category of castes/communities of working on metal. Many castes/ communities of this category found place in the central list of OBCs as shown in table 5.2.

Table 5.2

Statewise distribution of caste/communities working on metal

S. No.	State/UT	Caste/community	Traditional occupation
1.	Andhra Pradesh	Viswabrahmin or Viswakarma	Gold Smithy, brash Smithy and stone carving
2.	Assam	Maria	Making brass matel utensils
3.	Bihar	Kamar	working on matel
4.	Delhi	Sunar, Kasera, Tamera, Thathiar	Gold smithy
5.	H.P.	Chang	Working on brass
6.	Haryana	Sunar,Zargar, Soni	Gold smithy

	Rehar	Making ornaments of base matel
	Chang	Working on brass
7. Karnataka	Kasar, Kansar, Kachori, Kanchera, Kanchugara, Bogar, Otari,	Working on Matel
	Vishwakarma	Working on Matel
8. Kerala	Vishwakarma	
9. M.P.	Sonar, Sunar, Swarnakar, Jhhari, Jhhadi, Awedhiya, Audhiya	
	Thathera	Working on matel
10. Maharashtra	Tambat	Copper smithy
	Otari	
	Kasbi, Kasar, Kanchar, Kanchari	
11. Orissa	Thatari/Kansari	
	Pathuria	Stone-carving
12. Punjab	Rehar	Making ornaments of base metal
	Thathera	Working of matel
13. Rajasthan	Thathera, Kansara, Bharwa	Gold smithy
14. Uttar Pradesh	Kasera, Thathera, Tamrakar, Kalaikar	
15. West Bengal	Kansari	bell metal work

16.	Chandigarh	Thathera/Thethera	
		Rehar	Making ornaments of the base matel
		Chang	Working on brass
17.	Daman and Diu	Kasar	

The above table shows that the caste/communities traditionally working on matel are known as Vishwakarma or Vishwabrahmin in south indian states. Andhra Pradesh, Karnataka and Kerala while in the North Indian states. Sonar/ Sunar, Swarnakar, Soni, Karera, Thatera, Tamrakar etc. In Karnataka and Maharashtra 'Otari' caste is included in the central list of OBCs. Viswabrahmin or Viswakarma community of Andhra Pradesh is also known as Ansula or Kamsali, Kammari, Kanchari, Vadla or Vadra or Vadrangi and Silpi. While in Karnataka it includes Akkasale, Alingayat Akkasali, Achari, Davanga Brahman, Kammlan, Luhar (Kammari), Kamsal, Lingayat Kammasali. In Kerala it includes Assari, Kallassari, Kammala Karuvan, Kitaran, Kollan, Malayala Kammala, Pandi Kammala, Mossari, Perumkollan, Thattan, Padithattan, Vilkurup Villasan, Viswakarmala Thachan, Kalthachan, Kamsala, Kamsala, Kannan.

As mentioned earlier these artisanal castes/communities are not considered as non-polluting because of their traditional occupation. We can have an idea about the social status of this category through a brief discription of some of the castes/ communities.

Sunar

The traditional occupation of the Sunar community is the manfacturing of jewellery of silver and gold for their patron community. Many of them have now taken up cultivation. Sunars of Andhra Pradesh are reported to have migrated along with their patron from Rajasthan and Gujarat. In Madhya Pradesh most of the Sunar still depend on their traditional occupation of gold smithy. In the varna system, they place themselves under the varisya category. In Maharashtra they are also known as suvarnkar of Sonkar. The primary occupation of the Sunar is gold smithy and the secondary occupation is agriculture. Some of them taken up other occupations like tailoring, diamond-cutting and govt. jobs. In Uttar Pradesh they are also known as Swarnkar. Traditional and primary occupation is the business of gold and silver ornaments. Those who have land are settled cultivators besides being involved in the traditional occupation. In Delhi the Sunar claim themselves from Rajput ancesestors. Only some of them are engaged in their traditional occupation of making gold and silver ornaments, most of them serve in government and private organisations, sun shops and industries. In Punjab they are known as Sunar, Sonar, Sarag or Kwarnkar. Most of them now shifted to other highly technical jobs. In Himachal Pradesh they are also known as Jargar, largar, Kapila, Soni, Swarankar or Tank. They claim that they are from Kshathiya Varna. They are still engaged in their traditional occupation of the goldsmithy. Those are landowners are involved in agriculture and animal husbandary. Some among them are money lenders. In Bihar they are also known as Swarnakar. They are gold simth and money lenders but most of them are landlers. In Rajasthan they are known as Sonar, Soni or Swarnakar. They have adopted some other trades with traditional occupation. In Orissa they are known as Sonari Bania or Sonari. Traditionally the Sonar of Orissa were engaged as gold smiths. Now they are negaged in small business or service, teachers or daily-wage labourers. In Haryana they are also known as Swarnkar, Suniyara, Verma or Soni. They are an occupational community engaged in making gold and silver jewellery, some of them have taken up whitecollar jobs, they are teachers, administrators and in defence services. Many of them are traders and businessman. In Jammu and Kashmir they are Sanur, Sunar or Zargur, Shakish - primary occupation is goldsmithy in towns rural areas. They are Hindu and Muslims.

Kansari

Kansari caste/community found place in the central list of OBCs for West Bengal. It is also included for Orissa as Thatari/Kansari. This community is spriad over the states of West Bengal, Orissa, Gujarat, Maharashtra, Madhya Pradesh, Bihar and Goa. Risley (1891) refers to them as an offshoot of the Subarnabanik, who became degraded because they took to working in Kansa or bell -metal. They are also known as Kangabanik in West Bengal. They are known as Kansara in Gujarat and Twasta Kasar or Tambat in Maharashtra. They are known as Tamrakar in Madhya Pradesh. In Goa they call themselves Twashta Kasar Brahmin. In Bihar they are also known as Kanskar.

Traditional occupation of Kansari is working on bell-metal. Presently, agriculture, service, jewellery work and petty business are their subsidiary occupations. Most of the Kansara are engaged in making utensils and other objects of metal due to decline in the use of bell-metal utencils. A few of them are engaged in business also. They are mainly landless community.

Mohanti (1993) describes the social identity of Kansaris. According to Mohanti, Kansari occupy the middle range in the statified system. Kansari are widely known as an artisan caste all over the socio-cultural regional of Orissa. Mohanti in this study of Kansari also probes into the various other nonferrous metal craftsman in the socio-cultural and linguistics region of Orissa, such as the Tambara, Thatari, Khadura, Ghantara, Thentari (Rana)/ Sitala etc. for a comprihensive over-view of the social and craft boundaries of the Kansari caste. It is significant that the Tambara and the Kansari are intermarring ethnic groups and that Thatari and Kansari are almost interchangeable terms whereas the rest have separate identities as endogamous ethnic groups or castes. The Kansari, Thatari and Tambara serve the mainland of the state where as the rest known as the folk metal artisans serve the tribal and peasant groups on the periphery.

The Kansari as a functional caste with simple tools, equipments and craft technology manifest their dexterity and workmanship in producing domestic utensils and appliances, ritual objects, temple accessories, icons and artware. Their age old metal craft is vitalized by the induction of selective technological innovations from time to time.

Kansari politico-jural mechanisms with identifiable operational tiers during the pre-independence period have undergone transformation during the post-indendence period when merger into a wider political network was inevitable. The process of socialisation and education have enriched and paved the way to social mobility among them. Although the Kansari craftsmen and traders are accquinted with the urban situations in spite of rural anchorage the rural -urban situations are, for them, more a continuum rather than bipolar. The current trend towards economic diverstification is a prelude to economic development and consequential to statues elevation.[1]

Bhatiara

'Bhatiara' community is traditionally engaged in cooking and innkeeping. This community is also found place in the lists of OBCs. It is included in the central list of OBCs for Delhi, Bihar, Rajasthan, Uttar Pradesh and Madhya Pradesh. A brief discription of 'Bhatiara' community is given herewith to have understanding about it. They trace their origin to the reign of Sher Shah Suri and his son, Salim Shah. According Risley (1891) the Bhatiara are a class of Mahammedans whose traditional occupations are keeping inns or eating houses and sailing tobacco.[2] Enthovan (1920) writes that the 'Bhatiara' are cooks from a 'Muslman' caste distributed in the districts and princely states of Gujarat. A widely dispersed community, they inhabit Madhya Pradesh, Rajasthan and Bihar. They are both the Hindu and Muslims. In Bihar they are also known as Farooqi which is also used as surname. Wage-labour, share cropping and petty business etc. are the main economic pursuits of the Bhatiara. They are a landless community whose traditional occupation was inn-keeping. The Bhatiara women sing songs during Chhathi marriage celebrations.[3]

Caste/communities engaged in tailoring also found place in the central list of OBCs as shown in table 5.3.

Table 5.3

Statewise distribution of caste/communities engaged in Tailoring

S.No.	State	Caste/community
1.	Andhra Pradesh	Devanga
2.	Bihar	Rangrez
3.	Delhi	Chippi, Tonk, Darzi
4.	Goa	Shimpi
5.	Gujarat	Chhipa Vanza (Darji), Darji/Sai Sutar
6.	Haryana	Chimba or Chimba, Chhipi, Chimpa, Darzi
7.	Karnataka	Darzi, Bhavsarkshatriya, Chippi, Chgippiga, Simpi, Shimpi, Lingayat Simpy, Sivasimpy, Sai, Mirai, Rangari, Rangrez, Nilari, Namdev, Namdev Simpy, Rangare, Neelagar, Lingayat Neelgar
8.	Madhya Pradesh	Chippa/Chhipa (Muslim) Darzi, Cheepi/Chhipi/Chipi, Shipi, Mavi (Namdev)
9.	Maharashtra	Chhipa
10.	Orissa	Darji
11.	Punjab	Chimba or Chmbe, Chippi or Fa-qir, Chhipi, Darzi, Tonk
12.	Rajasthan	Chipa (Chhipi), Name, Bhavsar Darzi
13.	Tamilnadu	Namdev Mahratta
14.	Uttar Pradesh	Chhipa, Chipe Darzi
15.	Chandigarh	Chhimba/Chimba

The caste/communities are traditionally engaged in fixing of horse shoe, horse-gnomering and farring also found place the lists of OBCs for Bihar, Delhi, Haryana, Himachal Pradesh, Madhya Pradesh, Punjab, Chandigarh, Tamilnadu and Uttar Pradesh. Other artisan/artisanal caste/communities with non-pulluting occupations of different kinds are also shown in table 5.4.

Table 5.4

Statewise distribution of artisanal/artisan caste/communities of clean occupation

State/UT community	Caste/ occupation	Traditional
Andhra Pradesh	Achukatiavandlu	Comb making for weavers
	Jingar	Making images of gods and animals
Bihar	Abdal	Fitting horse shoe and mak ing whips
	Kagzi	Making papers
	Nalband (Muslim)	Farrier and horse shoeing
	Tikulhar	Making tikli and pargles or glass piece which are put on forhead by women
Delhi	Nalband	Fixing of horse shoe
Goa	Dhangar	Masonary and Carpentary
Gujarat	Jhakudia	Neeting
Haryana	Nalband	Fixing of horse shoe
	Kuchband	Making brush for weavers
H.P.	Nalband	Fixing of horse shoe
Karnataka	Kotekshatriya	Carcuss carrying
M.P.	Chitari	Painting on walls
	Chunkar	Massion work
	Nalband	Fixing of horse shoe
	Sikligar	Cleaning and Sharpening of arms

	Kharol	Construction of mud houses
Maharashtra	Jatigar	Polishing the horses and clip ping the hair of cattle
	Jhadi	Making ropes from wabir (a creeper)
	Jingar	Saddlers
Orissa	Khodra	Making of Bengals
	Gudia	Making sweets
	Raneyar	Carry car cass
Punjab	Nalband	Fixing of horse shoe
Tamilnadu	Kudumbi	Pounding rice
	Rowthar	Horse-gnomers
	Yogeswarar	Garland making and selling
	Perumkollar	Making carts
Uttar Pradesh	Nalband, Sains	Fixing of horse shoe
	Halwai	Sweet making
	Atishbaz	Manufecturing of gun powder and explosives
West Bengal	Moira	(Halwai) Confectioners
Chandigarh	Nalband	Fixing of horse shoe

(B) Artisan/Aritsanal Castes/communities with Polluting Occupation

Certain hereditary occupations are polluting, lowly and undignified. For example 'Butchery' which is considered lowly because it is attached with killing of animals. 'Fishing' involves killing living creatures. 'Leather work' is a low occupation because handling hide is defiling and such defilement may be related to the taking of life. 'Hair-cutting' and 'Washing Clothes' involves handling dirt and makes these occupations unclean. Making and selling of liquor i.e. diselling of liquor and Toddy Tapping are also considered lolly and undignified occupations.

Mayer (1986) writes that the clearest division sets of four occupations as lowest. Any work which is connected with dead things or bodily emissions pollutes seriously. Hence the tanner and sweeper are the bottom of the scale-the sweeper is a little lower because he handles human excrement and receives a dead person's shroud. The drummer's work demeans him because he plays at the rites of Harijan castes. Higher still is the barber's work, for though it involves handling hair and nail parings which are impure things, the barber who works for the higher castes does not also serve the Harijans.[6]

Some of the existing polluting occupations can be as listed

Fishing, Washing of clothes, Hair cutting, Scavenging, Toddy-tapping, Butchering, Snack-charming and snake-play; Monkey-catching and Monkey-play, Pig-rearing, Grain-roasting, Bagging or mandicancy, Hunting, bird catching, foul-catching, Drnmming, Iron-shoe fastening, Saddle making, Knife-glinding, grass-cutting, Ferrying by boat or country craft, Oil-pressing, working on leather, pottry, black smithy, etc.

Many of the caste/communities engaged in the above listed occupations had got the SC/ST status while some of them also found place in the OBC list. Such caste/communities of the OBC lists can further be divided into sub-categories as under:

(i) **Service Castes**: The caste of washermen 'Dhobi' is included in 15 states and five UTs in the SC list. This caste is known by different names such as Rajaka or Chakali/ Chakkala in Andhra Pradesh, Tamilnadu and Pondicherry, Parit in Maharashtra, Agasa and Medivala in Karnataka, Peruvannan and Vellan in Kerala, Vannar in Tamilnadu and Hawari Dhobi in West Bengal. Dhobi caste/communy has been included in the list of Scheduled Castes for Bihar, Uttar Pradesh, Delhi, Rajasthan and parts of Madhya Pradesh while this caste other than SCs also found place in the list of OBCs for these states. The caste of Washermen is included in the central list of OBCs for Gujarat, Haryana, Punjab, Chandigarh, Dadar and Nagar Haveli, Daman and Diu, Bihar, Madhya Pradesh, Rajasthan, Uttar Pradesh, Delhi and Goa.

Dhobi's who are Muslims by religion constitute a caste or caste-like community, linked with the traditional hereditary occupation of washing cloths as in the case of Hindu Dhobis. This community still suffers from the stigma of untouchability in the rural areas. They are carrying out their traditional occupation of washing and cleaning clothes though mechanised laundries owned by the other caste people and Dhobis are working there as a wage labourers. They have lost access to water and open plots for carrying out their work. In other words this skilled caste became unskilled and unemployed.

Hajjam and Nai are the names of the caste which is associated with the service of hair-cutting. Russel and Hiralal (1916) have describes the caste as Nai, Nao, Mhali, Hajjam, Bhandari, Mangla- the occupational caste of barbers. In central India the caste is also known as Khawas which was a title for the attendant on a grandee and Birtiya or 'he that gets his maintance (viritti) from his Constitutents'.[5] Where he is Muhammadan he usually calls himself Hajjam. Rose (1919) writes that the cults of the Nais are in essentials much like those of the other artisan castes.[6]

The caste/community is included in the OBC lists for Bihar, Delhi, Haryana, Himachal Pradesh, Madhya Pradesh, Punjab, Rajasthan and West Bengal. The caste/community also found place in the OBC lists for Andhra Pradesh as 'Nayi-Brahmin' along with its sub-castes of Mangali, Mangla and Bhajanthari; 'Napit' for Assam; 'Nhavi' and its sub castes-Nai, Nabhik, Napit and Mahalo for Goa; Yayinda, Lingayat Nayinda, Lingayat Bhandari, Bhajantari, Lingayat Bhajanthari and Lingayat Hadapada for Karnataka. The caste/community included in the central list of OBCs for Kerala as 'Vilakkithala Nair' 'Pandithar'; 'Ezhavathi and 'Kavuthiyan' 'Navi' for Maharashtra; Barika, Bhandari, Napit, Nai for Orissa; 'Kavuthiyar' and Maruthuvar for Tamilnadu; 'Napit' and 'Shil' for Tripura; 'Hajjam (Nai)' along with its synonyms (Salmani and Sain) for Uttar Pradesh and 'Napit' for West Bengal; Nhavi for Daman and Diu.

Other caste/communities of this category are related to iron work, wooden work, pottery, massion, oil pressing etc. also found place in the OBC lists for many states from different names such as 'Kanmbhakar' (Potters) for Tripura Kulala (Potter) for Tamilnadu; Jhangra Brahman (carpenter) along with its sub-castes-Khati, Lohar, Ramgarhia, Turkhan for Punjab; 'Kusivan' (Potter) with its sub castes (Kulala, Kulala Nair or Andhra Nair) for Kerala; Luhar, Bhubalia, Saifi (blacksmith) for Delhi; Agariya (iron workers) for Bihar; Gandla and Teli Kula (oil pressing) for Andhra Pradesh; Ganiga (oil pressing) for Gujarat; Ganali or Gandali (oil pressing) for Maharashtra and Vaniyar (oil pressing) for Pondicherry; Gangai (Ganesh) for Bihar, 'Ronas' for Orissa, 'Kulala' and 'Salivagana' caste/ communities engaged in pottery also found place in the central list of OBCs. Similarly the caste/communities traditionally engaged in iron work such as 'Agaria' for Bihar, Kolla for Karnataka, Kamara for Kerala, 'Gadri' and ' Panchal' for Maharashtra, 'Kammra' and 'Muliya' for Orissa; 'Saifi' for Punjab, Gadia- Lohar for Rajasthan, 'Kammalar or Viswakarma' for Tamilnadu and 'Gara' for Tripura found place in the list of OBCs. The Caste/communities associated with carpentary and massion work are included in the central list of OBCs as Khat bune for Delhi, 'Me or Meta' and Sargara for Gujarat, Kuchband (making brush for weavers) for Haryana, Khatiya for Madhya Pradesh. Sutar, Gavandi, Khathar and Wadi for Maharashtra, Khati-Khatti for Orissa, Perumkollar for Tamilnadu, Sutradhar for Tripura and West Bengal and Ramgarhia for Chandigarh. Caste/communities with iron work are also reflected in the list of OBCs for instance Kolla for Karnataka, Kammara for Kerala, Gadri and Panchal for Maharashtra, Kammara and Muliya for Orissa, Saifi for Punjab, Gadia-Lohar for Rajasthan, Kammalar or Vishwakarma for Tamilnadu and Gara for Tripura.

There are other subsidiary professional castes the people of which are employed only on particular occassions such as feasts and celebrations of marriage etc. The castes of Bards and geneologists and Palanqui carriers and water carriers can be put under this category. Bards and geneologist are generally known as 'Bhat'. 'Bhat' caste/community is included in the OBC lists for Delhi, Bihar, Haryana, Himachal Pradesh, Chandigarh, Punjab and Madhya Pradesh. It is also known by different names such as 'Ganak' in Assam; 'Bhatraju' and 'Bhatraja'in Tamilnadu and Andhra Pradesh respectively 'Kanisan' and 'Helava' in Karnataka, Mirasi (Muslim) in Haryana, Bhat, Bhatta Ard Pop and Darpi in Himachal Pradesh; Bhat, Charan, Sawli, Sutiya, Rav, Jasondhi and Maru- Sonia in Madhya Pradesh; Badwa, Bhat, Rao, Charan Jachak and Jaga in Rajasthan.

Risely (1891) writes that the Bhat of Bihar, Bengal and Orissa are also known as Bhandi. They are geneologists and family bords.[7] Russsel and Hiralal (1916) states that Bhats are an term Brahman. But the caste is very mixed one, a large section the Charan are derived from Rajputs.[8] The total pupulation of Bhat, Brahmabhatt, Charan, Jasondhi according to 1931 census was 307,274. They were distributed in the United Provinces, Rajputana, Western India States, Central India, etc. In Haryana they are in two sub groups i.e. Brahman Bhat and Rajbhat or Jaga. The Brahma Bhat are considered superior to the Rajbhat on the basis of occupation and economy. In Maharashtra they are denotified tribe concentrated in Pune, Satara, Kolhapur and Sholapur districts. In Bihar, the section of the Bhat who have embraced Islam live in Madhubani, Darbhanga, Patna, Purnia and Samastipur districts; their traditional occupation is cultivation.

The castes of water carriers and palanqui carriers are generally known as Kahar. This castes is also found place in the OBC lists as 'Dhekaru' in Bihar, Bhoi in Gujarat, Dhimar in Haryana, Dhinwar or Jhiwar and Mehra in Himachal

Pradesh; Sakka-Bhishti-Abbasi in Rajathan; and Kahar in West Bengal, Bhisti or Pakhali in Maharashtra, Bhujal in Sikkim; Saqqa Bhishti in Uttar Pradesh.

The caste/communities traditionally engaged in Bengal selling are 'Churihar (Muslim)' in Bihar, 'Manhar' in Madhya Pradesh, 'Gajula Balija' in Andhra Pradesh, Lakhera/ Lakhwara/Laxhar in Gujarat, Lakhera and Manihar in Haryana and Rajasthan; Manihar, Kacher, Lakher, Lakhera and Churihar in Uttar Pradesh.

The caste/communities taditionally engaged in Grain Parchering are also included in the lists of OBCs such; as 'Dhimar' and 'Kanu' in Bihar; 'Kanu' in Delhi, 'Bhadbunja' in Gujarat, 'Bharbunha' in H.P., Bhadbhuja in Madhya Pradesh and 'Bhurji' in Uttar Pradesh. A brief description of some caste/ communities of this categories is given below:

Teli

Enthoven (1920) describes Teli of Deccan and Konkan region, who were recruited for the purpose of making oil, traces their origin to the Maratha.[9] the Teli are traditionally oil-pressers. Many of them have now acquired land and become cultivators. In Rajasthan they are also known as Ganchhi. They trace their origin to the Rajput of Mewar. Most of them have shifted to oil-trading and business. They are Muslim (Teli) also known as Turk teli or Turkia. They are a landowing community and depend on agriculture and still engaged in their traditional occupation of oil-pressing. Traditional and Primary occupations of Teli of Tripura are Agriculture and trade. In Assam they are also known as Taili and Tailik. Most of them have migrated from South. Their primary occupation is cultivation and business. In Madhya Pradesh they are also known as Sahu. Teli are agriculturist, businessmen, money lenders, petty traders and service holders. They have given up their traditional occupation of oil pressing. In Orissa Teli have two subgroups i.e. Ekadasi and Haldia. Land is the main economic source for them. The traditional occupation of the Teli is business. Teli (Ghana) are a large community called by different names as Ghana, Ghani, Gachhna and Johria Teli in Orissa, they are categorized under Vaisya Varna. Now majority of them are agriculturists. They have taken up oil-pressing and business as their secondary occupations. In West Bengal they are also known as Ekadash, Dwadash, Peno and Panta, Cultivation and business are their principal occupations. Their traditional occupation is oil trade. Some are engaged in service and a few are agricultural labourers. In Himachal Pradesh, the 'Teli' have got SC status. They are both Hindu and Muslims. They have been oil-pressers but now shifted to cultivation agriculture labour, service and business.

Oil pressing and selling is very old profession. The caste/communities engaged in this profession are also found place in the list of OBCs for many states such as Bihar, Gujarat, Madhya Pradesh, Karnataka, Andhra Pradesh. In Andhra Pradesh they are known as Gandla and in Gujarat as Ganchi (Muslim).

(ii) Artists and Magicians

Caste/communities are engaged traditionally in personal entertainment by singing and dancing, acting, acrobatics or jugglery, snake-charming and snake-play, monkey-catching and monkey-play etc. are also found place in the list of OBCs.

Some of these caste/communities have already been discussed under 'Nomadic and Semi-Nomadic' in this chapter. The caste/communities of this category could also be called professional castes. As these occupations are still considerd polluting and the caste/communities associated with these occupations are the most backward in the caste hierarchy. The caste/communities of this category found place in the central list of OBCs are given in table 5.5.

Table 5.5

Statewise distribution of castes/communities of Artists and Magicians

State/UT	Caste/Community	Traditional Occupation
A.P.	Pamula	Snake Charming
	Surya Balija (Kalavanthula)	Dancing and Singing
Bihar	Gulgaliya	Monkey-Playing
	Khelta	Dancing and Singing
	Pamaria (Muslim)	Dancing and Singing
	Madari	Jugglery
Delhi	Badi	Jugglery
Gujarat	Madari, Nath, Bharathari	Jugglery
	Mir	Musician
Haryana	Madari	Jugglery
	Nar	Magician
H.P.	Beda	Musician
	Mirasi	Entertaining and Atendent to rulers
	Madari	Entertaining
	Nar	Megician
J & K	Bhand	Story tellers
Karnataka	Bajania	Musician and Rope dancer
	Panika	Dancer
M.P.	Nat	Snake-Charming
Maharashtra	Bahurupia	Strolling dramatic play
	Kasbi	Singing and dancing
	Bhavaiya	Performing Commedies
	Bajania	Musician and Rope dancers

	Bajigar	--do--
	Bhand	Story tellers
	Sapaliga	Playing Music
Pondicherry	Maruthuvar	Musician
Punjab	Madari	Jugglery
	Nar	Magician
Uttar Pradesh	Madari	Entertaining
	Bhand	Dancing and Singing
	Naqqal	-do-

(iii) Fishermen, Boating and Porter Castes

In Indian Caste system we find the fishing and related Comminities exclusively related with their tradition occupation which is inherited from father to son. As a result it is formed and shaped not only their economy but also their social life. Presently the fishing community is almost in economic distress with the distruction of large ports of the forest, increasing population, increasing industrial contaimination of rivers and ponds. Traditional fishing community is being pushed out from their occupation or reduced to being wage labours on trawlers or at other stages of processing of the seafood.

Social position of this community is low as of the menial castes but they are not untouchables. The community, generally Known as 'Mallah' in Northern India; Kewats or Keyots (Kaivarta or Kaibartta) in North-western India; Dhimar and Bhoi in central India. It is known from different names in Southern India. Caste/Communities found place in the OBC lists are given in table 5.6.

Table 5.6

Statewise distribution of OBCs traditionally engaged in Fishing and related occupations

S.No.	State	Caste/community
1.	A.P.	Agnikula Kshatriya, Pallireddi, Vedabalija, Besthe, Jalari, Gangavar,

		Gangaputra, Goondla, Vanyakula-Kshtriya, Vannekapu, Vennereddi, Pallikapu, Palliredi, Nayyala, Pattapu, Kandra
2.	Assam	Mahishya Das, Mahisya
3.	Bihar	Bind; Chanin, Chayeen, Kaivartta/ Kaibartta; Kewat; Tiyar
4.	Goa	Pagi
5.	Gujarat	Bhoi, Bhoiraj, Dhimar, Zinga Bhoi, Kevat Bhoj, Bhanara Bhoi, Machhindra Bhoi, Palwar Bhoi, Kirat Bhoi, Kahar Bhoi, Pardeshi Bhoi, Shrimali Bhoi, Kharwa-Bhadela, Koli, Wagher
6.	Haryana	Dhimar, Mallah, Kashyap-Rajpoot, Kahar, Jhinwar or Jhimar, Dhiwar, Khewat, Mehra, Nishad
7.	H.P.	Dhimar or Dhimar or Dhiwar; Dhinwar or Jhinwar; Mehra; Mallah
8.	Karnataka	Gangakula, Gangemakkalu, Gangamatha, Gangaputra, Gowrimatha, Ambig, Ambiga, Bestha, Kabbaliga, Kabbili, Kabber, Kabbera, Kharvi, Bhoi, Bhoyi, Boyi, Thoreya, Harakanthra, Harikanthra, Kahar, Meenagar, Magareera, Kharia, Sunnagar, Siviyar, Parivara, Galadakon - Kani, Bakada, Beshtar
9.	Kerala	Dheevara (Araya, Arayavathi, Mukkuvan, or Mukaya, Mongevera, Valam, Bovi Mukayar, Nulayan, Valinijar and Paniakkal), Latin Catholic
10.	M.P.	Dhimar, Bhoi, Kahar, Dhiwar, Mallah, Nawda Turaha, Kewat, Kir, Britiya, Sondhiya

11.	Maharashtra	Bhoi/Boi, Zinga Bhoi, Pardeshi Bhoi, Raj Bhoi, Kahar, Gadia Kahare, Dhuria Kahar, Kirat, Machwa, Manzi, Jatia, Kewat, Dhiwar, Dhiwar Bhoi, Dheewar, Dhimar, Palewar, Machhendra, Navadi, Malhar, Madhav, Gadhav Bhoi, Khadi Bhoi, Khare Bhoi, Dhevra, Bestar, Koli, Christian Koli, Chumle, Machhimar Koli, Panbhare (Panbhari), Son Kali, Ahir Koli, Pan Koli, Bari
12.	Punjab	Dhimar, Mallah, Kashyap Rajput
13.	Rajasthan	Sakka-Bhishti, Saqqa-Bhishti, Bhishti-Abbasi, Dhivar, Keer, Kallah, Mehra
14.	T.N.	Aragyar, Arayan, Nulayar, Kabbera, Kharvi, Kurga Vellalar, Labbai, Latin Cathalic, Mapilla, Meenavar, Parvatharaja Kulam, Pattanavar, Sembadavar (including converts to Christianity), Valaiyar
15.	Tripura	Bin, Bind
16.	U.P.	Kahar, Tanwar Singhariya, Jhoja, Kewat or Mallah
17.	Pondicherry	Kadaiyan, Kandra, Valans
18.	Daman and Diu	Koli

(iv) Castes/Communities Work in Bamboo

Most of these castes are low castes. They lead a unsteady and nomadic kind of like due to their occupation. There is a more or less definite life is drawn between castes which work is bamboo and those who work in reeds, palm leaves and roots.

The bamboo workers seem to belong to the big Dom caste known by othernames as Bansphoras (bamboo splitters), Basors, Bansors, Bansos or Bansodies. In Rajasthan they specialise in manufacture of fans (pankha). They are known as 'Barera' in Himalayan hills, Kanjars and Basors in Northern India; Lohra in central India, Bantar in eastern India.

Occassionally they work as stone-cutters and makers of grinding mills. They also manufacture the brushes which weavers require for the cleaning of cotton yarn for example 'Achukatlavandlu' of Andhra Pradesh. They make baskets, dig tank and make cart wheels and other wooden agriculture implements.

A few caste/communities found place in the list of OBCs such as Achukatlavandlu', 'Ayyaraka', 'Godaba' 'Gudala' and Medari or Mahendra for Andhra Pradesh; Manipuri (Muslim), Basor and Basphor for Assam; 'Bari and Dhankar for Bihar; Mahar for Goa; Dhosali and Dosal for Himachal Pradesh; Medari for Karnataka, 'Bari' for Rajasthan; Katesar for Tamilnadu; Manipuri and Kapali for Tripura; Bind for Uttar Pradesh; Korga for Orissa; Buttal for Maharashtra; Narikoravan for Pondicherry; Paraiyan for Orissa.

(v) Toddy Tappers and Distillers

The castes which live by tapping the palm for its juice take usually a position between the lower artisans and the field labourers. These castes are found along the coasts. It is not a full time occupation, at the same time they are cultivators as land holders or tenants or field labours.

In Punjab the distiller and seller of liquor is called Kalar or Kalwar Chief castes of the taddy tappers are Parsis in Uttar Pradesh and Bihar, Bhandari in Maharastra, Idigas in Andhra Pradesh, Ezhavas/Thiyya in Kerala, Sunri is distliller and liquor sellers in West Bengal.

Some of the caste/communities of this category which found place in the central list of OBCs are shown in Table 5.7

Table 5.7

Statewise distribution of castes/communities of the central list of OBCs traditionally engaged in Toddy Tapping/Distilling

S.No.	State	Caste/Community
1.	A.P.	Ediga, Gowda (Gammalla, Kalalee), Goundla, Settibalija (of Vishakhapatnam, Godavari and Krishna Districts), Lodh, Lodha, Lodhi, Srisayana (Segidi), Yata
2.	Bihar	Kalwar, Kalal, Eraqui
3.	Delhi	Kalwar
4.	Gujarat	Bhandari, Kalal
5.	Karnataka	Kalkari, Kelkari, Khelkari, Idiga
6.	Kerala	Billava, Ezhuvan, Ezhavathi, Nadar
7.	M.P.	Kalar, Kalal
8.	Maharashtra	Bhandari, Kalal, Kalar, Sav Kalar
9.	Orissa	Kalwar, Sunri, Sundi
10.	Rajasthan	Kalal (Tak)
11.	T.N.	Ezhavathy (in Kanniya Kumari and Tirunelveli Districts), Gounder, Idiga
12.	U.P.	Kalal, Kalwar, Kalar, RaiSikh (Mahatam)
13.	W.B.	Kalwar
14.	Pondicherry	Idiga

(vi) Earth Workers, Stone, Salt and Lime Workers

These occupational castes are known by different names though they may have the same origin. In many regions the stone, salt and lime workers were orginally fishermen.

Odh or Oudhia or Oudh or Odari the Orissa caste of earth workers is originally belong to Rajasthan and distributed over the Punjab. Koras or Khairas of Bihar and West Bengal are earth worker's caste while they are known as Pathrat in Maharashtra, Upparas in Andhra Pradesh; and Uppalinga/ Uppiliyens, Ottar or Otte in Tamilnadu.

A few of the caste/communities of this category also listed as OBCs in different states as shown in Table 5.8.

Table 5.8

Statewise distribution of caste/communities of Earth Workers, stone, Salt & Lime Workers in the central list of OBCs

S.No.	State	Earth Workers	Stone, Salt & Lime Workers
1.	A.P.	Nagaraddilu Kummara or Kulala or Salivahana	Vannia
2.	Bihar	Beldar	Nunia
3.	Delhi		Agri, Kharwal
4.	Gujarat	Od	Sathwara,Agri
5.	Haryana		Noongar
6.	H.P.		Labana, Thawin
7.	Karnataka		Uppara,Lonari (sub caste of uppara), Takankar
8.	Kerala	Kudumbi, Kumbaran Odde, Boyan	
9.	M.P.	Tarhe, Tirwali, Waddar	Chunkar, Loniya/ Luniya, Odh, Muraha
10.	Maharashtra	Nonia	Agri, Kaikadi
11.	Orissa		Nuniya, Pathuria
12.	Punjab		Noongar
13.	Rajasthan		Odd

14.	T.N.	Kharvi, Oddar, Chakkala
15.	Tripura	Nunia
16.	Daman and Diu	Agri, Mitna
17.	Chandigarh	Noongar

C. **Untouchable Caste/Communities**

A few Caste/Communities of this category found place in the Central list of OBCs. For instance 'Halalkhore, 'Hela,' 'Dohar' and 'Lal begi' for the state of Uttar Pradesh. 'Hela' for Madhya Pradesh; Methar (Muslim) for Andhra Pradesh, 'Mochi' for Rajasthan, Delhi, Haryana and Uttar Pradesh; 'Paky' for Orissa.

'Halalkhar' is a community which in the traditional Caste system, has been identified with sweepers work. They Crook (1919) describes 'Lal Begi' and 'Hela' under the title 'Bangi' as the sub castes of Bhangi tribe of Hindustan. Census classified them under five main sub-castes i.e. 'Balmiki', 'Dhanuk', 'Hela', 'Lalbegi' and 'Patharphor' (Stone breaker).

'Dohar' caste is similar to Chamars' according to Russel and Hiralal, (1916) The caste is included in SC list for Uttar Pradesh and Madhya Pradesh also included in the central list of OBCs for Uttar Pradesh.

The Caste/Communities traditionally engaged in drum beating, piggary working on leather, scvanging butchery etc. also found place in the central list of OBCs can be listed in this category (see table 5.9)

Table 5.9

Distribution of Untouchable caste/ communities in the central list of OBCs

S. No.	State	Name of the Caste/community	Occupation
1.	A.P.	Arekatika	Butchery
		Pambala	Drum-beating
2.	Assam	Hari	Scavenging

3.	Bihar	Madar	Removal of dead cattle from the villave, scvanging & sweeping
		Khatik	Pig rearing
		Kasab (Kasai) (Muslims)	Butchery
		Chik (Muslim)	"
4.	Delhi	Kasai	Butchery
		Chak	----do--
		Katik	
5.	Gujarat	Khatik	Scarenging
6.	J&K	Doom	Scarenging
7.	Karnataka	Kasai	Butchery
8.	M.P.	Dafaali	Drum-beating
		Kasabi/Kisbi	----do--
		Hela (Muslim)	Scarenging
9.	Maharashtra	Khatik	Buchery
		Ladia	Leather work
		Dabgar	Working on hide & leather
10.	Orissa	Paky	Scarenging
		Paniyandi	Piggary
		Mahla/Mahlar	Butchering
11.	Rajasthan	Kasai	Butchering
		Damami	Drum-beating
		Hela, Janwa, Sirvi	Scarenging
12.	U.P.	Sheikhsarvari (Pirai)	Drum beating
		Halalkhor, Hela, Lalbagi	Scarenging
13.	West Bengal	Kasai-Quraishi	Butchering
14.	Daman & Diu	Dhor	Tan Cattle skin

D. Peasantary and other castes/communities related to Agriculture

There are three classes of farmers i.e. the land owners, the tenant and the agricultural labourers. Generally the uppar castes own the land and the lower castes help to cultivate it as tenants or agricultural labourers. This position in the agricultural system is partly reflexes of the caste's traditional occupational positions. Majority of people of the certain castes now engaged in cultivation as landowners were previously cattle rearers, oil-pressers, goldsmiths, petty traders, etc. Yadavs of Uttar Pradesh and Bihar, Telis of Madhya Pradesh and Sunars of many states are no more landless. The people of these castes farmed quite a lot of land at this time and now can be considered as land owning. Their traditional occupations either leftout or reduced to a great extent. Thus the connection of economic activity with the caste group is less clearcut where an occupation is not followed exclusively by one caste. The position is rapidly changing due to modernisation, free economy and globalization process. Jajmani practices had changed intomarket economy. Even then allied castes are prominent as landowners.

There is a widely quoted probers 'Uttam Kheiti, Madhyam Vyapar, Nikhid Chakri, Bheek Nidan' (highest in agriculture, in the middle is trade, next is service, most worthless is begging). This illustrated both the regard in which independence is held, and the way in which the cultivators, who cultivate the largest occupational group, have put themselves at the top of the scale.

In economic and occupational terms the backward classes by and large, comprise of peasants, artisanal communities and those who provide various traditional services. In caste terms the owner and tenant can be of the same caste. Many marginal farmers (of whatever caste) lease their holdings, not having the capital or equipment needed to farm them. Tenants are also found in many castes. Some are upper caste without sufficient land. There is also a rapid turnover in tenants and contract labourers. Table 5.10 shows the peasantry as occupational class:

Table 5.10

Peasantry as an Occupational Class

Land Owners	Tantants	Labourers
1a. Cultivators (Rich farmėrs or big peasants)	c. Marginal farmers (Small peasant)	e. Contact labourer (seasonal labourers)
2b. Non Cultivators (absentee land lords.)	d. Share Croppers (landless or having less than 2-3 acre of land)	f. Majdoor (hired on a daily wage basis)

a. Rich farmers are either higher caste people or upper strata of the intermediatly caste.

b. Non-Cultivators are socially and economically advanced castes.

c. Under share coropping system tanant and owner divide the crop. The owner contributes the land, tax and the seed, the tanant give half the seed, bulucks, equipment and labour. The proportion in which the crop is divided vary. If the owner gives every thing except labour he receives three-forth of the crop.

d. In the system of Sikmi/Jins, a fixed sum in cash or kind is paid annually as rent. It also vary from individual to individual quantity is fixed in advance, generally ¼ of the total goes to tenant.

e. Contact labourers works in the fields of others in the harvasting season (March-April), they are also called Laba or Labourers or Naukar.

f. Majdoor are hired on a daily wage basis.

In view of the above the caste/communities engaged in farming may be divided into two categories i.e. Land owning cultivators (Peasantary castes) and agricultural labourers which also includes the tenants. In this section we will discuss the peasantry castes and agricultural laboures which found place is the list of OBCs. As cattle reering and Pastoral castes and the Caste communities traditionally associated with gardening, growing and selling of vegetables, fruits and betal leaves are associated with Agriculture also discussed in this section. The caste with cultivation as a sole traditional occupation have more population in companinion to other castes. Numerical strength of the peasentaly castes makes a lot of difference in respect of inter-caste relationship. These castes tend to predominanate generally in Andhra Pradesh, Bihar, Karnataka, Gujarat, Haryana, Madhya Pradesh, Maharashtra, Punjab, Rajasthan and Uttar Pradesh. The following table shows the distribution of peasantly castes engaged in cultivation cattle rearing, gardening and found OBC status.(see table 5.11 to 5.13)

Table 5.11

Statewise distribution of Peasant Caste/Communities in the central list of OBCs

S.No.	State	Peasants	Agricultural Labourers
1.	Andhra Pradesh	Atirase	Agaru
		Gavara	Mathura
		Koppulavelama	
		Munnurukapu (Telengana)	Passi
			Nagaralu
		Vannia, Vanniar, Vannikula, Kshatriya	Vanjara (Vanjari)
		Neeli (Nelli)	Ayyaraka
		Nagavamsa	Mudiraj
		Pala-Ekari	Gudala
		Palinativalivelana	Poosala
		(of Srikakulam &	Lodh
		Vishakhapatnam districts)	Gajula Balija
2.	Assam	Moran,	
		Bhuyan	

		Keot	
		Kharia	
		Shut	
		Ghosh	Mali
		Nagbansi	Kachi/Kachhia
		Nath	
		Saloi	
3.	Bihar	Amaat	Chopota (Sub Caste
		Rajbhar	of Julha)
		Bagdi	Dhanuk
		Chain	
		Chandrabanshi	Kadar
		(Kahar)	
		Chanou	Korku
		Gangota, Gangoth	
		Ghatwar	Namshudra
		Gorh, Gourh	
		(only in Saran and	Rauttiya
		Rohtas districts)	Kulahia
		Kawar	
		Khetauri Khataur	Markande
		Kochh	
		Kurmi Mahto	
		Shershahbadi	
		Tharu	
		Sukiyar	
		Nagar	
4.	Delhi		Ark, Arakvanshiya
			Qassar, Lodhi
5.	Goa	Velip	Pagui, Mahar
		Kunbi	Gowda
			Nathjogi
6.	Gujarat	Bharwad, Thakarda	Mali Bhar, Defer
		Sandhi (Muslim)	
		Rathodia, Sathwara	Kathi Rajbhar, Sidhi
		Sindhi (Muslim)	Mahia (Maiya),

		Khant, Miyana	Galiara (Muslim)
		Makarani (Muslim)	
7.	Haryana	Meo	Lodh Gorkha, Mina
		Gujar	Gadaria
		Saini	
		Kamboj	Ghasi
		Ghirath or	Gwaria
		Ghidath	Dewala
			Kurmi
8.	Himachal Pradesh	Kurmi	Gorkha
		Ghirath	
9.	Karnataka	Balasanthoshi	
		Gatti/Gattiyavaru	
		Halawakki-Wakkal	
		Nadora,	Balija
		Uppina Kolaga	Nairy
		Vokkaliga	Koyava
		(Rural area).	
		Lingayat Gowli/	Kulvadi (Sudra)
		Gauli/Kawadiga,	Kurma
		Lingayat Kuruba/	Hanabaru
		Kurubaru	Sudir
		Kanvi Maratha	
		Rajput	
10.	Kerala	Gatti, Hegde, Marati	Sadhu Chetties
11.	Madhya Pradesh	Agharia	Meru, Mer
		Asara	Kunjara
		Dangi	Rajwar
		Rautiya	
		Deshwali	
		Kirar	Mankar
		Lodh, Lodha, Lodhi	
		Rajwar	
		Ghoshi	
		Mewati, Meo	

		Mirasi	
		Tadavi	
		Patidar	
		Lodhi, Lodha, Lodh	
		Powar	
		Rauttiya	
12.	Maharashtra	Baria, Kali Baria	Alitkar
		Kunbi	
		Dode Gujar, Dore Gujar	
		Kohli	
		Sangar	
13.	Manipur	Meite, Meetei (including Meitei Brahman, Sanamahi, Rajkumar)	
14.	Orissa	Alia	Bhanja Puren
		Arue	Mahla/Mahlar
		Bhogta	
		Chasa	Paiko
		Godda	
		Kalandi Baishanaba	Pal
		Kalanga, Kaslanji/	Pulayan
		Kalingi	Holeya
		Khetauri	
		Koppula Vellama	Koraga
		Manna Dhora	
		Paliyan	
		Palli	
		Suda	
		Shudra (in Puri district only)	
		Telaga	
15.	Punjab	Ghirath	
		Kamboj	Bhar, Rajbhar

		Kachhi	Kurmi
		Rahbari	
		Saini	
16.	Rajasthan	Dhakad	
		Janwa	Lodhi (Lodha, Lodh)
		Kirar	
		Lodha, Lodha, Lodhi	
		Mer	
		Rawat	
		Sirvi	Saini
		Jat (except in Bharatpur and Dhaulpur dist.)	Chungar
		Kachhi	Rai Sikh
		Kalbi	
17.	Sikkim	Sanyasi	
		Manger	
		Thami	Jogi
18.	Tamilnadu	Agamudayar including Thozhn or Thulava Vellala	Moopanar/Nainar
		Ambalakarar, Ambalakaran	Thoraiyar of Nilgiri, Parkavakulam
		Badagar	Pulavar
		Billava	
		Bondil	
		Hegde	
		Kalingi	Savalakkarar
		Kalveli Gounder	
		Kongu Vellalar	
		Koppala Velana	
		Kunchidigar	
		Kunnuvar Mannadi	
		Labbai	
		Mappila	
		Moundadanchetty	

		Nangudi Vellalar Pooluva Gounder Urali Gounder Vallambar Vanniyakula- Kshatriya Wynad Chetty	
19.	Tripura	Bhar, Rajbhar Bishnupriya Manipuri	Giri, Pangal Nayak Kandh
20.	Uttar Pradesh	Ahir, Yadav Arakh, Arakvan-shiya Bhar Bhot Kisan Kuthaliya Bora Murao or Murai Lodh, Lodha, Lodhi, Lodhi Rajput Nayak	Bot Rai Sikh (Mahatam)
21.	West Bengal	Bhar Bhujel Chamling Dhanuk Dhimal Hela/Halia/Chasi-Kabartha Das Kalbartta Kapali Kurmi Nagar Raju Sarak Satchasi	Bhujel Nambang Thami

22.	Dadra and N. Haveli	Kapadi	
23.	Daman and Diu	Kunbi, Sagar	
24.	Pondicherry	Ambalakaran, Gatti, Kalingi, Urali Goundan Vadukan	Parkavakulam

Table 5.12

Statewise distribution of Cattle rearing and Pastoral Caste/ Communities

S.No.	State	Cattle rearing	Postoral
1.	Andhra Pradesh	Kuruba or Kuruma Pondara	Yadava (Golla)
2.	Assam	Chutia, chutiya	Ghosh, Gope, Gwala, Goal, Goala
3.	Bihar	Yadav, Gope, Gwala, Ahir, Ghosi	Pal (Bherihar-Gaderi)
		Gaddi (Muslim)	Gadaria
4.	Delhi	Ahir (Yadav)	Gwala, Gujar
5.	Gujarat	Ahir	Bharwad, Gadhai (Muslim) Jat (Muslim)
6.	Haryana	Ahir	Gawala, Gujjar, Gadaria
		Rahabari	
7.	H.P.	Ahir	Gadaria, Gaddi Gujjar or Gujar (in merged area only)
8.	Karnataka	Golla	Yadav, Gouli, Gujar

9.	Kerala	Yadava (Kolaya, Ayar, Mayar, Maniyani and Iruman)	
10.	M.P.	Ahir Banjara Bhurtiya Ghoshi Goojar/Gurjar	Gadariya Hatgar Dhangar
11.	Maharashtra	Yadav, Ahir	Dhangar/Dhanwar Gavli, Hatkar/Hatker Gopala, Kurmar
12.	Orissa	Goala	
13.	Punjab	Ahir Rahabari	
14.	Rajasthan	Ahir (Yadav)	Gadaria (Gadri), Gaddi, Gujar Ghosi (Gvala)
15.	Sikkim		Limboo (including Tsong, Subbna and Yakthungba)
16.	Tamilnadu		Krishnan Vaka (in Kanyakumari and Tirunelveli districts) Kurumba (where they are not STs)
17.	Tripura	Goala	Gareri
18.	Uttar Pradesh	Yadav Gadaria	Gaddi, Gujar Ghosi
19.	West Bengal	Goalas and Sadgopa	Gope
20.	Chandigarh		Gadaria

Table 5.13

Statewise distribution of Caste/Communities associated with Garderning, growing and selling of vegetable, fruit, flowers and betal leaves

S.No.	State	Gardening (including vegetable, fruit and flowers growing & selling)	Growing & Selling of Betal leaf
1.	A.P.	Kurakula Mali (other than STs) Pondara	
2.	Assam		Baroi
3.	Bihar	Khatik Kushwaha	Tamali Barai Turha
4.	Gujarat		Kachhia, Kachhi, Kachi-Kushwaha Maurya-Koria Mali
5.	Haryana		Barai, Tambali
6.	Karnataka		Gurav, Tambli
7.	Kerala		Sanai Thalavar
8.	M.P.	Mali (Saini), Marar Kunjra, Raine, Murai Pemdi Kachhi	Barai, Tamali, Wari Kumavat
9.	Maharashtra	Badia Mali Kachhi/Kachhia Phulari	Bari or Barai Tamboli

10.	Orissa	Mali	Bariji, Barmi, Tambuli Tamali
11.	Punjab		Barai
12.	Rajasthan	Mali, Saini, Bagwan, Rayee/ Rayeen, Kunjra	Tamali
13.	Tamilnadu	Male, Kurumba Yogeswarar	Senaithalaviar
14.	Tripura		Barui, Baruijibi
15.	Uttar Pradesh	Kachhi, Kush-waha, Shakya Tanwar, Singhariya Mali, Saini, Kunjra/ Rayeen	Tamoli
16.	West Bengal	Malakar Rayeen (Kunjra) Turha	Barujibi Tamali/Tamali

A brief description of some caste/communities of this category may help in understanding the categorisation of caste/ communities included in the OBC lists mainly on the basis of their traditional occupation. Thus an account of certain caste/ communities highlighting their primary and secondary, occupations in which they are engaged traditionally, is given herewith:

Jat

A dominant peasant caste of North-West India. They are distributed in Haryana, Uttar Pradesh, Punjab, Rajasthan, Himachal Pradesh and Jammu and Kashmir, Madhya Pradesh and in UTs of Chandigarh and Delhi. It seems that the Jat were a section of the pastoral communities whno migrated from Central Asia to Western India. In the course of time, the Jat settled down as peasants and emerged as a dominant caste and founded a state in the later medieval period. A section of the Jat in Gujarat (Jat-Muslim) are still pastoral. According to 1931 census the population of Jat was 8,377,819. On the basis of religion, the community is divied into three segments, Hindu Jat, Sikh Jat and Muslim Jat. Hindu Jat are concentrated in northern Rajasthan, Haryana, Part of Punjab, Delhi and Western Uttar Pradesh. The Sikh Jat live in Punjab and Chandigarh.

As diversification of occupations is concerned that they are engaged in a combination of traditional occupations as agriculture, animal husbandary and cattle breading with a number of modern occupations. The Jat are mainly a landowning community and their primary and traditional occupation is agriculture. Jats of Uttar Pradesh Claim that Punjab and Rajasthan to be their original homeland. Majority of them are agriculturist. A good number of them are in the military and police service. The traditional & primary occupation of Jats of Rajasthan is agriculture, followed by animal husbandary. Many of them have joined the civil services and are engaged in business. In Jammu and Kashmir the Jat are also called Jant, Jhat or Jit. The majority of them are Sikh migrants from Pakistan. Most of them are landowneres and their primary occupation is agriculture. Jats of Madhya Pradesh are traditionally land owning but have also gone through a process of occupational diversification, some of them involved in business also.

Yadav/Ahir

As pastoral castes mixed with local cattle breeding groups and gradually settled down in many parts of the country, they also became peasants. However, the pastoral elements continued to flourish in their economy, In fact agriculture and cattle breeding went together. Some of them acquired political power. The Yadava and Gauli Kingdoms emerged in Western India. Their aristocratic strata in the north-west were recognised in the colonial period. Large sections of the Yadavas emerged as small peasants in many parts of north and central India, a few of them also acquired large tracts of land in the newly reclaimed areas of eastern Bihar and were recognised as bigh landholders.

According to 1931 census, the population of Ahirs was 71.75 lakh and Yadav was 17.10 lakh, Golla/Yadava 17.40 lakh. The first were concentrated in Uttar Pradesh (37.45 lakh), Bihar (17.50 lakh) and Madhya Pradesh (10.74 lakh) followed by Gujarat (1.32 lakh), Punjab, Maharashtra, Assam, Orissa, etc. and three Southern States of Tamilnadu (6.7 lakh), Karnataka (1.73 lakh) and Andhra Pradesh (1.73 lakh).

In Uttar Pradesh Yadav are also known as Ahir. In Bihar also known as Ahir, Goala, Rai, Sar-gope, Gope. In Andhra they are called Golla or Kanarulu. In Pondicherry as Idainyan, Idaiyar or Golla. They are known as Konar, Idayar, Golla or Idaiyar in Tamilnadu. In Kerala they are also known as Erumakar or Gosangi. In Maharashtra known as Gwalvanshi, Nandavanshi and Denusevak. They are considered as one of the subgroups of Gauli.

Yadavas of the North and South have reported common origin from Yadu and Krishna. They depend on agriculture and animal husbandary. Now many of them are businessmen, government servants.

Gadaria

The caste/community is included in the list of OBCs for Himachal Pradesh, Uttar Pradesh, Haryana, Chandigarh, Delhi, Rajasthan, Madhya Pradesh. The Gadaria are largely shepherds and blanket weavers.

In Haryana they are also known as Pal. In Himachal Pradesh, Dhingar, Nikhar and Ochre are subgroups among the Gadaria. In Madhya Pradesh they are also known as Gadri, Dhanger, Kurmar, Hatgar and Gayari. In Maharashtra they are also known as Kurumar, Gadri and Dhangar. In Rajasthan the Gadaria are commonly known as Gairi or Gadri.

The Gadaria subsist primarily on animal husbandry and sheep and goats comprise their livestock. They sell wool, milk and animals, agriculture is a subsidiary occupation. Some of them are still engaged in their traditional occupation of grazing sheep and goats and weaving blankets from sheep's wool. Some of them have become agricultural labourers. The Gadaria have abandoned their traditional occupation of rearing sheep and goats in Haryana and Punjab. They are now mainly engaged as labourers in masonary work, while some are involved in animal husbandary.

E. Priestly Caste

The Caste/ communities traditionally engaged in astrology, palmistry, temple service, exoreeistry, religious mendicancy can be categorise as Priestly caste. We find one thing common among these castes/communities i.e. Begging (alms-taking). But begging as an occupation is not adequate. For instance Nath, Jogi Sanyasi, Parsai, Gosain, Bairagi, Babaji, Fakir etc. cannot be termed simply as beggars because they are more or less priests and alms given them are in some way a return for the services rendered by them such as 'Naths' tend the shrine of Hanuman, Gosains tend the shrine of Siva, Bairagi sings devotional songs in praise of Nar Singh (Vishnu) and Fakir build of Tazia at Moharam festival. They perform such rites as marriage, sacred readings, performing festival rites, martuary rites, incharge of shrines, etc. Among the castes/ communities of this category we find different ranking for example most of the Gosains are land owners while Naths and Babajis are tenants or labourers. Priests and temple servants are considered the most highly respected members in the society. Their social status is as high as of Brahmins while the Charge Maha Brahmin and Acharaj, Beduva, Dakaut etc. caste/ communities are still considered as they are associated with such occupations which are still considered polluting castes lowely. The Caste/Communities of this category found place in the OBC lists on the basis of their traditional occupation further be divided into sub-categories as (i) Priest (including those who perform death rites) (ii) Astologers/Palmist/Exorcist (iii) Temple servants (iv) Religious Mendicants as shown in table 5.14.

Table 5.14

Statewise distribution of Priestly caste in the central list of OBCs

S.No.	State	Priest (including those who performed death rites)	Astrologers, Palmist,	Temple servant	Religions Mendicants
1.	Andhra Pradesh	Jangam	Tammali	Satani (Chattadas- Chatadi Dasari	Veearmushti (Netti-rivaishnava, Kotala) Bandara Chopemari Dasari Jogi Kanjara-Bhatta Pariki Muggula, Mandula
2.	Assam	Ganak (in Cachar, Karimganj and Haila Kandi districts)		Manipuri	
3.	Bihar				Aghori, Kapadia, Sayee (Muslim)
4.	Delhi				Bairagi Dakaut, Prade Fakir, Jogi, Goswami
5.	Goa				Gosavi
6.	Gujarat	Charam Gadhvi Mir, Dhadhi, Langha,			Bawa Fakir or Faquir (Muslim) Shrawan, Sarwan, Vahivancha Charan

7.	Haryana	Nar			Bairagi, Faquir Jogi, Nath, Jangam-Jogi Dakaut
8.	Himachal Pradesh	Ard Pop Bhat, Bhatta, Darpi Nar Sanyasi			Baragi, Faquir Bhjhrus, Dakaut
9.	Jammu & Kashmir	Mirasi			Dambali Faqir
10.	Karnataka	Kanisan	Satani, Chattada- Shri Vaishnava, Vashnava, Ghadi Sanyasi,		Nandiwala Durgamurga Gondali
11.	Kerala		Ambalakkaran		
12.	Madhya Pradesh	Bhar, Charan (charahm), Sawli, Sutiya, Rav, Jasondhi, Maru-sonia Dholi (Priest)	Gusai/gosai/gasain, Gosaib, Goswami/ Gowsami	Bairagi Garpagari Vasudev, Harvala, Kapadia, Kapdi, Gondhli, Joginath, Nathjogi	Devadigi
13.	Maha-rashtra	Bhute, Bhope Jajak	Bhavin	Jogi, Jogin Guruv/Gurav	Nandiwale, Tirmal Pangul, Chitrakathi Dawari/Davari Gondhali, Jangam

14.	Orissa	Sanyasi, Membram	Jyotish	Damal Muni, Ranla (of Ganjan district only) - Sub-castes of Mali	Bairagi Matangi
15.	Punjab	Darpi, Nar		Dakaut	Jogi Nath
16.	Rajasthan	Rao. Sad Swami Dhadi		Dakaut, Deshantri Faqir/Faquir Jogi, Nath	
17.	Tamilnadu	Odiya Dasari Kambar	Male Veerasaiva	Andi Pandaram Dasari Jangam Jogi	
18.	Uttar Pradesh			Jangama Bairagi Jogi Faqir	
19.	West Bengal			Fakir, Sain Yogi, Nath Jogi	
20.	Chandigarh	Nar		Dakaut/Dahakaut, Faquir	
21.	Pondicherry		Dasari		

A brief description of the caste/community of this category is also given herewith as under:

Jogi

Jogi caste/community is found place in the central list of OBCs for Andhra Pradesh, Kerala, Maharashtra Sikkim, Uttar Pradesh, West Bengal, Pondicherry, Tamilnadu, Delhi, Karnataka, Bihar, Orissa, Haryana, Punjab, Chandigarh and Rajasthan. The caste/community is also known as Nath, Giri and Gosawin in Uttar Pradesh; Padha Jogi or Nath in Haryana; Padha or Upadhya Jogi or Jangam Jogi in Delhi; Judi, Juginath, Jugiswain in Orissa; Joger, Sanjogi and Jogar in Karnataka; Jogishwaran, Uogi, Yogeshwaran and Purush. The Jugi of Tripura and West Bengal are also called as Jogi or Tanti.

Jogi of Himachal Pradesh found place in the SC list. Jogi of Tamilnadu and Pondicherry are traditionally pig-rearers and scavengers. The traditional occupation of Jogis of Karnataka are seeking alms and selling medicines. The ancestors of the Jugi of Tripura were the weavers of the famous muslin, jamdani and hazarbuti saris and also various superior quality linens and calicos. The traditional occupation of Jogis in Delhi is preaching and teaching in ashrams and living on alms.

Jogi caste/community covers a variety of occupations. Early accounts identify two very distinct classes among them. First are the Jogi proper a regular religious order of Hindus, which includes both the Anghar Jogis and the Kamphatta Jogi ascetics who are followers of Gorakhnath and priests and worshippers of Shiva. The second class is that miscellaneous assortment of low-caste faquirs and fortune tellers, both Hindu and Muslim but mainly muslim, who are commonly known as Jogis (Rose 1901).

Now the caste/community in engaged in cultication, priesthood, petty business, skilled and unskilled wage labour, tailoring, poultry farming etc. The community is mainly a landless.

F. Others:

SC Converted to Christianity found place in the central list of OBCs for Assam, Kerala, Madhya Pradesh, Maharashtra, Gujarat, Orissa and West Bengal states.

'Ahom' (Assam)– They were Shan tribes and converted to Hinduism.

'Choudang'–They have been the gaurds of Ahom Kings.

'Katipadala' (Andhra Pradesh)– Employed as watchmen at burrial grounds.

'Mukhari Saraswat Non-Brahmin' (Kerala)– This is Devdasi community a demeaning profession.

'Kotwar/Kutwar' (Madhya Pradesh)–They are village watchmen.

'Mirdha (excluding Jat Muslim)' (Madhya Pradesh)– They are watchmen cum personal messangers.

Bandi (Maharashtra)–Domestic servants.

Hatua (Orissa)–Hawking.

Jhetty (Tamilnadu)–They are wrestlers and gymnasts.

'Karuneegar' (Tamilnadu)–Those who are employed as village accountant..

'Koteyar' (Tamilnadu)–They were soldiers to Lingayat Kings.

'Panisaivan' (Tamilnadu)–The persons belonging to this community are those who carry death news to the relative of deceased.

Bhamta (Maharashtra)–Preparing hemp (tak).

Koteyar (Kerala and Tamilnadu)–Guarding Forts.

Kalanga (Orissa)–Military Caste.

Kannada Saineegar (Tamilnadu)–Military caste.

Makra (Muslim) (Dadra and Nagara Haveli)–Military caste.

Saiees (Madhya Pradesh)–Negotiating Marriage.

Mogia (Rajasthan) – Guards of Agricultural Farms.

Raneyar (Orissa) – Carry Carcass.

Mappila (Kerala) – Trade and Business.

Reddiar/Reddian (Kerala) – Business Community.

Kanghera (H.P.) – Mendors of the nose, ears and tongues of the culprits whose lims were amputted as punishment for their crimes.

Depala (Maharashtra) – Carvan traders and Hawkers.

Sahis (Maharashtra) – Quacks of cattle.

Moopan (Tamilnadu) – Coolies.

Aheria (Haryana and Uttar Pradesh) – Hunters.

Nyria (Rajasthan) – Collection of dust of Gold and Silvar.

Daroga, Daroga-Rajot, Ravana-Rajput, Hazuri, Wazir (Rajasthan) – Servant of Rajput Kings.

Tamang (West Bengal and Sikkim) – Horse trading.

The people of this category are mainly involve in manual labour as wage labourers. They are traditionally engaged in petty work which are low paid. Some of the caste/communities of this category are migrant labourers such as 'Kurmi' and 'Gorkha' in Haryana and Punjab, Mina in Haryana. Some of them are domestic servants and others are engaged in petty job such as Hawkers, Helper to massion collis, Rickshaw pullers etc.

References

1. Mohanti, S.K., 1993, Social Mobility and Caste Dynamics.
2. Risley, H.H., 1891, The Tribes and Castes of Bengal (Calcutta; Bengal Secretariat Press, rpt. 1981, Firma Mukhopadhyay).
3. Enthovan, R.E., 1920, The Tribes and Castes of Bombay (Bombay: Government Central Press, 1920, rpt. 1975, Delhi, Cosmo Publications).
4. Mayer, Adrian, C., 1986, Caste and Kinship in Central India, Routledge and Kegan Paul, London.

5. Russel, R.V. and Hiralal, 1916, Tribes and Castes of the Central Provinces of India (London: Macmillan and Company; rpt. 1975, Delhi, Cosmo Publications).

6. Rose, H.A., 1919, Glossary of the Tribes and Castes of Punjab and N.W.F. Province (Lahore, Civil and Military Gazette Press; rpt. 1980, Delhi, Amar Prakashan).

7. Risley, H.H., 1891; op.cit.

8. Russel, R.V. and Hiralal, 1916; op. cit.

9. Enthovan, R.E., 1920, op. cit.

6

Emerging Trends

In this chapter we will discuss the distribution of caste/communities which found place in the central list of OBCs during the recent years on the recommendation of the NCBC separately. It may help to understand the latest trend in identification of caste/communities of OBCs. Occupation wise distribution of such caste/communities is given in table 6.1

The analysis of table 6.1 shows the highest number of castes/communities of artisan/artisanal category. It comes to 43 percent alone. Other categories 'service cates' and 'Agricultural labour' consist of 18 percent and 15 percent respectively. If we take these three categories together, it comes to 76 percent of the total. The category of 'Peasantary castes' covers 17%, 'Ex- criminal, nomadic and semi-nomidic' 5%, Priesly castes' covers 1% and 'others' 1%. The Nomadic, Semi-Nomadic and Denotified tribes constitute genuinely backward classes and their position in no way better of then that of SCs and STs are 5%. The basis of inclusion of these 235 new caste/communities clearly shows the latest trend in identification of castes/communities and their listing as SEBCs for the purpose of Article 16(4).

The Classification based on occupation can help in identification of more backward and most backward among the backward castes/communities. The categories shown in

Table 6.1

Occupatian wise distribution of number of castes/communities included in the central list of OBCs during 1999 to 2001 (till 14th November)

S.No.	States/Union Territory	Peasantary	Artisan/Artisanal	Lowely labour (Service Caste)	Excriminal Nomadic & Semi Nomadic	Agricultural Labour	Priestly Caste	Others	Total
1.	Andhra Pradesh	—	3	3	1	4	—	—	11
2.	Arunachal Pradesh	—	—	—	—	—	—	—	—
3.	Assam	—	—	—	—	—	—	—	—
4.	Bihar	2	2	1	—	1	—	—	6
5.	Delhi	—	1	1	—	—	—	—	2
6.	Goa	1	9	—	—	1	1		12
7.	Gujarat	3	5	1	—	9	—	—	18
8.	Haryana	2	7	3	—	2	—	—	14
9.	Himachal Pradesh	—	2	—	—	—	—	—	2
10.	Jammu & Kashmir	—	1***	—	—	—	—	—	1
11.	Karnataka	1	6	3	4	—	—	—	14
12.	Kerala	—	2	6	—	—		1*	9
13.	Madhya Pradesh	2	6	2	1	2	—	—	13

14.	Maharashtra	2	2	1	—	1	—	—	6
15.	Manipur	—	—	—	—	—	—	—	—
16.	Meghalaya	—	—	—	—	—	—	—	—
17.	Mizoram	—	—	—	—	—	—	—	—
18.	Nagaland	—	—	—	—	—	—	—	—
19.	Orissa	7	5	1	—	5	—	—	18
20.	Punjab	2	1	1	—	—	—	—	4
21.	Rajasthan	2	5	2	1	1	1	—	12
22.	Sikkim	1	—	—	—	2	—	—	3
23.	Tamil Nadu	1	3	2	2	—	—	1**	9
24.	Tripura	4	1	—	—	3	—	—	8
25.	Uttar Pradesh	1	14	4	1	1	—	—	21
26.	West Bengal	7	23	8	1	—	1	—	40
	Union Territories								
1.	A & N Island	—	—	—	—	—	—	—	—
2.	Chandigarh	1	1	1	—	2	—	—	5
3.	Dadra & Nr. Haveli	—	—	—	—	—	—	—	—
4.	Daman & Diu	—	—	—	—	—	—	—	—
5.	Lakshadweep	—	—	—	—	—	—	—	—
6.	Pondicherry	—	1	1	—	—	—	—	2
	Total	39	100	41	11	34	3	2	235

* Erstwhile Devadasi Community of Kerala

** Panisaivan of Tamil Nadu who carry death news to the relatives of the deceased.

*** Included on the recommendation of State Government of J&K.

table 6.1 can further be classified into sub classes to put the caste/communities in the proper categories. This task should be done very carefully and the following conclusions may be kept in mind while doing such Classification:

It can be concluded that occupations are regarded as having distinguised, and in others varying in the general prestige attached to them. For example Brahmins are taditionally priest and got the highest prestige in the socity white Bairagi, Nath, Jogi, Gosain, Babaji, Modha etc. Were also attached with priestly occupations. These castes developed from sects and now enjoy the status of OBCs.

'White Coller Occupations' need to be seen according to the socital status attached with it, for example 'School teacher' and 'Village accountant' both are white coller jobs but school teacher get respect like land lords in the villages and village accountant get respect but less than school teacher.

As traditional occupation of warrior caste or military cast is concerned that many caste/communities claim their origin from Kshatriyas and associate themselves with the military caste. The problem comes when the caste/community is traditionally linked with more than one occupation for example Rajputs were rulers, warriors and landlords.

Where there is no clear traditional occupation of any caste/community or any caste/community people can adopt such occupation are linked in separate category of 'others'. Some caste/communities have a tribal derivation and got the SC/ST status, while others are included in the list of OBCs. One can say that the caste/communities partly SC or ST or partly OBC.

There are occupations for which no generic name is given but there occupations includes crafts for which piece work payments are made usually in cash such as Tailoring, Tabacco-curring, cotton cardering etc. There are occupations which are not connected with crafts at all such as goatherd, milk-making and milk vending, gardening, farming trading but these are herditary occupations.

Occupations like Chowkidari, Patwari, well diggers etc. is not limited to any caste though there is some identification with caste rank.

Though Jajmani system is almost eliminated but the relationship between certain castes as 'Kamin-Jajman' can be seen even today. Kamin are those to whom payment is given in kind on an annual basis in return of their services. Most of these services are related to crafts and those who follow them are called Kamin such as Barber, Carpenter, Blacksmith, Potter, Tanner, Mochi, Drum Beater, Sweeper. The tailors now augemanted by men of other castes who learned tailoring.

Certain caste/communities also found place in the OBCs in the Central list be classified into three categories (Most backward, more backward and generally backward), based on different degrees and levels of backwardness.

The following traditional or hereditary occupations considered to be undignified. Castes/communities arising out of these occupations can be considered "Most Backward" out of the OBCs.

1. *Pack-Carriers*
2. *Carpenters*
3. *Grain Parchers*
4. *Dyers and Printers*
5. *Astronomers and Ghost exercisers*
6. *Drum Beaters*
7. *Personal attendants*
8. *Tailors*
9. *Fisherman*
10. *Waterman and Palanquin bearers*
11. *Boatsman (Ferrying by Boat)*
12. *Leaf Plats makers*
13. *Wandering Blacksmiths*
14. *Oil Processers*

15. *Weavers*
16. *Religious mendicants*
17. *Distillers*
18. *Cotton scutchers*
19. *Salt makers*
20. *Potters*
21. *Masons*
22. *Lac Bangle makers*
23. *Blacksmiths*
24. *Singers and dancers*
25. *Barbers*
26. *Distincters of Gold and Silver from dust*
27. *Earth diggers*
28. *Silk braid makers*
29. *Sharpners of iron implements*
30. *Armour makers*
31. *Grass and Bamboo curtain makers*
32. *Brass and Copper vessel makers*
33. *Butchers*
34. *Muslim cooks (Bhatiyara)*
35. *Stone masons*
36. *Katha makers*
37. *Washerman*
38. *Snake charmers*
39. *Acrobats, Jugglers and gipsies*
40. *Horse Trainers*
41. *Lime burning*
42. *Toddy tapping*
43. *Painting on leather*

7

Protective Discrimination: An overview

The Constitution of India provided protection for Backward Classes to help them overcome their social disabilities. A certain proportion of seats in the Parliament and in the state legislatures was reservered for SCs and STs as were jobs in the Government and seats in educational institutions. The Constitution abolished untouchability through The Untouchability Act, 1955. Protection of Civil Rights Act of 1976 and Prevention of Atrocities Act 1989 also were passed. These redical measures were a right begining to eliminate caste-like discrimination and to help the Backward Classes overcome their social disabilities.

Backward Classes other than SCs and STs were also brought under the protective discrimination policy with the dicision of the Government of India in 1990 to implement the recommendations of the Mandal Commission report and recommendations regarding the benifits to be extented to the socially and educationally backward classes. Accordingly orders were issued for 27 percent of the vacancies in civil posts and services under the government of India to be reservered for Socially and Educationally Backword Classes in case of direct recruitment.[1] After this decision of implementation of recommendations of the Mandal Commission there was wide spread protest against it. Writ petitions were filled in the Supreme Court challenging this decision of the government. The judgement in the Writ petition (civil) No. 930 of 1990, Indira Sawhney and others V/S Union of India and others was delivered on 16-11-1992 by the Supreme Court of India. In this judgement the Supreme Court went into several basic questions including those relating to reservation. Some of the issues dealt with by the Supreme Court is reproduced as under:

1. Creamy layer can be, and must be excluded. Government of India specify the basis of exclusion– whether on the basis of income, extent of holding or otherwise of 'Creamy Layer'. (Vol. I, Para 86)

2. A backward class of citizens cannot be identified only and exclusively with reference to economic criteria. It is, of course, permissible for the government or other authority to identify a backward class of citizens on the basis of occupation cum income, without reference to caste, if it is so advised. (Para 90 and 91 Vol.I)

3. There is no constitutional bar to classify the backward classes of citizens into backward and more backward categories. (Para 92, Vol.I)

4. The rule of 50% should be applied to each year. It cannot be related to the strength of the class, category, service or cadre, as the case may be (Para 96, Vol. I)

5. The reservation of 10% of the posts in favour of 'other economically backward sections of the people who are not covered by any of the existing schemes of the reservation' made in the impugned office memorandum dated 25.9.1991 as constitutionally invalid and is accordingly struck down. (Para 115)

6. Under the Constitution, the reservations in employment in favour of backward classes are not intended either to be indiscriminate or permanent. Article 16 (4) which provides for reservations, also at the same time

> prescribes their limits and conditions. In the first place, the reservations are not to be kept in favour of every backward class of citizens. It is only that backward class of citizens which, in the opinion of the State, is 'not adequately represented' in the services under the State, which is entitled to the benefit of the reservations. Secondly, and this follows from the first, even that backward class of citizens would cease to be the beneficiary of the reservation policy, the moment the State comes to the conclusion that it is adequately represented in the services. (Vol. II Para 24)

Following the decision of the Superme Court, the Government of India has decided that the benefit of reservations intended for the OBCs will not be extended to persons/ sections falling under the category of the Creamy Layer.[2]

The Government of India has taken many steps such as notification of central list of OBCs on the basis of principal of commonaly, setting up the National Backward Classes Finance and Development Corporation, setting up the National Commission for Backward Classes for recommending upon requests for inclusion of more caste/communities in the lists of OBCs, etc.[3]

It is worth mentioning here that no provision for reservation of seats was made in the Parliament and legislatures and educational institutions for Other Backward Classes (OBCs) as for SCs and STs because OBCs were in superior position than SCs and STs. OBCs do not suffer the same social handicaps inflicted upon SCs and STs, though OBCs are socially and educationally not forward. Thus the objective of reservation for the SCs and STs is to bring them into the mainstream of national life, while the objective of reservation for OBCs is to remove their social and educational backwardness. As a result, OBCs are treated dissimilarly and they do not form an integrated class with SCs and STs.

The Reality

From that time onwards continous efforts have also been made to assess the success and failures of such protective discrimination. Many social scientist, political parties, caste/ community organisations have participated in such debates and argued in many ways. Many social scientists claim that such efforts have benefitted only the creamy layer of the caste/ communities so protected. Other say that reservation should not be made a permanent phenomenon as it appears today becouse it is neither in the interest of the OBCs nor the nation. Similarly, other issues raised like the caste has lost its traditional sanctions and functions but caste continues to occupy the central place in regard to the policy of reservation. The provisions made under the protective discrimination policy attracts criticism as no scientific criterion is evolved to assess the backwardness of castes/communities and thus the genuine OBCs are not benefitted from the existing reservation policy.

As protective discrimination has taken a political turn and become very complex and lost its relevance. The reservation has now become a politically senstive issue. Political parties and caste/community organisations are utilizing the reservation issue for their vested interest upto a great extent. They are engaged in extending reservations to more and more castes which is building resentmant among the castes. Representatives of the castes/communities complain that the more educated and socially advantaged castes in the reserved categories have monopolised the privilages of reservation and a new trend to demand separate quotas for each of the castes within the reserved categories has started. This trend is sharpening the identity of castes and of even sub-castes within castes.

Approach Towards Mobilization of OBCs

The understanding of the concept of Backward Classes in India is complicated by the influence of the western thinkers who mixed up issues of caste and culture, caste and language, caste and class. Moreover, the existence of caste system and dominance of certain higher castes prepared the mentalaty of the anthropologists in India coming from the higher castes and classes. In all the system of classifications we see a mixing up of the issues, but there was an ideological struggle also going on in the Indian anthropologists and socialogists against these tendencies.

The term 'Backward Classes' is used by the leaders of the Backward Class movement with varying emphasis. It pertains to the OBCs although the SCs are not clearly excluded. We find in the history that the differences between the touchable and untouchable *sudras* were not clearly recognised and the depressed classes did not exclude the touchable *sudras*. With the Poona Pact (1932) there was a clear line of demarcation between the touchable Sudras and the untouchables. Untouchable *sudras* were recognised into a distinct group, while the touchables sudras began to organise themselves under the general term Backward Classes particularly in North India.[4]

Colonial administration from the mid 19th century had realised the divisive potential of castes and religion and done an ethnological mapping as a resource base for effective social control. Bagchi (1990) in 'Caste, Politics and Raj' writes that largely as a result of British appointment policy, political and administrative innovations, the caste dichotomy was successfully turned into a political dichotomy. The colonial regime in the consciousness of many among the disadvantaged sections of the Hindu society, appeared to be their most trusted friend, may their liberator. Frankel and Rao (1990) argue that British rule in India opened the door to educated *Sudras* and untouchables who had hitherto been bound by the order of the religious hierarchy. But the traditional order was too entrenched to be displaced completely. Caste associations cropped up all over India and were used to lobby governments for specific caste based concessions. Quite paradoxically, economic differentation enhanced primordial caste loyalities. The Backward Classes too found their own identity as separate from the other, Scheduled Castes. "Thus all of these factors taken together help explain why despite growing economic differentiation, region, religion, caste cluster or tribal group remained the primary identity through which economic discontent was articulated."[5]

Dumont (1970) says "The notions of dominance, or rather of dominant caste, represents the most solid and useful acquisation of the studies of social anthropology in India". The dominance of certain Castes is being questioned politically and for that matter in almost all realms of life. Whatever may be the basis of the prevailing dominance, whether structural or functional, the fact is that it is getting challanged in one or the other ways.[6]

M.S.A. Rao (1978) described that the backward classes movements varied in their support base, goals and means. He had identified four types of such movements. In Madras, Karnataka and Maharashtra the Brahman, Non-Brahman cleavage appeared and the movement had the aim of reducing the dominance of the Brahmans in politics and profession. The second pattern prevailed in the North, where the cleavage appeared between the generally forward and twice born castes of Brahman, Bhumihar, Kayastha and Rajput on the other hand and the intermediate castes of Ahir, Kurmi, etc. on the other. The third pattern is that of a conflict between the depressed castes and the forward castes. The tribal movements constituted the fourth type.

The root of this phenomenon can be seen in the historical context, as hierarchisation of the Hindu society along the caste lines more or less corresponded with the political and economic ones before the British came in India. The self-assertion movements of the intermediate castes become particularly pronounced since the middle of the last century. The British rule and modernization entailed aggravated the status difference between various castes, particularly the Brahmans, the Kayastha on the one hand and the peasantry on the other. In the beginning of the ideas of equality of opportunity, or meritarian principles of justice, came in handy for the literate castes, who almost monopolized the Govt. jobs and professional opportunities in the name of full and free competetion. But the meritarion principle of justice was soon challenged as the equal treatment of the unequals. The purity- pollution concepts and the social disabilities suffered by different castes.

The agrarian castes were in the forefront of agitations demanding more concessions while after independence rich peasants and better-off tenant cultivators became owner proprietors. Marathas in Maharashtra strike alliances with lower peasant castes while Jats of Western Uttar Pradesh make alliances with other cultivating castes like Gujars, Rajputs, Ahirs and Sainis (all of them considered themselves from the same Kshatriya varna). That is why this alliance was given name as AJGAR by politicians to mobilize vote bank during the elections. Many land owning farmer's castes like Gujar, Ahir, Jat and Saini are included in the list of backward classes in most of the States while these castes have been exploiting the SCs and STs and most backward classes, namely, Nai, Khati, Chhipi, Lohar, Kumbhar, etc. for centuries and now grab the chunk of reservation in the Government jobs. The question comes in mind that why and how these castes have been identified as socially and educationally backward? Are they socially and educationally backward? If not, then what was the criterion by which these could be included in the list of OBCs?

It was also argued for long time that the caste system, far from being a hindrance to democratic polity, was in fact providing peasants with a ready made grouping from which they could put forward their interests within a competitive political structure. It may be concluded that caste and communities remained the primary identity for all groups and there is no political will for removal of caste or for the gradual lessening of its importance in the public sphere but there is a great enthusiasm for caste based political mobilizations in every areana of state craft.[7]

Since the goverment's capacity for giving employment is limited, reservations are thought of as a way of access to employment. It is both economic compulsions and political weight that impel the agricultural castes to demand reservations. Hence it is clear that improved economic and political situation is related to a demand for reservations. The political might of the Jats makes the demand pressing or at least gives them the boost to make such a demand. Otherwise, most of the really deserving backward castes are unable to put pressure for their demand as nobody hears them. It is only with improved economic and political power that any caste can make an effective demand for reservations. Otherwise such a demand goes uncared.

Padhy and Mahapatra (1988) point out a similar trend indicating that caste-based political mobilisation with the vested interests of politicians has procreated strong parochial and chauvinistic tendencies threatening the unity of the nation. Those who are once designated as 'backward' resist any attempt to eliminate them from the list of backward castes. The Lingayats and Vokkalingas of Karnataka, the Izhavas and Nayars of Kerala, the Reddies and Kammas in Andhra Pradesh, Nadars and Vaniyars in Tamil Nadu, Kurmis, Ahirs and Koeries in Uttar Pradesh and Bihar, and Kunbis and Aghis in Maharashtra have always exerted pressure for their continual recognition as backward castes. The dominant castes are able to strike a political bargain with those in power for being classified as backward castes.

Thus, backwardness in this context has become a privilege to be fought to consolidate political power.

Maheshwari (1991) says that under the logic of reservations, the backward castes would press for their recognition. During the period when no reservation culture prevailed in the Indian society, the so-called lower castes tried to move upward socially in order to enhance their social status. The following observation in the Census Report of 1921 in instructive that the opportunity of the census was seized by all but the highest castes to press for recognition of social claims and to secure, if possible, a step upwards in the social ladder.

Now, with the advent of reservations, the reverse is happening—the upper castes want to be classified as lower castes.

Recapitulating, it can be said that a majority of the respondents of both the caste categories expressed the belief that their caste was under-represented in the government sector and modern professions. However, this belief was more pronounced among the backward castes. A three-fourth majority of the backward caste respondents expressed the belief that the greater the representation of a caste in government services and professions, the more powerful the caste. A majority of the forward caste respondents also expressed a similar belief. Regarding benefits of government service a majority of the backward caste respondents perceived 'livelihood' as the greatest benefit. While a mojority of the forward caste respondents perceived 'power and status' as the greatest benefit of government service. Besides, a majority of the respondents of both the categories expressed the wish to raise the status of their caste. Almost half of the backward caste respondents answered in the affirmative when they were asked if reservation could fulfill the purpose of enhancing the status of their castes. In this regard only a minority (15.62 percent) of the forward caste respondents answered in the affirmative. A further analysis revealed that a majority of these forwards belongs to the peasant castes. With regard to reservations as an avenue for upward social mobility, it was observed that there were significant backward-forward difference. The backward caste respondents took reservations as a very high avenue for upward social mobility. A deeper analysis revealed that a majority of the forward caste respondents who took reservations a very high avenue for upward social mobility belonged to the middle peasant castes.

With regard to improvement in economic and political conditions, it was observed that the forward castes have gained more than the backward ones. Among the forward castes, the peasantry has gained substantially. Interestingly, it is the same section which wanted reservations for upward social mobility.

In the 70's in A.P. the Congress Party responded to increasing Backward Caste pressure by providing reservations of upto 25 percent for these castes and reduced the number of congress tickets to Kamma and Reddy castes after 1972. Similarly in Karnataka the then chief minister Devraj Urs also reduced the proportion of upper caste Lingayat and Vokkaliga aspirants to the state government on the Congress tickets. In Gujarat, the Patidars deserted the Congress in 1975 but the Congress strategy of bringing together the Koli-Kshatriyas, Harijans, Adivasis and Muslims (Kham) brought it back to power in the elections of 1980. the Patidars who wanted to be included among the Backward castes, though they also claim Kshatriya status, have successfully lobbied for an increase in reservation for the Backward Castes from 10% in 1978 to 28 percent in 1985. Thus 'caste and community remained the primary identity for all groups'.

In Eastern Uttar pradesh the Kisan Sabha and Eka movements in the 1920s, against indebtedness and low wages led at times by low caste leaders such as Baba Ramchand and Pari Madari and second a spontaneous rural agitation by dalits in 1946, against the exploitative practice of begar (unpaid labour). After independence, both the Socialist and the Communist parties had a strong base in the eastern districts of Uttar Pradesh and supported land distribution, lower land ceilings, abolition of land revenue on small holdings, etc. in the 1960s. Following the decline of the Left and Socialist parties, the lower castes shifted their alliance to the congress, and in more recent years, the Bahujan Samaj Party (BSP).

Thirunavukkarasu (2001) writs that in the last assembly elections in Tamilnadu the dominating OBCs like 'Vanniyars' in Northern Tamilnadu were supporting PMK, while TMC had support in the 'Kallars' in Kaveri delta and the Nadars in Southern Tamilnadu. Dominating castes like Telugu-speaking Naidus are the base of MDMK. Newly formed 'New Justice Party' launched as an exclusive platform for one of the dominant OBC caste group i.e. Mudaliars. The support base for DMK,

AIADMK and Congress comes from numerically as well as economically dominant OBCs such as Kallars, Udayars and Vellalas. The AIADMK's support base is OBC, Thevar community in Madurai, Theni and Dindigul districts and Yadavs in urban areas. Dominant OBC community Gounders have always been supporters of AIADMK.

Thus, the caste has been the rallying point for political mobilisation in the state. The emergence of Dravidian politics in the state began with zeal and enthusiasm with the progress of non-brahmin castes. If the DMK had the support of some sections of non-brahmin communities, so was the case with all other offshoots of the Dravidian movement. Therefore, politicisation of caste is neither something new nor an anathema in the State.[8]

Emerging Pattern of Mobility

The social gradation of the caste in India appears to be based broadly on the traditional occupational pursuits of the castes, castes whose traditional occupations necessarily involve learning appear to take precedence over the castes who are primarily land owners, the land owning castes take precedence over the trading castes, the trading castes over castes engaged in manual labour over those engaged in noxious labour, etc. There are also many local variations and sometimes trading castes supersede the landowning castes and artisans precede the petty traders. There are also numerous other small castes. Generally Denotified Nomadic and Semi Nomadic tribes who are outside the reckoning of caste hierarchy, rank lower than other castes. It is also broadly noticed that whenever a member of a caste moves socially upward there is generally a total or partial abandoment of his traditional occupation. A land owner who acquires learning moves up in the social scale, traders who acquires land similarly moves up, as also the craftsman who becomes a trader, the mannual worker who becomes a craftsman and a person engaged in noxious work who become a manual worker. As such, there can be occassional upward or downward movement of the caste/community, depending in the change of vocation.

Presently, OBCs comprise the caste/communities who were traditionally engaged in agriculture, animal husbandary, artisanal work and functional services. Social change and mobility has also taken place in their traditional occupation and socio-economic and political standing, despite of this many cast/communities still remained socially and educationally backward. Caste rank and occupation are the main criteria by which most of the OBCs are considered backward. The following studies shows the trends of social mobility and change that have taken place.

A study of a village in the East Godavari district in A.P. (Reddy and Murthy, 1978) shows that the backward castes have a highly differentiated land tanure system corresponding to their economic status and caste rank. The pure tenant category essentially comprises low castes from the OBCs. In terms of size of landholdings they are divided into three: (i) small; (ii) Medium; and (iii) big. In terms of tenurial category they are divided into four: (i) pure-tenant cultivators; (ii) Owner-cum-tenant cultivators; (iii) pure-rent receivers and (iv) Owner-cum-rent receivers.[9]

Harry W. Blair (1980) observes that the Karpoori Thakur's reservation policy changed Bihar's political economy and initiated the process of replacing the forward castes by the backward castes as the dominant stratum in the system of social stratification. The upper strata of OBCs (Bania, Yadav, Kurmi, Kahar, Kandu, Kumhar, Mallah, Tatwa, Teli) i.e. 19.3 percent of the total population in Bihar dominating political economy and inproved their social status remarkably. some of the conclusions of Blarir's study are as under:

(i) The transfer of power to the upper strata of the OBCs might be expected to continue at the local level along political lines.

(ii) Noticeable transfer of economic power in the country side to the backwards as the forward are not able to face the fury and aggressiveness of the upper Strata of OBCs.

(iii) There is a continuing struggle between the forward and the backwards.

(iv) The condition of landless agricultural labour is weakened and would be weaken further because of inroads of capitalism in Bihar's economy.[10]

Hooda in his book 'Contesting Reservations, (2001) under the head Economic Prosperity and Political Ascendance, describes that there are significant backward - forward differences with respect to change in their socio-economic status since 1950. He writes that not much change in the socio-economic position of backward classes has taken place and the most backward castes still continue to be either artisans or labourers. The peasantry castes improved their position by military, paramilitary and police services in a big way. The peasantry is over represented in these avenues in Haryana. Land reforms introduced two major changes: (i) distribution pattern favoured the tenants and cultivators and (ii) scientific farm management introduced by way of consolidation of landholdings. Green Revolution brought the changes in the status of different castes in Haryana. This brought about prosperity to landowning castes. The change in the economic position affected all occupational groups. Artisans could get better wages for their services. He further mentions that political power has been in the hands of agriculturists castes alone in Haryana.[11]

K.C. Yadav (1992) in his book *Haryana: Itihas Evam Sanskriti,* Vol.I under the title "Hindu Castes in Medival Period", put agriculture caste in the middle category as Rajput (5 percent), Ahir (8 percent), Jat, Gujar (5 percent), Saini (2 percent), Rod (2 percent), Kambo, Ranghad, Thethar, Badai, Sunar. Small traders, Rich peasants, Government servants, Mulla, Kazi, Hakim, Vaidh, etc. are listed in the higher category. Small peasants, labours, etc. Bawaria, Balmiki, Chamar, Julaha, Dhanak, Khatik, Kahar, Kumhar, Lohar,

Mirashi, Nai, Ramdasiya, Sonsi, Teli, Manihar are categorise as the lower ones.[12]

Chakravarti (2001) in his study 'Caste and Agrarian Class' of Bihar finds that both the traditional and new dominant castes have privileged access to material and political resources, and constitute the dominant class. As a consequence, those who belong to the depressed social groups are denied access to such resources. The circumstances of birth into a low-ranking caste, therefore, tend to determine their social and material condition.[13]

Rudra (1978) describes 'agricultural labours' as comprise landless labourers, poor tanents, as well as labourers possessing small amount of land who do not hire in labour to any considerable extent. Among the non-antagonistic groups are small land holders who, because of caste taboos, indulge in cultivation almost exclusively through hired labourers, and small farmers whose dependence on hired labour is minimal. Rudra also discribes that the upper caste landholders (i.e. other than Bhumihar) comprised of Brahmin, Rajput and Kayasth; those from middle castes comprised Yadav, Kaesarbani Vaish, Halwai, Teli, Hajjam, and Markande. Prasad (1991) also observes that the upper stratum of the OBCs in Bihar comprise of Yadav, Kurmi and Koeri, among whom the well to do sections are prominent in the agrarian economy and politics. He finds that several among these castes were tenants of Zamindars (Bhumihar and Rajput and Kayasth) and later become landholders following the land reform programme in Bihar. It should be noted, though, that in certain parts of Patna, Nalanda and Rohtas districts in central Bihar, the Zamindars were Kurmis.[14]

Blair (1980) writes that since the late 1970s the Yadavs in particular, among the OBCs have a presence, especially in politics. According to him, Yadavs held 35 percent of the general seats in Bihar assembly in 1977, where as the Bania, Kurmi and Koeri together held only 14 percent of the seats.[15]

Blair and Prasad (1980) describe that the beneficiaries of development are mainly the upper stratum of the OBCs. The rich and the middle peasants have been on the rise simply becouse they have access to modern benefits occuruing to the countryside. In the two decades after independence the major beneficary groups consolidated their economic gains, and from the late sixties began their effective entry into electoral politics. They took nearly a decade to put it to the wider political forces that they could not be ignored or sidelined becouse numerically they were a formidable segment and economically they stood on a sound footing.[16]

Caral Upadhya (1988) in a study of farmers in coastal Andhra Pradesh found that a new class of businessmen has arisen from the class of capitist farmer in costal Andhra Pradesh. These farmers turned businessmen belong to many castes, for whom agriculture and not trade was traditional occupation.[17]

Rajender Singh (1988) in a study of rural society in eastern Uttar Pradesh found that the emerging elites, partly displacing the established elites, are the new entrants and they are the beneficiaries of certain social, political and agrarian reforms. The electoral process, open competition and achievement ideal are the main basis of the positions which they hold under the new dispensation. They are not necessarily from the Uppar Castes, aristocratic and priestly families.[18]

Jan Breman (1985) lists factors which stimulate mobility and also those which retard it thereby resulting into immobility. Out migration is taken as the main yardstick of social mobility. According to Breman the villagers are driven, not by a higher level of aspiration than their non-migrating fellow villagers, but by economic necessity. Inter-generational differences in occupations indicate such a pattern of social mobility.[19]

Desai (1984) is of the view that the rural middle castes which have gained access to political and economic dominance are in a position to take advantage of education for further upward social mobility. These middle castes comprise the upper stratum of the backward castes.[20]

Rajendra Singh in a recent study of the Basti district in Uttar Pradesh wrote that ownership of land and support of people (numerical strength of castes) together have made it smooth for the middle peasant castes to reach the corridors of power. Since the upper castes have lost control over land and were never numerically preponderant, they could not continue with their traditional supremacy in the changed circumstances in the post-independence era.[21]

Ray and Kumpathe (1987) in a study of the Zila Parishad presidents in Karnataka suggests that the caste composition of the local government leadership does not seem to have significantly changed. The Lingayats and the Vokkaligas, the two dominant land-owning castes, dominate the rural political scene even now as they did in the past.[22]

Gaurang Ranjan Sahay Conducted a study of four villages of Buxar (Bhogpur) district of Bihar (1991-93). A paper titled caste system in contemporary Bihar: A study of selected villages based on the above study, published in *Sociological Bulletin*, 47(2) Sept. 1998. It focusses the linkages between Caste and occupation as well as the status of the jajmani system today. Sahay pointed out that the concept of class denotes a category of people who occupy the same position in the economic structure within a social formation. The position is determined by the quentity of passession of the most important means of production in the villages, i.e. land. on the basis of their ownership of land people have been categorized into five classes as under:

(i) Big peasants (those families own more than twelve acres of land.

(ii) Upper-middle peasants (families having more than seven acres of land but not exceeding twelve acres.

(iii) Lower middle peasents (families with three to seven acres of land).

(iv) Small peasants (families owning between one to three acres of land).

(v) Landless and near landless people (families are either landless or owning not more than one acre of land).

Sahay examines that there are four general types of occupations in the villages: (i) agriculture farming; (ii) monthely paid government or non-government services; (iii) business and (iv) hiring out labour power or working as wage labourers. He has concluded that agriculture farming is an occupation in which the majority of the families from different castes are involved. Agricultural farming is the most extensively practised occupation in the villages. It is an occupation practised by almost all castes belong to forward, backward and Scheduled Castes.

Another finding of the study is that a majority of the families belonging to the forward castes such as Brahmin, Rajput and Bhumihar have access to monthly paid jobs. Other castes, with the exception of the Bari and Bind, do not have as much access to similar opportunities. Although all families belonging to Bari and Bind are attached to agricultural farming, their members perform meagerly paid jobs. Among the backward classes a good percentage of families belong to the Yadav, Koeri, Kamkar and Sonar have access to monthly paid jobs whereas the representattion of Bania, Rajbhar, Bhar, Gond, Paneri, Nonia, Lohar, Nalband and Kahar in government and non-government services is very minimal. Families belonging to Scheduled Castes such as the Dhobi, Chamar, Dusadh and Dom, have very limited access to such jobs. Thus, a highly uneven pattern emerges, if the representation of various castes in government or non-government monthly paid services is taken into account. The finding of the study is that Bania, Paneri, Nau, Dhobi, Dom and Sonar have commercialized their caste related occupations. In the villages studies not all purohits (priest) were Brahmins. There is a family belonging to the Koeri caste which also acts as purohit. This is a new phenomenon. This happend due to Arya Samaj movement. Koeris wanted to oppose and change the system and designated one of the families belonging to their own caste as a purohit family to perform all the rituals for them.

Pardeep Kumar (Reservations within Reservation, Economic and Political weekly September 15, 2001) describes that many castes which were once termed as the *Sudra* Castes have ceased to be so far all practical purposes. Many of these included some of the peasant castes of today, which have attained an 'upper caste' status and have even become politically dominant in the politics of some states, during the last five decades of the post colonial politics in India. Under several developments such as Zamindari abolition, land reform, land ceilling, tenancy reforms, consolidation of land holdings, etc., agricultural land holdings were transformed to these castes from the erstwhile dominant Zamindari castes. The subsequent introduction of given revolution package and the grass roots institutions of the panchayati raj, reinforced their economic and political power, more particularly in view of their number, which in an electoral democracy made all the difference. The Awadhias, the Mahatos, the Dhanuks and the Kamarias of the 1920s gradually became the more numberous Kurmis or the Kurma Kshetriyas or the Lodha Rajputs, etc. and the Gwalas, the Goapals, the Gopes, the Yadavas, the Mandals, the Ahirs, the Abhirs, the Dharonds, the Dhusias, the Goalis and the ones associated with the rearing of the milch cattle came to be identified as the politically powerful and socially dominant Yadavas. One may characterise the politics of the last few decades as Yadavisation and Kurmiaisation of politics in Bihar and Uttar Pradesh. This reminds one of Padayachis and the Shanars of the erstwhile Madras province eventually turning to become Vannikula Kshatriyas and the Nadars respectively; and the Valemas, the Telagas, the Naidus, the Toorpukapus and the Kondas, all becoming part of the larger group of Kapus in Andhra Pradesh, subsequently fighting for reservations and constituting themselves into a powerful party Kapunadu in the 1980s.

The Yadavas, the Kurmis and the Koeris who constituded the triveni (trio) to fight the zamindari system in Bihar in the 1920s today constitute about 20 percent of the population of the state but corner most political positions assigned to the backward castes, leaving little for the remaining 35 percent backwards.

A similar pattern may be observed where the Vokkaligas and Lingayasts of Karnataka, the Kunbis of Maharashtra and the Kapus of Ahdhra Pradesh have consequently succeeded in capturing political and economic power.

The original occupation basis of most caste categories which are no logner relevant in mobile castes continue to be so in case of these really backward communities i.e. Telis, Kahars, Dhobis, Gadarias, Nats, Mangs, Lohars, Sunars, Kumhars, Sansis, Lakarharas, Baheliyas, Barhais, Nais, Kewats Madaris and the Snake Charmers, etc.[23]

A study in Meerut and Azamgarh districts of Uttar Pradesh on segmentation arising out of caste/class divisions as a significant contextual variable in determining the development of trust, social capital between groups and democratic functioning (1996-1999) conducted by Sudha Pai, concluded that the hierarchical arrangements of the divisions of caste and class especially at the top and the bottom level has created social animosities, which are not easily overcome. Undoubtedly conflicts exist in all societies, and it is arguable that positive attitude to democracy are not part of norms inherent in social capital.

The study examines that the post colonial period has witnessed beginning is the mid 1960s, successive wares of caste-based horizontal mobilisation in UP leading to the fomation of political parties such as the BKD, BLD, JD and more recently the BSP, representing the backward, other backward castes and dalits, as there large coglomerations are now called. These groups by constituting distinct social identities and joint political action were able to effectively challange the dominant position of the Congress party. By these means, the middle and lower castes developed networks and shared values, which allowed them to function as a collective social group in politics.

One of the findings of the study is that the Ahirs and Kurmis, clean cultivating castes (OBCs), but roughly equivalent to the Jats in the west and constituting about 15 percent of the population of Azamgarh still form the dominant caste. They share their dominant status with upper castes Muslim Siddiquis in Azamgarh.

Education has not substantially contributed to assertion against the dominant castes. Despite rise in literacy, land remains the major source of livelihood with little diversification of the occupational structure, apart from small business such as poultry farming, sheep and pig rearing.

The analysis of the functing of the gram and block panchayats revealed that despite changes in their social composition due to reservations and questioning of the dominant position of the Jats and Rajputs, there has been little increase in participation in decision-making and implementation of programmes by the large majority of villages.

The study also indicates that an ongoing process of conflict resolution, through intervention by state officials and local caste leaders, is present in the functioning of the new Panchayats. This suggests that a broad-based social capital, capable of bringing together different caste/class groups may evolve over a period of time out of an interplay of both conflict and consensus, negotiation and bargaining, leading to more democratic functioning of panchayats.[24]

It can be concluded that the Indian society is undergoing a continous process of change and social scientist confronted with a number of problems when attempting to trace the ongoing processes of mobility in the socio-economic, political and ideological spheres. The castes, which are ever mobile, are adopting suitable adoptive mechanisms in the arena of interacting process concerning demographic migrations, socio-economic transformations, political upheavals, religions and ideological changes, etc. The major changes which have been brought about in the past decade in the Indian society:

> May be mentioned as modernisation and Urbanisation increased rapidly,

Modernisation of agriculture,
Industrilization,
Growth of trade and Commerce,
Political instability,
Free economy and globalization,
Emergence of new occupations and
shifting in traditional occupations.

These developments have changed the overall correlation of social forces. In the process, socio-economic status of certain caste/communities have changed. For instance some of the peasant castes have become rich peasants and landlords due to modernization in agriculture. Occupational castes either maintained their status or have found their status reduced. Thus significant changes took place in the socio-economic status of the OBCs during the last five decades which reflect the expansion of certain civic amenities like education, communication, transportation, medical facilities, expansion of government semi-government and private agencies and creation of multi-dimensional interest groups in the society.

On the other hand certain negative aspects of these developments may be mentioned as poverty, unemployment, competion between different sections of OBCs, caste conflicts process of caste politization, etc.

We find that Artisan/landless labours are going mainly downword mobility ladder. Those who are educated whose families are engaged in higher status occupations are economically well off and got the maximum benefit of the reservation while those who are illiterate, involoved in lower status occupations and belong to economically poor sections are deprived of reservation.

As representation in the elected bodies such as Panchayat, Zila Parishad, Municipalities etc. is concerned that the leadership is still with the higher sections of OBCs. There is an increase in caste conciousness. with increase of caste conciosness, caste consolidation has been utilized for political purpose and thus caste/communities are politicized the maximum. In this process a number of caste/communities of most backward section are getting alienated.

The political affiliation of caste/communities with the political parties is mainly responsible for caste consolidation in the country which not only give chance to caste conflict but also against the norms of the constitutional provisions. This trend will be very harmful for the unity of the nation and development.

Notes and References

1. G.I.Deptt. of Per. and Trg. O.M.No. 36012/31/90-Estt. (SCT), dated 13-8-1990.
2. G.I.Deptt. if Per. Trg. O.M. 36012/22/93-Estt. (SCT), dated 8- 9-1993.
3. National Backward Classes Finance and Development Corporation (NBCFDC) was set up on 13th January, 1992 with the objective to promote economic and developmental activities for the benefit of OBCs and to assist the poorer section of these classes in skill development and self employment ventures.

   The National Commission for Backward Classes (NCBC), set up by a special Act passed by Parliament on 2nd April 1993, viz., the National Commission for Backward Classes Act, 1993, was intended to take care of such genuinely backward castes/sub-castes/communities/synonyms which did not find place in the central list of backward classes prepared on the principle of commonality, provided requests came from or on behalf of such castes/sub-castes/communities/synonyms.
4. Poona Pact is a historical agreement which was signed on 24th September, 1932 between Dr. Ambedkar and the Hindu leaders at Poona. The Scheduled Castes through this agreement got representation in legislature, facilities in education and reservation in government servies.
5. Frankel, Francise and M.S.A. Rao 1990, *Dominance and State Power in Modern India: Decline of a Social Order*, Delhi, Oxford University Press.

6. Dumont Louis, 1970, Homo Hierarchicus, London: Paladin, Granada Pub. Ltd.

7. Rao, M.S.A. 1978: Introduction (p ix-xxiv Social Movement in Kerala Vol. I (ed.) M.S.A. Rao, Manohar Publications,New Delhi.

8. R. Thirunavukkarasu 2001; 'Election 2001: Changing Equations' EPW, Vol. XXXVI, No. 27, PP. 2486-89.

9. Reddy, V.N. and C.S. Murthy, 1978, 'Backward Castes and Tenancy: A Village study', EPW, Vol. XIII No. 26, pp. 1061-76.

10. Blair, Harry W.; and Prasad, 1980, Rising Kulaks and Backward Classes in Bihar, Social change in the Late 1970's, EPW, Vol. XV, No. 2 pp. 64-74.

11. Hodda Sagar Preet, 2000, 'Contesting Reservation's Rawat Publications, Delhi.

12. Yadav, K.C.; 1992, 'Haryana: Itihas Evam Sanskriti: Hindu Castes in Medival Period. Manohar Publishers, Delhi, Vol.1.

13. Anand Chakravarty, 2001, 'Caste and Agrarian Class: A view from Bihar', EPW, Vol. XXXVI, No. 17, pp. 1449-62.

14. Rudra, A; 1978, Class Analysis and its Relevance to the study of Indian Society', State and Society, pp. 96-106.

15. Blair, H.W; and Prasad, 1980, op.cit.

16. Ibid.

17. Upadhya, Carol Bayack, 1988, 'The Farmer-Capitalists of Coastal Andhra Pradesh', EPW, Vol. XXIII, No.27,28; pp. 1376-82; 1433 42.

18. Singh, Rajendra, 1988, Land Power and People: Rural Elite in Transition, 1801-1970, New Delhi, Sage Publications.

19. Breman, Jan, 1985, Of Peasants, Migrants and Paupers: Rural Labour Circulation and Capitalist Production in West India, Delhi, Oxford University Press.

20. Desai, I.P., 1984; 'Should Caste be the basis for recognising backwardness', EPW, Vol. XIX.

21. Singh, Rajendra, 1988, op.cit.

22. Ray, Amal and Jayalakshmi, Kumpatla, 1987, 'Zila Parishad President in Karnataka', EPW, Vol.XXII, Nos.42 and 43, pp. 1825-30.

23. Pardeep Kumar, 2001, 'Reservation within Reservation', EPW, Vol. XXXVI, No. 37 pp. 3505-7

24. Pai Sudha, 2001, 'Social Capital, Panchayats and Grass Roots Democracy: Politics of Dalit Assertion in Uttar Pradesh, EPW, Vol. XXXVI, No.8 pp. 645-54.

8

A Postscript: Towards a Class Cohesion

The process of identification and listing of Backward Classes has started long back. It was started in the provinces and princely states and then taken up in the States/UTs at different points of time. After independence, a debate on reservation to those sections of the Indian society who were deprived of their rights had started. Constituent Assembly debate and the provisions made for removal of untouchability, reservation to SCs, STs and OBCs were thought to be proved as milestone for upliftment of BCs. This has been conceptualized as protective discrimination policy. It is found that though considerable efforts have been made over several decades, the gains of development following protective discrimination policy have not reached the genuine backward castes/communities to the desired level. In fact, the process of social engineering after independence by the Government has become more complicated and the society has become more fragmented and anti-cohesive politically and socially. Reservation policy has generated competition among the BCs for the limited job opportunities and are available to them and thus promoted the flowing of individuality and breaking caste cohesion. It was motivated more by political exigencies rather than by truly uplifting the backward and deprived.

The Supreme Court verdict on identification of Social Education and Backward Classes was kept aside and identification of OBCs on caste basis continues. This practice results in each caste being treated as backward or not in its entirety; and the social class has been understood narrowly by the Government to reckon only castes.

The reservation policy was introduced with a view to achieving equal social status to a section of population which has been oppressed, exploited and socially degraded to a large extent for centuries together. It was not a vote bank and not a poverty alliviation programme as it seems today. When we see the landowning castes are included in the list of OBCs, the question comes in mind that what was the crietia for inclusion of castes. One aspect i.e. political influence which has contributed to the intensification of the offensive against agricultural labourers, marginal farmers, sharecroppers and others. In the caste-based reservations the maximum benefits is taken by the more powerful castes and by the more powerful families within a caste.

The nation fought against the evil of caste during the struggle of independence. For example, the caste columns were removed from the census after 1931 and mark of caste was deleted from application froms and other documents. Despite these efforts, then why we want to raise the caste consciousness, caste conflict and caste system by continuing with reservation based on caste model?

It maybe because the caste-based reservation is helping political parties to consolidate their position in the short term. It maybe because bureaucracy finds it easy and convinient. It maybe because the caste/community people are not made aware about the facts and consequencies of baste-based reservation; for them it is still a false dream.

Infact the caste system is a part of the structure of Indian feudalism. The caste factor in Indian politics manifests itself in two ways: (i) Acts to divide the oppressed masses; and (ii) Caste oppression which is inhuman and medieval form of outrage on a deprived section of the society. The success of the struggles against feudalism has been only partial because of the failure to grasp this point and apply it conscientiously. The age-old mistake be rectified and proper reservation policies formulated.

The 'Caste' as a category seems to be inadequate in the case of artisan, agriculture labour, tea garden labour, denotified tribes, nomadic and semi-nomadic tribes. They belong to a deprived class in real sense.

The evolution of the caste system is directly related to the growth of an exploitative agricultural economy where a class of people who controlled land and political power, needed caste to keep a large section of the society enslaved. In feudal India, land was the main means of production. Those who controlled the land constituted the feudal exploiting classes, those who cultivated the land and related other occupations belonged to the exploited class. The caste system provided a division of labour which was necessary to sustain the political-economic system. Caste and class were not synonymous but caste system played important role. The uninterrupted history of caste over thousands of years has given it a resilience and autonomy of its own, which has its own impact holding back the process of change.

India's backward classes (other than SCs and STs) is estimated 52 percent of the total population of the country and there is an enormous range of diversity among OBCs in terms of occupations, customs and level of development. Social formation and the pace of development might be slow but it has taken place in different forms because change is an inevitable phenomenon.

New norms of status evaluation signifying change in the traditional 'composite status' system have acquired legitimacy and acceptance. Caste has become weak and yet it has revitalized giving the impression of its entrenchment in new spheres of social life. Class, occupation, income, power and mobilization capacity are accepted today as the effective channels of upward social mobility.

The caste/communities appear in the OBC list mainly found place on the basis of their traditional occupation. About 80 percent caste/communities belonging to occupational caste group; denotified, nomadic and semi-nomadic and service castes groups. Most of the caste/communities of these categories could not raise their socio-educational status during the last 50 years, Some of the families of caste/communities of these categories may have obtained upward mobility but caste/community as a whole remains the same or reached to downward mobility. It is true in case of Artisanal/artisan caste/communities because cottage industries are ruined, traditional arts and crafts are lost, moderanisation, urbanisation, free economy and globlization have left no place to the traditional occupational services such as tailoring, hair cutting, washing of clothes, pressing of oil seeds, pottery, etc. Most of these service classes either have become agricultural labourers in the village or doing other manual work in the towns and cities as most of them are landless.

Caste/communities belonging to rich peasantary, priestly, trading, and military caste have found place in the OBC lists and those number is 10 percent of the total number of caste/communities of the central list of OBCs. The caste/communities of these categories have a scope of improvement in their status during the last 50 years. The peasantary caste and particularly rich farmers have taken the benefits of land reforms and modern technology and able to increase their agriculture production and land holdings. Many of these caste/communities have become cultivators-cum-traders. Peasantry castes are politically strong. In many states, political power has been in the hands of these castes alone. The caste/communities of this category are ever represented in the military, para-military and police services after independence and such advanced caste/communities found place in the list of OBCs on the basis of *principle of community*.

Secrutiny of the central list of OBCs shows that certain caste/communities are not socially and educationally backward but found place in the lists on the basis of principle of commanility. Some non-existance castes also found place in the central list of OBCs. Such caste/communities can be identified and suggested for exclusion from such lists.

Generally, Artisan and landless labourers downward mobile because lake of opportunities while those who are educated, whose families are engaged in higher status occupations are economically well-off and got the maximum benefits of the reservation while those who are illitrate, involved in lower status occupations and belong to economically poor sections and deprived of reservation benefits.

From the distribution of the caste/communities of OBC lists, it can be concluded that the caste/communities traditionally engaged in weaving occupation are more in number in the category of Artisanal/Artisans, while the largest number of caste/communities under sub-category of 'caste/communities with polluting occupation' of the same category is fishing caste then follows by castes/communities engaged in Toddy Tapping and distilling of liquor, Artists and Magicians.

In the category of Peasantary we find more number of castes in Andhra Pradesh, Bihar, madhya Pradesh and Tamilnadu in comparison to Punjab, Maharashtra, Gujarat and Rajasthan. In many states peasantry castes have shifted to other occupations. Similarly the caste/communities were engaged in animal husbandry have also shifted to other occupations to a great extent.

A few caste/communities particularly those who belong to minority religious groups are also found place in the OBC lists in good number. Mainly the artisanal caste/communities and the communities of tribal origins are more in number. Caste/communities distributed under de-notified, nomadic and semi-nomadic category generally have the same rank as of Scheduled Castes and Scheduled Tribes are found in the largest number in Maharashtra.

Among the priestly castes the number of Religions Mendicants is found the highest. There are some castes Sub-castes also known as castes of traders or money lenders. A few of such castes as 'Mappila' and 'Reddiar/Reddian' of Kerala, 'Tamang' of Sikkim and West Bengal and 'Wynad Chetty' of Tamilnadu found place in the central list of OBCs. Trading is not limited to any caste but there are certain commodities of which trading is done by certain castes such as trading of liquor by Kalars. Caste/communities selling commodities at a small scale should not be mix up with the trading communities of big business men. Petty business is done by certain castes traditionally such as betel leaf selling, cattle trade, trade in crops and live stocks, selling of vegetables by Kachis and flowers by Malis, etc.

A few military castes such as 'Kalinga' for Orissa, Kannada Saineegar for Tamilnadu and Makrana (Muslim) for Dadra and Nagar Haveli also found place in the cental list of OBCs.

As class exists in caste, caste can be seen in different classes. It can be seen clearly in the category of occupational castes particularly peasantary and artisan and artisanal castes which have some common features of a class. In this era of globalization, moderanisation and free-economy traditional occupations either eleminated or disappearing fast. As a result, due to rapid occupational mobility the caste is not only loosing identity but changing into different forms and these existing forms ara nothing but classes.

As analysis of social stratification and mobilization of Backward Classes is concerned that the emerging trends shows that class is the right term to understand the staus of the Backward Classes. For instance, in the category of artisanal partisan caste/communities most of the groups and sub-groups belong to a class of labourers which a few group or sub-group of this category ball in the category of a class of middle strata of businessmen and industrialist and thus make a separate class. Similarly in the category of peasantary some of the castes are holding political and economic power and now belong to rich peasantary section and sharing political power in many states and in the centra as well. Caste organisations/associations of this class are also emerging an effective political organisations and serving the interest of this class against the inerest of centain deprived classes. In this process, caste groups and alliances based on caste have become centres to share the political power.

On the other hand the category of denotified, Nomadic and Semi-Nomadic tribes; ogricultural labourers; and those who are involved in menial work, service castes remains backward. Their economic condition is datorating day by day and socially and politically still work. They are logging behind in the development process becouse they are generally rasourceless and uneducated.

Occupational structure in the Indian society can also be seven without caste which have created a non-traditional basis. In other words, the tradition basis of determining the identity, of caste/communities is no more relevant in changing world. Thus caste factor for identification of Backward Classes in general and traditional occupation in particular have become outdated and inadequate. In the present circumstances, economic and political factors seem appropriate for determination of backwardness of any caste/community.

Bibliography

Adhyapak, Gajey Singh, 1999, Karpoori Formuley Koo Bhool Gayey, *Hindustan Daily*, 31 March, 1999.

Aggarwal, Pratap, 1986, *Halfway to Equality,* Manohar, New Delhi.

Beteille, Andre, *Inequality and Social Change*, Oxford, New Delhi,1972.

Benjamin, J., *Scheduled Caste in Indian Politics & Society*. Ess Ess Publications, New Delhi, 1989.

Bhambhri, C.P., On the Problem of Minorities: The Muslim Question, *The Hindustan Times,* 4 December, 1997.

Bhashan, L.I.: *Casteism: A Socio-Psychological Study*. New Delhi. Classical Pub. Co.1996.

Bisht, Bhagavan Singh: *Backward Communities*, Gyan Books, 1999.

Blunt, E.A.H.: *The Caste System of Northern India*, 1931.

Breton, Roland J.L.: *Atlas of the Languages and Ethnic Communities of South Asia*. Sage India, 1997.

Burman, B.K. Roy, *Beyond Mandal and After*. Mittal Publications, New Delhi, 1990.

Chalam, K.S., 'Caste Reservations and Equality of Opportunity in Education', *Economic and Political Weekly,* 13 October, 1990.

Campbell, J.M.: Gujarat Population: Hindus *Gazetteer of the Bombay Presidency,* Vol. IX, Bombay, 1901.

Chanran, F.: *Issues in Reservation Caste Versus Economic States.* New Delhi, Cosmos Book Hive, 1990.

Charsley, S.R. and Karanth (GK): *Challenging Untouchability.* Sage India and Vistaar, 1998.

Chatterjee, S.K.: *Scheduled Castes in India.* Gyan Pub., 1996.

Chaudhary, S.N.: *Changing Status of Depressed Castes in Contemporary India.* Daya Pub. House, Delhi, 1988.

Chaurasia, B.P. : *Scheduled Caste and Scheduled Tribes in India.* Allahabad, Chugh Publication. 1990.

Chetty, VBK: *Scheduled Caste and Development Programmes in India.* New Delhi. Vohra Publishers. 1991.

Chitralekha V/s State of Mysore: AIR 1964 SC 1823.

Crooke, W.: *Tribes and Castes of the North-West Provinces and Oudh*, Calcutta, 1896.

Devi S.: *Caste System in India.* Pointer Publishers. Jaipur, 1999.

Dushkin, Lelah, 1979, 'Backward Class: Benefits and Social Class in India', 1920-70, *Economic and Political Weekly,* 14, Annual Number, April.

Dutt, N.K.: *Origin and Growth of Caste in India*, Calcutta, 1931.

Enthoven, R.E.: *The Tribes and Castes of Bombay*, Bombay, 1920-2.

Frankel, Francine, 1988, Middle Classes and Castes in Indian Politics, Prospects for Political Accommodation, in Atul Kohli, ed.; *India's Democracy: An Analysis of Changing State Society Relations*, New Delhi, orient Longman.

Ghurye, G.S.: *Caste and Class in India.* Popular Book Depot, Bombay, 1957.

—— *Caste and Race in India.* Popular Prakashan.

—— *Caste, Class and Occupation*. Popular Book Depot, Bombay, 1961.

Gupta, Rajesh Kumar, 2000, *Bharat mein Arakshan Neeti*, Manak Publications.

GOI, *Report of the First Backward Classes Commission*, 1955, Part I and II.

—— *Report of the Second Backward Classes Commission*, Part I & II, 1980.

Hammerton, J.A. (Ed): *An Encyclopaedia of Human Races all Over the World* (7 vols). Gyan Books, 1997.

Hasan, Zoya, 1989, *Dominance and Mobilization: Rural Politics of Western Uttar Pradesh*. 1930-1980, New Delhi, Sage.

Hasnian, N. (Ed). *Weaker Section*. Gyan Books 1997.

Havanur, L.G.: 'Backward Classes, Juridical Meaning' Bangalore, *Socio-Legal Services*. 1991.

Hellwald, Von and AN. Keane (ed): *World Encyclopaedia of Continents, Communities and Cultures*. (Set of 7 vols) Commonwealth Publishers, 1998.

Hill, S.C.: 'Origin of the Caste System in India', March-October, 1930, Bombay.

Hocart, A.M.: The Basis of Caste in India, in *Acta Orientalia*, XIV. Lexden, 1936.

Hunter, W.W., *Annals of Rural Bengal*, 1868.

—— *Annals of Orissa*, 1872.

Hutton, J.H., *Caste in India: Its Nature, Function and Origins*, Oxford University Press, London, 1963.

Ibbetson, D.: Panjab Castes, Being a reprint of the chapter on 'The Races, Castes and Tribes of the People' in the Report on the Census of the Punjab Published in 1883 by the late Sir Dezil Ibbetsou, K.C.S.I., Lahore, 1916.

Iliah, Kancha, 1990, Reservations: 'Experience as Framework of Debate', in *Economic and Political Weekly*, vol.25.

Imam Ali A.F.: *Social Stratification Among the Muslim and Hindu Community*. Commonwealth Publications, 1992.

Indu, Dharti, 'The Bihar Formula.' *Economic and Political Weekly,* November 3, 1990.

Iyer, L.A.K.

—— *The Cochin Tribes and Castes*, Madras, 1909-12.

—— *The Travancore Tribes and Castes* Trivandrum. 1937-41.

Iyer, L.A.K. and Nanjundayya, H.V.: *The Mysore Tribes and Castes*. Bangalore, 1928-35.

Jain, S.K.: *Caste and Politics in Bihar*. Commonwealth Publications, 1989.

Jha, Gulab: *Caste and the Communist Movement*. Commonwealth Publications, 1990.

Karunanithi, G.: *Caste and Class in Industrial Organisation*. Commonwealth Publications, 1991.

Ketkar, S.V.: *History of Caste in India Ithaca*, N.Y. 1908.

Khanna, S.K.: *Castes in Indian Politics*. Commonwealth Publishers, Delhi, 1998.

Khanna, S.N.: *Children and Human Rights*. Commonwealth Publishers, 1998.

Kothari, Rajni, 1986, 'Master, Classes and the State', in *Economic and Political Weekly*, vol.21.

Leach, E.R.: *Aspects of Castes in South India, Ceylon and North-West Pakistan*. Cambridge University Press, 1962.

Lohia, Rammanohar.: *The Caste System*. Nav Hind, Hyderabad, 1964.

Mahadevia, Darshini : *Sagmentation of Metro Cities: a case study of Mumbai and Chennai*. Allied Publishers 1999.

Mahala, N.K., Sociological Understanding - Exploration in Social Diversities. Classic Publishing House, Jaipur, 1991.

Manor, James, 1989, 'Karnataka: Caste, Class Dominance and Politics in a Cohesive Society', in Francine Frankel and M.S.A. Rao, eds, *Dominance and State Power: Decline of a Social order*, Vol.1, Delhi. Oxford University Press.

Mazumdar, D.N.: *Caste and Communication in an Indian Village.* Asia Publishing House, Bombay, 1956.

Michael, S.M.: *Dalits and Modern India:Vision and Values.* Saga India and Vistaar 1999.

Misha, R.B.: *Caste and Caste Conflicts in Rural Society.* Commonwealth Publications, 1989.

Muslim, *Law of Marriage, Divorce and Maintenance.* Deep and Deep Publications, 1995.

Nesfield, J.C.: *Brief View of the Caste System of the North-West Provinces and Oudh*, Allahabad, 1885.

Northey, W.B. and Morris, C.J.: *The Gurkhas, their Manners, Customs and Country,* 1928.

O'Malley, L.S.S.: *Indian Caste Customs*, 1932.

Omvedt Gail: *Dalits and the democratic revolution Sage India,* 1994.

Painandikar, V.A.Pai, 1997, *The Politics of Backwardness-Reservation Policy in India*, Delhi, Konark Publication.

Pal, R.M.: *Human Rights of Dalit Societal Voilation.* Gyan Books, 1999.

Pandian, J.: *Caste, Nationalism and Ethnicity an Interpretation of Tamil Culture.* Popular Prakashan.

Pant, V.K., *Backward Communities: Identity, Development and Transformation*, Gyan Publishing House, 1999, New Delhi.

Parvathamma, C:1986, 'Should Caste be a basis for recognising backwardness', *Guru Nanak Journal of Sociology* 7 (2) October.

Prasad, Anirudh, 1997, *Reservational Justice to Other Backward Classes (OBCs)-Theoritical and Practical issues.* New Delhi. Deep and Deep Publications.

Prasad Anirudh: *Reservation Justice to Other Backward Classes*. 1997, Deep & Deep Publications.

Raha M.K.: *Tribal India*, Gyan Books, 1996.

Ramaswamy, Uma, 1986, 'Protection and Inequality and Backward Group', *Economic and Political Weekly*, May 21.

Rao, H.: *Indian Caste System*. Bangalore, 1931.

Rao, H.: *Scheduled Castes and Tribes*. New Delhi, 1994.

Rao, S.R.L: *Caste System in India: Myth and Reality*. New Delhi, Reliance Pub. House. 1989.

Ravi Prasad L.M.: *Dalit Youth: A Sociological Study*. A.P.H.

Report of the Karnataka First Backward Classes Commission (4 volumes), 1975.

Report of the Karnataka Third Backward Classess Commission (2 volumes), 1990.

Report of the Karnataka Third Backward Classes Committee (Nagan Gauda), Final Report, 1960.

Risley, H.H.: *Tribes and Castes of Bengal*.

—— Ethnographic glossary, Calcutta, 1891. Tribes and Caste of Bengal.

—— Anthropometric Data. Calcutta, 1891.

—— The People of India, 1908.

Roy, S.C.: *Caste, Race and Religion in India in Man in India*. Vol. XIV, no.2. XVII, no.4, XVIII nos 2 and 3, Ranchi, 1934, 1937, 1938.

Russel, R.V. and Lal Hira: *The Tribes and Castes of the Central Provinces of India*. 1916.

Sahay, K.N.: *Dynamics and Dimensions of Tribal Societies*, 1993.

Sangwan, Om Prakash (Ed): *Dalit Society and Vice Challenge of Development*. Commonwealth Publications, 1996.

Sen, Sipra : *Tribes and Castes of Assam*. Delhi, Gyan Books 1999.

Shah, Ghanshyam, 1990, 'Caste Sentiments, Class Formation and Dominance in Gujarat', in Francine Frankel and M.S.A. Rao, eds., *Dominance and State Power: Decline of a Social Order.* Vol.II, Delhi: Oxford University Press.

Sharma, Anuradha: *Castes and Tribes in India*. Commonwealth Publishers, 1998.

Sharma, K.L., 1998: *Caste and Class in India*. Jaipur, Rawat Publications.

Sharma, K.L.: *Social Stratification in India*: Jaipur, Rawat Publication, India, 1997.

Shashi, S.S.: *Encyclopaedia of Indian Tribes* (12 vols), Anand Pub. Delhi, 1994.

Sher, Sher Singh, 'Ex- criminal tribes of Northern India need reclassification on more authentic and scientific grounds.' *Journal of Social Research* 3(2) Sep. 1960.

Sherring, M.A., *Hindu Tribes and Castes*. Delhi, Cosmo Publications 1987.

Sheth, D.L.: 'Muslim Reservation: No Provision for Communal Quotas', *Times of India*, 20 September, 1997.

Sheth, D.L.,: Political in Caste Conflict, *Seminar*, 233, January 1979.

Shourie, Arun, 'The Mandal Report - 'This Way Lies Not only folly, but disaster', *Indian Express*, 25 August, 1990.

Shukla, K.S.: *Development of Scheduled Castes and Administration*. New Delhi, Uppal Pub. House. 1993.

Siddiqui, M.K.A.: *Inter Caste and Inter Community Relationship Developing Patterns*. Commonwealth Publications, 1993.

Singh, K.S.: *Scheduled Castes* (2v). New Delhi, Oxford University Press. 1993.

Singh, V.P. (Ed): *Caste, Community and Conflict in Social Change*. Commonwealth Publications, 1992.

—— *Caste, Culture and Society Series* (Set of 6 vols). Commonwealth Publications, 1992.

—— *Caste System and Social Change.* Commonwealth Publications, 1992.

—— *Class Structure and Culture Dynamics.* Commonwealth Publications, 1992.

—— *Country Prospective in Class and Society.* Commonwealth Publications, 1992.

Srinivas, M.N.: *Caste in Modern India and other essays.* Asia Publishing House, Bombay, 1960.

Srinivas, M.N., *The Dominant Caste and Other Essays.* Oxford University Press, Delhi, 1987.

Thakur, Bimla: *Socio-Economic Analysis of the Weaker Sections: Rural Urban Comparative study in H.P.* Daya Pub. House, 1991.

Thakur, D.: *Tribal Education.* Deep and Deep Publications, 1995.

Thirunavukkarasu, R.,2001,'Tamil Nadu: Election 2001- Changing Equations', *Economic and Political Weekly,* July 7.

Thurston and K. Rangachari.: *Castes and Tribes of Southern India.* Madras, 1909.

Tod, James.: *Annals and Antiquities of Rajasthan.* 1829-32.

Topo, S.R., *Caste - A Social Evil.* Rajat Publications, New Delhi, 2000.

Yadav, K.C.; 1994, *India's Unequal Citizens-A study of Other Backward Classes.* Delhi, Manohar Publishers.

Appendix-I

Andhra Pradesh

Group - 'A'

Aboriginal tribes Vimuktha Jathis Nomadic and Semi Nomadic tribes etc.

1) Agnikulakshatriya, Palli, Vadabalija, Bestha, Jalari, Gangavar, Gangaputra, Goondla, Vanyakula-Kshatriya (vannekapu, Vannereddi, Pallikapu, Pallireddi, Neyyala & Pattapu)
2) Balasanthu, Bahurupi
3) Bandara
4) Budabukkala
5) Rajaka (Chakalivannar)
6) Dasari (formerly engaged in Bikshatana) (amended vide G.O.Rt.L. No. 32, BCW (MI) Dept., dated 23-2-1995.
7) Dommara
8) Gangireddlavaru
9) Jangam, whose traditional occupation is Begging.
10) Jogi
11) Kalipapala
12) Korcha
13) (Lambada or Banjara in Telangana area (deleted and included in S.Ts list) vide G.O.Ms. No. 149, S.W., dt. 3-5-1978)
14) Medari or Mahendra

15) Mondivaru, Mondibanda, Banda

16) Nayee Brahmin (Mangali), Mangala and Bajantri (amended vide G.O.Ms. No.1, BCW (M1) Dept., dated 6-1-1996).

17) Nakkala

18) Vamsharaj (amended vide G.O.Ms. No.27 BCW (M1) Dept. dated 23-6-1995)

19) Pamula

20) Pardhi (Mirshikari)

21) Pambala

22) Peddammavandlu, Devaravandlu, Yellammavandlu, Mutyalammavandlu.

23) Veeramusthi (Nettikotala), Veerabhadreeya (amended vide G.O.Ms. No.62, BCW (M1) Dept., dated 10-12-1996.

24) Valmiki, Boya (Boya, Bedar, Kirataka, Nishadi, Yellapi, Peddaboya) Talayari and Chunduvallu (G.O.Ms. No.124, S.W., dated 24-6-1985) Yellapl and Yellapu are one and the same (amended vide G.O.Ms. No.61, BCW (M1) Dept. dated 5-12-1996.

25) Yerukulas in Telangana area (deleted and included in the list of S.Ts).

26) Gudala

27) Kanjara-Bhatta

28) Kalinga (Kinthala deleted vide G.O.Ms. No.53 S.W., dated 7-3-1980.)

29) Kepmare, or Reddika

30) Mondipatta

31) Nokkar

32) Pariki Muggula

33) Yata

34) Chopemari

35) Kaikadi

36) Joshinandiwalas

37) Odde (Oddilu, Vaddi, Vaddelu)

38) Mandula

(Govt. Memo. No.40-VI/70-1, Edn., dated 10-2-1971)

39) Mehtar (Muslim) Govt. Memo. No.234/V1/72-2, Edn., dt. 5-7-1972)

40) Kunapuli

(Govt. Memo. No.1279/P1/74-10, E & SW, dated 3-8-1975)

Group - 'B'

Vocational

1) Achukatlavandlu

2) Aryakshatriya, Chittari, Giniyar, Chitrakara, Nakhas.

(Muchi (Telugu speaking) deleted vide G.O.Ms. No.31, BCW (M1) Dept., dt.11-6-1996).

3) Devanga

4) Goud (Ediga, Gouda (Gamella), Kalalee Goundla, Settibalija of Visakhapatnam, East Godavari, West Godavari and Krishna Dists. and Srisayana (Segidi)

(amended vide G.O.Ms. No.16, BCW (A1) Dept., dated 19-6-1997).

5) Dudekula, Laddaf, Pinjari or Noorbash.

6) Gandla, Telikula, Devatilakula (amended vide G.O.Ms. No.13, BCW (A1) Dept., dated 20-5- 1997).

7) Jandra

8) Kummara or Kulala, Salivahana (Salivahana Added vide G.O.Ms. No.28, BCW (M1) Dept. Dated 24-6-1995).

9) Karikalabhakthulu, Kaikolan or Kaikala (Sengundam or Sengunther)

10) Karnabhakthulu

11) Kuruba or Kuruma

12) Nagavaddilu

13) Neelakanthi

14) Patkar (Khatri)

15) Perika (Perika Balija, Puragirikshatriya)

16) Nessi or Kurni

17) Padmasali (Sali, Salivan, Pattusali, Senapathulu, Thogata Sali).

18) Srisayana (Segidi) deleted and added to Sl. No.4 of Group-B)

19) Swakulasali

20) Thogata, Thogati or Thogataveerakshatriya

21) Vishwabrahmin, Viswakarma (Ausula or Kamsali, Kammari, Kanchari, Vadla or Vadra or Vadrangi and Silpis)

(Viswakarma added vide G.O.Ms. No.59, BCW (M1) Dept., dated 6-12-1995).

Group - 'C'

Harijan Converts

1) Scheduled Castes converts to Christianity and their progeny (G.O.Ms. No.5, S.W. Dept., dated 24-1-1981).

Group - 'D'

Other Classes

1) Agaru

2) Arekatika, Katika

3) Atagara

4) Bhatraju

5) Chippolu (Mera)

6) Gavara

7) Godaba

8) Natkar

9) Jakkala

10) Jingar

11) Kandra

12) Koshti

13) Kachi

14) Surya Balija (Kalavanthulu), Ganika (amended vide G.O.Ms.

No.20, BCW (P2) Dept., dated 19-7-1994.

15) Krishnabalija (Dasari, Bukka)

16) Koppulavelama

17) Mathura

18) Mali

19) Mudiraj, Mutrasi, Tenugollu

20) Munnurukapu (Telangana)

21) Nagavamsam (Nagavamsa)
(amended vide G.O.Ms. No.53, BCW (M1) Dept., dated 19-9-1996).

22) Nelli

23) Polinativelamas of Srikakulam & Visakhapatnam districts.

24) Poosala

25) Passi

26) Rangrez or Bhavasara Kshatriya

27) Sadhuchetty

28) Satani (Chattadasrivaishnava)

29) Tammali confined to five districts of Nalgonda, Mahaboobnagar, Karimnagar, Nizamabad & Adilabad of Telangana Region only and not to other parts of A.P. (amended vide G.O.Ms. No.29, BCW (A1) Dept., dated 21-7-1997).

30) Thurpukapus of Gajulakapus of Srikakulam & Visakhapatnam districts who are subject to social Customs of divorce and re-marriages among their Women (G.O.Ms. No.65, E & SW, dt. 18-2-1974).

31) Uppara or Sagara

32) Vanjara (Vanjari)

33) Yadava (Golla)

Assam

1. Ahom
2. Baria

3. Baruj
4. Barjabi
5. Baroi
6. Chutia
   Chutiya
7. Cheudang
8. Ganak in Districts of Kachar
   Karimganj and Hailakundl
9. Ghosh
   Gop
   Gowala
   Gawala
   Goal
   Goala
10. Rumai, Rudra Paul of district of Cashar
   Karimganj and Hailakandi
11. Kupadhar
   Kushiari,
   Path
12. Mahisya Das,
   Mahisya
13. Manipuri, including
   Manipuri Brahmi and
   Manipuri Muslim
14. Moran
   Matak
15. Mukhi
16. Napit
17. Nepali (i.e.
   Thapa,
   Gurung,

Lama,

Gains,

Rai,

Chetri, Chatri, Chhctri,

Lihu,

Magar,

Lohar,

Dami

Sark i.e. (Cobbler)

18. Rajbanshi

Koch

19. Sudra Das, Dey

20. Saloi

21. Sut, Seet

22. Scheduled Caste persons converted to Christianity

23. Tantripal,

Tanti,

Tantri

24. Tea Garden Lobouress.

Tea Garden Tribes,

Ex-Tea Garden Labourers

& Ex-Tea Garden

Tribes as listed below :

1. Ahitgroala
2. Arya Mala
3. Asur
4. Barhai
5. Basphor
6. Bhokta
7. Baurl
8. Bowrl
9. Bhayan
10. Bhumij
11. Bedia
12. Beldar
13. Bharaik
14. Bhatta
15. Basor
16. Baiga
17. Baijara
18. Bhil

19. Bondo
20. Binjia
21. Birhar
22. Birjia
23. Beddi
24. Chamar
25. Chowdhari
26. Chero
27. Chick Banik
28. Dandari
29. Dandasi
30. Dusad
31. Dhanwar
32. Ganda
33. Gonda
34. Gond
35. Ghansi
36. Gorait
37. Ghatowar
38. Hari
39. Holra
40. Jolha
41. Keot
42. Koiri
43. Khonyor
44. Kurni
45. Kawar
46. Karmali
47. Korwa
48. Kol
49. Kalabandi
50. Kalihandi
51. Kotval
52. Kharia
53. Kumhar
54. Kherwar
55. Khodal
56. Khond
57. Koya
58. Kondpan
59. Kohar
60. Kormakar
61. Kashan
62. Lahar
63. Lodha
64. Lodhi
65. Madari
66. Mahli
67. Mohali
68. Modi
69. Mahato
70. Malpatharia
71. Manki
72. Majwar
73. Mirdhar
74. Munda
75. Nonia, Nunia
76. Nagasia
77. Nagbansi
78. Nath
79. Oraon
80. Pasi

81.	Paidi	82.	Pan
83.	Panika	84.	Parja
85.	Patratanti	86.	Pradhan
87.	Rajwar	88.	Sahora
89.	Santhal, Santal	90.	Sarvera
91.	Turi	92.	Telenga
93.	Tassa	94.	Tantubai
95.	Teli	96.	Tanti

25. Teli
26. Yogi, Jogi, Jugi Nath
27. Maimal (Muslim Fisherman)
28. Maria

Bihar

अनुसूची-1 (अत्यन्त पिछड़े वर्गों की सूची)

1.	कपरिया	1.	Kapadia
2.	कानू	2.	Kanu
3.	कवार	3.	Kawar
4.	कलन्दर	4.	Kalandar
5.	कोछ	5.	Kochh
6.	कुर्मी (महतो) (झारखंड स्वशासी क्षेत्र)	6.	Kurmi (Mahto) (Jharkhand Autonomous Council)
7.	केवट (कउट)	7.	Kewat (Kaut)
8.	कादर	8.	Kadar
9.	कोरा	9.	Kaura
10.	कोरक	10.	Korku
11.	केवर्त	11.	Kaibart
12.	कुमार भाग पहाड़िया	12.	Kumar Bhag Paharia
13.	खटवा	13.	Khatwa

14.	(विलोपित)	14.	(Delated)
15.	खतौरी	15.	Khatouri
16.	खंगर	16.	Khangar
17.	खटिक	17.	Khatik
18.	(खेलटा)	18.	Khelta
19.	खतवे	19.	Khatwe
20.	(विलोपित)	20.	(Deleted)
21.	गोड़ी (छावी)	21.	Gorhi (Chhabi)
22.	गगाई (नगेश)	22.	Gangai (Nagesh)
23.	गंगोता	23.	Gangota
24.	गोड़ या गोंड़	24.	Gour or Gonr
25.	गंधर्व	25.	Gandharb
26.	गुलगुलिया	26.	Gulgalia
27.	गौड़	27.	Gour
28.	चांय	28.	Chain
29.	चपौता	29.	Chapota
30.	चन्द्रवंशी (कहार)	30.	Ghandrabansi (Kahar)
31.	टिकुलहार	31.	Tikulhar
32.	ढेकारु	32.	Dhekaru
33.	तांती (ततवा)	33.	Tanti (Tatwa)
34.	तमरिया	34.	Tamaria
35.	तुरहा	35.	Turha
36.	तियर	36.	Tiar
37.	धारु	37.	Dharu
38.	धानुक	38.	Dhanuk
39.	धामिन	39.	Dhamin
40.	धीमर	40.	Dhimar
41.	धनवार	41.	Dhanwar
42.	नोनिया	42.	Nonia
43.	नइया	43.	Naiya
44.	नाई	44.	Nai

45.	नामशूद्र	45.	Namsudar
46.	पाण्डी	46.	Pandu
47.	पाल (भेडिहार गड़ेरी)	47.	Pal (Bherihar) (Gareri)
48.	प्रधान	48.	Pradhan
49.	पिनगनिया	49.	Pingania
50.	पहिरा	50.	Pahira
51.	वारी	51.	Wari
52.	बेलदार	52.	Beldar
53.	बिन्द	53.	Bind
54.	(विलोपित)	54.	(Deleted)
55.	सेखड़ा	55.	Shekhra
56.	बागंदी	56.	Bagdi
57.	भुईयार	57.	Bhuiyar
58.	भार	58.	Bhar
59.	(विलोपित)	59.	(Deleted)
60.	भास्कर	60.	Bhaskar
61.	माली (मालाकार)	61.	Mali (Malakar)
62.	मांगर	62.	Mangar
63.	मदार	63.	Madar
64.	मल्लाह (सुरहिया)	64.	Mallah (Surhia)
65.	मझवार	65.	Majhwar
66.	मारकन्डे	66.	Markandey
67.	मारियारी	67.	Moriyari
68.	मलार (मालहोर)	68.	Malar (Malhor)
69.	मौलिक	69.	Molik
70.	राजधोबी	70.	Rajdhobi
71.	राजभर	71.	Rajbhar
72.	रंगवा	72.	Rangwa
73.	बनपर	73.	Banpar
74.	(विलापित)	74.	(Deleted)
75.	सौंटा (सोता)	75.	Shota (Shota)

76.	संतराश (केवल नवादा जिले के लिए)	76.	Sangatrash (for Nawadah Dist.)
77.	अगरिया	77.	Agaria
78.	अघौरी	78.	Aghouri
79.	अबदल	79.	Abdal
80.	कसाब (कसाई) (मुस्लिम)	80.	Kasab (Kasai) (Muslim)
81.	चीक (मुस्लिम)	81.	Chik (Muslim)
82.	डफाली (मुस्लिम)	82.	Dafali (Muslim)
83.	धुनिया (मुस्लिम)	83.	Dhunia (Muslim)
84.	धोबी (मुस्लिम)	84.	Dhobi (Muslim)
85.	नट (मुस्लिम)	85.	Nut (Muslim)
86.	पमरिया (मुस्लिम)	86.	Pamaria (Muslim)
87.	भठियारा (मुस्लिम)	87.	Bhathiara (Muslim)
88.	भाट (मुस्लिम)	88.	Bhat (Muslim)
89.	मेहतर, लालवेगीया, हलालखोर, भंगी (मुस्लिम)	89.	Mehtar, Lalbegia, Halalkhor, Bhangi (Muslim)
90.	मिरियासीन (मुस्लिम)	90.	Miriasia (Muslim)
91.	मदारी (मुस्लिम)	91.	Madari (Muslim)
92.	मोरशिकार (मुस्लिम)	92.	Neershikar (Muslim)
93.	साई (मुस्लिम)	93.	Saeen (Muslim)
94.	मोमिन (मुस्लिम)	94.	Momin (Muslim)
95.	अमात	95.	Amat
96.	चुड़ीहार (मुस्लिम)	96.	Churihar (Muslim)
97.	प्रजापति (मुस्लिम)	97.	Parjapati (Kumhar)
98.	राईन या कुंजरा (मुस्लिम)	98.	Raeen or Kunjara (Muslim)
99.	सोयर	99.	Soyar
100.	ठकुराई (मुस्लिम)	100.	Thakurai (Muslim)
101.	नागर	101.	Nagar
102.	शेरशाहवादी	102	Shershahbadi
103.	बक्खो (मुस्लिम)	103	Bakkho (Muslim)
104.	अदरयी	104	Adarakhi

105.	छीपी	105	Chhipy
106.	तिली	106.	Tili
107.	इदरीसी/दर्जी/ (मुस्लिम)	107.	Idiris or Darzi (Muslim)
108	सेकलगर (सिकलगर) (मुस्लिम)	108.	Saikalgar (Sikalgar) (Muslim)

नोटः- (उन जाति तथा वर्गो को जिन्हे मुस्लिम नही लिखा गया है हिन्दू तथा मुसलमान दोनो जाति का समझना चाहिए । जैसे तेली मे दोनो हिन्दू तथा मुसलमान तेली).

अनुसूची-२ (पिछडे वर्गो की सूची)

1.	(विलोपित)	1.	(Deleted)
2.	कागजी	2.	Kagji
3.	कमार (लोहार और कर्मकार)	3.	Kamar (Lohar & Karmkar)
4.	खुशवाहा (कोइरी)	4.	Kuswaha (Koiri)
5.	कोस्ता	5.	Kosta
6.	गददी	6.	Gaddi
7.	घटवार	7.	Ghatwar
8.	(विलोपित)	8.	(Deleted)
9.	चनउ	9.	Chanau
10.	जदुपतिया	10.	Jadupatia
11.	जोगी (जुगी)	11.	Jogi (Jugi)
12.	तमोली	12.	Tamoli
13.	तेली	13.	Teli
14.	देवहार	14.	Dewhar
15.	नालबंद (मुस्लिम)	15.	Nalband (Muslim)
16.	(विलोपित)	16.	(Deleted)
17.	परथा	17.	Partha
18.	बढई	18.	Barhi
19.	बड़ई	19.	Barai
20.	बनिया (सुढी, हलवाई, रोनियार,	20.	Bania (Sundi, Halwai, Roniar, Pansari, Modi,

	पंसारी, मोदी, कसेरा, केशरवानी, ढढेरा, कलवार, (कलाल / एराकी) (वियाहुत कलवार), पटवा, कमलापुरी वैश्य, सिन्दुरिया बनिया, माहुरी वैश्य, (वंगाली बनिया), बर्नवाल, अग्रहरा वैश्य, पोददार, कसौधन, गंधबनिक)		Kasera, Kesarwani, Thathera, Kalwar, (Kalal/ Araqi) (Bihayut Kalwar), Patwa, Kamlapuri Vaishya, Sinduria Bania, Mahuri Vaishya, Awadh Bania, Bangia ,Vaishya, (Bengali Bania), Barnwal,Agrahari Vaishya, Poddar, Kasaodhan, (Gandhbanik).
21.	मुकरी (मुकेरी) (मुस्लिम)	21.	Mukri, (Mukeri) (Muslim)
22	यादव (ग्वाला, अहीर, गोरा, घासी, मेहर)	22.	Yadav (Gwala, Ahir, Gora, Ghasi, Mehar sadgope).
23.	राजवंशी (रिसिया या पोलिया)	23.	Rajbansi (Rasia or Polia)
24.	रंगरेज (मुस्लिम)	24.	Rangrej (Muslim)
25.	रौतिया	25.	Rautia
26.	(विलोपित)	26.	(Deleted)
27.	लहेड़ी	27.	Laheri
28.	शिवहरी	28.	Shivhari
29.	सोंनार	29.	Sonar
30.	सूत्रधार	30.	Sutardhar
31.	सुक्रियार	31.	Sukriar
32.	(विलोपित)	32.	(Deleted)
33.	ईसाई धमावलम्बी (हरिजन)	33.	Ishai Dharmawalambi (Harijan)
34.	ईसाई धर्मावलम्वी (अन्य पिछड़ी जाति)	34.	Ishai Dharmawalambi (Pichari Jat)
35.	कुर्मी (महतो)	35.	Kurmi (Mahto)
36.	भाट (हिन्दु)	36.	Bhat (Hindu)

37. दांगी
38. कुल्हैया

37. Dangi
38. Kulhaiya

नोटः- उन जाति तथा वर्गो को जिन्हे मुस्लिम नही लिखा गया है, हिन्दु तथा मुसलमान दोनो जाति का समझना चाहिए जैसे तेली मे दोनो हिन्दू तथा मुसलमान तेली ।

Delhi

1. Abbasi, Bhishti, Sakka
2. Agri, Kharwal, Kharol Khariwal
3. Ahir, Yadav, Gwala
4. Arain, Rayoo, Kunjra
5. Badhai, Barhai, Khati, Tarkhan Jangra-Brahmin, Vishwakarma, Porichal, Mathul-Brahmin, Dheeman, Ramgarhia-Sikh.
6. Badi
7. Bairagi
8. Bairwa, Berwa
9. Barai, Bari, Tamboli
10. Bauria/Bawria (excluding those in SCs)
11. Bazigar, Nat., Kalandar 9excluding those in SCs)
12. Bharbhooja, Kanu
13. Bhat, Bhatra, Darpi, Ramiya....
14. Bhatiara
15. Chak
16. Chippi, Tonk, Darzi, Terishi
17. Dakaut, Prade
18. Dhinwar, Jhinwar, Nishad, Kewat/Mallah (excluding those in SCs) Kashyap (Non-Brahmin), Kahar
19. Dhobi (excluding those in SCs)

20. Dhunia, Pinjara, Kandera-Karan, Dhunnewala, Naddaf, Mansoori
21. Fakir
22. Gadaria, Pal, Baghel, Dhangar, Nikhar, Kurba, Gadhori, Gaddi, Garri
23. Ghasiara, Ghosi
24. Gujar, Gurjar
25. Jogi, Goswami, Nath, Yogi, Jugi Gosain
26. Julaha-Ansari (excluding those in SCs)
27. Kachhi, Koeri, Murai, Murao, Maurya, Kushwaha, Shakya, Mahate.
28. Kasai, Qassab, Quraishi
29. Kasara, Tamara, Thathiar
30. Khatguna
31. Khatik (excluding those in SCs)
32. Kumhar, Prajapati
33. Kumri
34. Lakhera, Manihar
35. Lodhi, Lodha, Lodh, Maha-Lodh
36. Luhar, Saifi, Bhubhalia
37. Machi, Machhera
38. Mali, Saini, Southia, Sagarwan, Shimali, Nayak
39. Memar, Raj
40. Mina/Meena
41. Merasi, Miras
42. Mochi (excluding those in SCs)
43. Nai, Hajjam, Nai (Sabita), Sain, Salmani
44 Nalband
45. Naggal
46. Pakhiwara
47. Patwa

48. Pathar, Chera, Sangtarash
49. Rangrez
50. Raya-Tanwar
51. Sunar
52. Teli
53. Rai-Sikh
54. Jat

Goa

1. Kumbhar including Christian Kumbhar
2. Teli
3. Shimpi
4. Christian Mahar
5. Kalaikar/Blacksmith/Tinsmith
6. Pagui/Gabit
7. Christian Barber
8. Satarkar
9. Bhandari Naik

Gujarat

1. Agri
2. Ahir
   Ayar-Boricha

2.A Yadav

3. Bafan (Muslim)
4. Barot
   Vahivancha Charan-Gadhvi.
5. Bavcha (now S.T.)
6. Bavri or Baori.
7. Bawa,

Atit Bawa,
Goswami,
Gosai,
Dashnam Goswami,
Ramanandi/Ramanandi Bawa/Ramanandi Sadhu.
Puri,
Bharti,
Kapdi,
Nath Bawa,
Bharathari,
Margi,
Gangajalia,
Dashnami Baws,
Giri

8. Bhalia.

9. Bhamta,
Pardesi Bhamta

10 Bharwad,
Motabhai Bharwad,
Nanabhai Bharwad

10.A Kabari Baria Motabhai,
Chosla,
Janpda. (where there are not S.T.)

11. Bhil (now S.T.)

12. Bhoi,
Bhoiraj,
Dhimar,
Zinga-Bhoi,
Kevat Bhoi,
Bhanara Bhoi,
Machhindra Bhoi,

Palewar Bhoi,
Kirat Bhoi,
Kahar Bhoi,
Pardeshi Bhoi,
Srimali Bhoi

13. Charan, Gadhvi or Charan
13-A Bhat
14. Chhara,
Adodia,
Sansi
15. Chunara
16. Chuvalia Koli
17. Dabgar
18. Divecha Koli
19. Dafer (Hindu And Muslim)
20. Dhobi
21. Fakir or Faquir (Muslim)
22. Gadhai (Muslim)
23. Gadalia or Gadiluharia
23.A Luhariya/Luvaria
24. Galiara (Muslim)
25. Ganchi (Muslim)
25.A Teli,
Modh Ganchi
26. Ghedia Koli
26.A Gola-Rana
27. Hingora (Muslim)
28.A Hingora (Hindu)
28. Julaya,
Garana,
Taria and Tari (all Muslim)
29.A Jilaya (Muslim)

29.B Tariya-Tai/Tariya (Muslim)
Tariya-Tai (Muslim)
30. Jat (Muslim)
31. Kaikadi
32. Kambadia Bhagat
33. Kangasia
34. Katki or Kasai,
Chamadia Khatki,
Halari Khatki (all Muslims)
35. Khatki
36. Khant
37. Kharwa-Bhadela
38. Kristi
Gujarati-Christian
(converts from S.C only)
39. Koli
Idaria Koli,
Kharwa-Koli,
Rathwa-Koli,
Baria-Koli,
Dhebaria-Koli
39.A Koli-Malhar,
Koli-Mahadev or Dongar
Koli (where they are not S.T.)
40. Labana
Mehravat,
Goti,
Hadkashi,
Zod,
Dhinga,
Pelya,
Shatbe,

Baman

41. Lodha

42. Mir, Dadhi,
Langha, Mirasi (all Muslim)

43. Machhi (Hindu)
Kharwa,
Khalas,
Dhimar,
Dhivar,
Bitna,
Tandel,
Mangela,
Khalasi,
Sarang,
Kahar

44. Mandari,
Nath,
Bharathari,

45. Majothi Kumbar,
Darban or Darbar Majothi (all Muslim)

46. Makrani (Muslim).

47. Matwa or Matwa-Kureshi (Muslim),
Gavli (Hindu).

48. Me or Meta.

49. Mena (Bhil).

50. Mer

51. Miyana (Muslim)

51.A Miana, Miyana (Hindu)

52. Mochi (now S.C.)
Jansali,
Sivania,
Myanagar.

Jingar,
Dasania,
Chamadia
Bharatbhara,
Chandlia,
Sonara,
Aari Bharatbhara

53. Nat,
Nat-Bajania, Bajania,
Bajigar,
Natada or Bajania

54. Od

55. Padhar (now S.T.)

56. Padmashali-Patushali

57. Pinjara, Ganchi,
Mansuri-Pinjara (all Muslim)

57.A Mansuri (Muslim)

58. Rabari,
Bhopa,
Kodiatar
Sorathiya Rabari,
Champya

58.A Charalia,
Charmta,
Luni,
Kushar,
Tank,
Muchhal,
Kadiya Kumbhar
(where they are not S.C.)

59. Rathodia

60. Raval-Ravalia,
Jati or Raval Yogi
Raval Jati, Jagaria

60.A Padat,
Ravar,
Rawalia

61. Salat (excluding Sompura Salat)
Salat Ghera

62. Sandhi (Muslim)

62.A Sandhi (Hindu)

63. Sarania

64. Sargara

65. Shrawan
Sarwan

66. Shikligar

67. Siddi

68. Sipai, patni Jamat or Turk
Jamat. (all muslim)

69. Talpada Koli/Tarbada Koli

70. Tankar

71. Targala,
Bhavaiya,
Nayak,
Bhojak,

72. Thakarda,
Thakore,
Patanwadia,
Dharala,
Barieya
Baria

72.A Palanwadia

73. Theba (Muslims)
74. Vadi
74.A Jogi Vadi
75. Vahivancha Charan-Gadhavi of Harijan Vankar and Chamar
76. Valand
Nayi and Barbar (Hindu)
Hajam (Hindu)
Khalipha (Muslim)
76.A Vale (Hindu)
77. Vankar/Sadhu
78. Vansfoda,
Vansfodia or Vanza
78.A Vanza (Saurashtra)
79. Vanzara,
Shinagwala (Hindu)
Kangasiwala (Hindu) and
Vanzara (Muslim) of Dang district only
79.A Ra,
Charan Vanzara,
Mathura Vanzara,
Maru Vanzara,
Bhagora Vanzara,
Kangashiya Vanzara,
Bamania Vanzara,
Ladonia Vanzara,
Gavaria Gawalia,
Rohidas Vanzara,
80. Waghari,
Dataniya Vaghari,
Vedu Waghari,
Talpada Waghari,
Gamacniya Waghari,

Godadia Waghari,
Chibhadia Waghari,
Marwada or
Marwada Waghari,
Marwadi Waghari,

80.A Waghari Gamichiya,
Wedva Churaliya,
Jakhudia
(where they are not S.T.)

80.B Wadva Waghari or Velva Waghari

81. Wagher (Hindu & Muslim)

82. Wandhara

83. Arab (Muslim)

84. Bhand

85. Burud

86. Chakrawadya Dasar

87. Chaudhari of Hindu Anjana,
Chaudhari or Hindu Aanjana,
Chaudhari or Aanjana,
Aanjana Patel, Aanjana Patidar,
Aanjana Desai, Aanjana Kanbi,
Chaudhari Patel, Chaudhari Patidar
(where they are not S.T.)

88. Chamtha

89. Dakaleru

90. Depala

91. Ghantia

92. Ghancha

93. Galkada

94. Gavli

95. Hati

96. Jachak

97. Kalodhia
98. Kotwal
99. Kumbhar,
(Biyar,
Kadra Patel,
Lathiya,
Potmaker,
Prajapati
Variya
Varia
or Sorathiya Prajapati,
Kadia Kumbhar,
Vataliya Prajapati,
or Gujjar Kshatriya Kadia
Gurjar Prajapati,
Kshatriya Kadia, Kadia
100. Kharak
101. Khavas
102. Karadiya-Nadoda,
Bhati Rajput,
or Karadiya Rajput,
or Nadoda Rajput.
103. Kasiya
104. Mistri,
Gujjar,
Mistri Rathod
Mistri Suthar
Suthar,
Sutar,
Suthar Gurjar,
Gujjar Suthar,
Gurjar,

Mistri Sutar, Luhar, Panchal, Kadiya
Suthar
Sai-Suthar

105. Munda
106. Madhaviya
107. Mali/Mali Rami,
Marwadi Mali
108. Maiya or Mihiya
109. Palwadia
110. Padhariya
111. Pakhali
112. Sangheda
113. Shingdav or Shingadiya
114. Sochi
115. Sumra (Muslim)
116. Sagar
117. Sathvara/Satvara,
or Kadiya-Sathwara or
Kadiya Satvara Dalwadi or Kadiya
118. Thakur (Non Rajputs)
119. Timali,
120. Tarak (Muslim)
121. Vajir
122. Kathi
123. Lakhara/Lakhavara/Lakshakar
124. Kalal (Muslim)
125. Jagri
126. Jogi
127. Bahvaiya (Muslim)
128. Nizama (Hindu)
129. Gadriya
130. Kamaliya-Pujara
131. Gari

7. Haryana

Block - 'A'

1. Aheria, Aheri, Heri, Naik Thori or Turi, Hari
2. Barra
3. Beta, Hensi or Hesi
4. Bagria
5. Barwar
6. Barai, Tamboli
7. Baragi, Bairagi
8. Battera
9. Bharbhunja, Bharbhuja
10. Bhat, Bhatra, Darpi, Ramiya
11. Bhuhalia Lohar
12. Changar
13. Chirimar
14. Chang
15. Chimba, Chhipi, Chimpa, Darzi, Rohilla
16. Daiya
17. Dhobis
18. Dakaut
19. Dhimar, Mallah, Kashyap-Rajpoot, Kahar, Jhiwar, Dhinwar, Khewat, Mehra, Nishad
20. Dhosali, Dosali
21. Faquir
22. Gwaria, Gauria or Gwar
23. Ghirath
24. Ghasi, Ghasiara or Ghosi
25. Gorkhas
26. Gawala, Gowala
27. Gadaria, Pal
28. Garhi Lohar
29. Hajjam, Nai, Nais, Sain

30. Jhangra-Brahman, Khati, Suthar, Dhiman, Tarkhan, Barhai, Baddi
31. Joginath, Jogi, Nath, Jangam-Jogi
32. Kanjar or Kanchan
33. Kurmi
34. Kumhars, Prajapati
35. Kamboj
36. Khanghera
37. Kuchband
38. Labana
39. Lakhera, Manihar
40. Lohar, Panchal
41. Madari
42. Mochi
43. Mirasi
44. Nar
45. Noongar
46. Nalband
47. Pinja, Penja
48. Rehar, Rehara or Re
49. Raigar
50. Rai Sikhs
51. Rechband
52. Shorgir, Shergir
53. Soi
54. Singhikant, Singiwala
55. Sunar, Zargar, Soni
56. Thathera, Tamera
57. Teli
58. Banzara, Banjara
59. Weaver (Jullaha)
60. Badi/Badden
61. Bhattu/Chattu

62. Mina
63. Rahbari
64. Charan
65. Chaoraj (Mahabrahman)
66. Udasin
67. Ramgarhia

Block - 'B'

68. Ahir/Yadav
69. Gujjar
70. Lodh/Lodha
71. Saini
72. Meo

Throughout the Himachal Pradesh

(A)

1. Aheri, Ahori, Neri, Haik, Thori, Turi
2. Ard pop
3. Beda
4. Bahti
5. Bata, Hensi, or Hosi
6. Bagria
7. Batoerha
8. Baragi, Bairagi,
9. Bharbunha, Bharbhuja
10. Bhat or Bhatta (whether with or without the appendage-Brahman), Darpi
11. Bhuhalia
12. Chang
13. Changar
14. Chirimar
15. Dhimar
16. Dhosali, Dosal

17. Daiya
18. Faguir
19. Ghirath including Chang & Bhati
20. Ghasi, Ghasiara or Ghosi
21. Gorkha
22. Ghai
23. Gowala, Gwala
24. Gadaria
25. Gawaria, Gauria or Gwar
26. Hajam, Nai
27. Jhiwar, Dhiwar, Jhinwar, Dhinwar, Jheur, Jheer
28. Keshap Rajput
29. Kahar
30. Kumhar
31. Kangehra
32. Kanjarokanchan
33. Kurmi
34. Labana
35. Mahatam
36. Madari
37. Mirasi
38. Mallah
39. Mehra
40. Nai (Kullen Brahman)
41. Nalband
42. Nar
43. Pinja, Panja
44. Roolband
45. Soi
46. Tarkhan, Badhai, Ramgarhia, Dhiman (excluding Lohar), Vishwakarma, Thawins
47. Vanzara

(B) In Merged area only

1. Keer
2. Gaddi
3. Gujjar

Karnataka

Category- I

Sl. No. Name of the Caste

1. Agamudi
2. (a) Ambalakaran
   (b) Ambalakarma
3. Bavandhi
4. (a) Bavaji
   (b) Atit
   (c) Bairagi
   (d) Bavani
   (e) Byragi
   (f) Daurigosayi
   (g) Davari
   (h) Gosayi
   (i) Gusai
   (j) Helava
   (k) Helova
   (l) Holeva
   (m) Nandiwala
   (n) Nathapanthi
   (o) Pichigunta
   (p) Pichguntala
   (q) Pichiguntala
   (r) Bava
   (s) Byaragi

5. (a) Bestha
   (b) Ambiga
   (c) Barki
   (d) Besthar
   (e) Bhoyi
   (f) Bunde-Beshtar
   (g) Daaiji
   (h) Daavat
   (i) Gabit
   (j) Galadakonkani
   (k) Gangemakkalu
   (l) Gangakula
   (m) Gangamatha
   (n) Gangamathastha
   (o) Gangaputra
   (p) Gowrimatha
   (q) Bunde Bestha/Gunde Bestha
   (r) Harakanthra
   (s) Jalagara
   (t) Kabbera/Kabber
   (u) kabbaliga
   (v) Kabbili
   (w) Kahar
   (x) Kharvi
   (y) Koli
   (z) Kolimahadev
   (aa) Maddar
   (ab) Meenagar
   (ac) Mogaveera
   (ad) Moger
   (ae) Mukkavan
   (af) Parivara

	(ag)	Siviyar
	(ah)	Sunagara
	(ai)	Thoreya
6.	(a)	Bhamta
	(b)	Bhompta
	(c)	Paradeshi-Bhampta
	(d)	Takari
	(e)	Bhomptra
	(f)	Uchillan
7.	Bhatraju	
8.	(a)	Bogad
	(b)	Begadi
	(c)	Bagali
	(d)	Bogadi
9.	(a)	Budubuduki
	(b)	Bududki
	(c)	Chhetri
	(d)	Devari
	(e)	Garadi
	(f)	Gidakoni
	(g)	Joshi
	(h)	Kichagara
	(i)	Killikyata
	(j)	Modiga
	(k)	Pansa
	(l)	Panasa
	(m)	Pingale
	(n)	Sadajoshi
	(o)	Budbudkala
10.	Chunchar	
11.	(a)	Dasari
	(b)	Chakravadya-Dasa

	(c)	Dang-Dasar
	(d)	Dombi-Dasaru
12.	(a)	Devadasi
	(b)	Basavi
	(c)	Bhavin
	(d)	Bogam
	(e)	Ganika
	(f)	Kalavant
	(g)	Nat
	(h)	Natuva
	(i)	Patramela
13.	(a)	Ghisade
	(b)	Ghisadi
14.	(a)	Goniga-Mane
	(b)	24 Mane Telugu Shetty
	(c)	Goni Chetty
	(d)	Sadusetty
	(c)	Salaparu
15.	(a)	Gurav
	(b)	Tamballa
	(c)	Tambli
16.	Gurkha	
17.	(a)	Halawakki Wakkal
	(b)	Halakki Vakkal
	(c)	Atte Vokkalu
	(d)	Gam Gawada
	(e)	Gam Vokkal
	(f)	Grama Vokkalu
	(g)	Halakki Vokkalu
	(h)	Kare Vokkalu
	(i)	Kunchavakkal
	(j)	Shilwakkal

	(k)	Vakkal
	(l)	Gavada
	(m)	Gam Gawda
	(n)	Gram Vakkal
18.	(a)	Hawadiga
	(b)	Hawgar
	(c)	Howgar
19.	(a)	Jogi
	(b)	Brahma Kapali
	(c)	Jogar
	(d)	Jogtin
	(e)	Kapali
	(f)	Raval
	(g)	Ravalia
	(h)	Sanjogi
	(i)	Sanyasi
	(j)	Joger
20.	(a)	Kanjlibhat
	(b)	Kanjar
	(c)	Khanjar Bhat
21.	(a)	Kashikapadi
	(b)	Kashikapdi
	(c)	Tirumali
22.	(a)	Katabar
	(b)	Katabu
23.	(a)	Katik
	(b)	Aray
	(c)	Are Kasal
	(d)	Ari Katikelu
	(e)	Kalal Khatik
	(f)	Kasab
	(g)	Kasai

(h) Maratti
(i) Suryavamsha Kshatriya

24. (a) Kolari
(b) Kalayiri
(c) Koleri

25. (a) Kolla
(b) Kollala

26. Kotari

27. Kudubi

28. (a) Kurma
(b) Kurmi

29. (a) Ladaru/Ladara/Ladar
(b) Lad
(c) Yelegal

30. Malaya

31. (a) Medara
(b) Batter
(c) Burned
(d) Gauriga
(e) Gouriga
(f) Gowri
(g) Gowrimaratha
(h) Gowriga
(i) Medari
(j) Burud

32. Mudhar

33. Otari

34. Pamtor

35. (a) Pangual
(b) Pangusal

36. Panika

37. (a) Raya Rawath
 (b) Ravat
38. Reinudas
39. Sansia
40. Satarkar
41. Siddi
42. (a) Sikkaligara
 (b) Shikalgar
 (c) Shikkaligar
43. (a) Somavamsa Arya Kshatriya
 (b) Chitara
 (c) Chitragar
 (d) Digwan
 (e) Jeeragara
 (f) Najabund
 (g) Nalabund
 (h) Tambat
44. Takankar
45. (a) Tewar
 (b) Kalari
 (c) Kallar
 (d) Maravar
46. (a) Tilari
 (b) Tirali
47. (a) Uppara
 (b) Beldar
 (c) Chunar
 (d) Gavadi
 (e) Goundi
 (f) Kallu Kutiga Uppara
 (g) Lonari
 (h) Melu Sakkreyavaru

(i) Melusakkare
(j) Namada Uppara
(k) Padit/Padti
(l) Padithi
(m) Padi
(n) Sagara
(o) Sunnagara
(p) Sunna Uppara
(q) Uppaliga
(r) Uppaliga Shetty
(s) Uppaliyan
(t) Uppera
(u) Yakalara
(v) Yekkali

48. Vaidu

49. Vasudev

50. (a) Veer
(b) Veeramasti
(c) Vir

51. Yeralu

52. (a) Yerkala
(b) Erakala
(c) Kaikadi
(d) Koragar
(e) Kormasetty
(i) Kunchi
(g) Korwari
(h) Yerukala

53. (a) Bailpatar
(b) Bailapatar
(c) Bilapatar

54. (a) Bajania
    (b) Bajenia
55. Balasanthoshi
56. Bazigar
57. Deria
58. (a) Bhardi
    (b) Bhargi
59. (a) Chara
    (b) Chhar
    (c) Chhara
60. (a) Chapper Band (Muslim)
    (b) Chapper Banda
61. Chitrakathijoshi
62. Darvesu
63. Dholi
64. (a) Durgamurga
    (b) Burburcha
65. (a) Modikara
    (b) Modikar
66. (a) Gondali
    (b) Ghondali
    (c) Gondaliga
    (d) Gondhali
    (e) Gondhalli
67. Vagri
68. (a) Javeri
    (b) Jawari
69. Johari
70. (a) Kamatti
    (b) Kaman
71. (a) Kanjari
    (b) Kanjir

72. (a) Kalkari, Kelkari
    (b) Khelkari
73. (a) Kolhati
    (b) Kolhatigi
74. (a) Masania Yogi
75. Full Mall
76. Sarania
77. (a) Sarordi
    (b) Saroda
78. Vadi
79. Bedaru
80. (a) Golla
    (b) Yadav
    (c) Asthanagolla
    (d) Yadava
    (e) Adavigolla
    (f) Gopala
    (g) Gopali
    (h) Gouli
    (i) Gauli
    (j) Gavali
    (k) Gavli
    (l) Anubaru
    (m) Atanabaru
    (n) Hanabar
    (o) Kavadi
    (p) Kolayan
    (q) Konar
    (r) Konnur
    (s) Krishna Golla
    (t) Maniyani
    (u) Urali

81. (a) Banjari
(b) Brinjari
(c) Vanjara
(d) Wanjari
(e) Lambaid
(f) Gore or Goria

82. (a) Bendar
(b) Berad
(c) Boya
(d) Naikamakkalu
(e) Naikwadi
(f) Palegar
(g) Remoshi
(h) Talawar/Talwar-Boya
(i) Valmikimakkalu
(j) Vedan
(k) Parivara Nayaka
(l) Myasa Nayaka
(m) Urs Nayaka
(n) Byada
(o) Haranshikari
(p) Chigari Betagar
(q) Vaghri
(r) Wagiri
(s) Nirshikari
(t) Bargi
(u) Baori
(v) Phasachari
(w) Hirshikari

83. Daveri

84. (a) Garudi
(b) Garudiga

(c) Garadiga

85. Paradhis

86. (a) Girni Waddar
(b) Tudug-Woddar
(c) Kallu Vaddar
(d) Mannu Voddar
(e) Bhandi Voddar

87. (a) Bhot
(b) Boyi
(c) Harikanthra
(d) Kharia
(e) Bovi

88. Pinjara

89. S.C. Converts to Christianity

Category-II (A)

1. (a) Agasa
(b) Chakala
(c) Dhobi
(d) Madivala
(e) Mannan
(f) Parit
(g) Rajaka
(h) Sakala
(i) Vannan
(j) Velluthedan
(k) Sakalavadu

2. (a) Devadiga
(b) Devali
(c) Moyili
(d) Padiar
(e) Seregara

	(f)	Servegar
	(g)	Sheregar
	(h)	Suplig
3.	(a)	Idiga
	(b)	Bandhari
	(c)	Belehad
	(d)	Billava
	(e)	Deevar
	(f)	Desha Bhandari
	(g)	Devar
	(h)	Devaramakkalu/Divara Makkalu
	(i)	Ediga
	(j)	Eliga
	(k)	Ezhava
	(l)	Gamalla
	(m)	Goundla
	(n)	Halepaikaru
	(o)	Hale Paik
	(p)	Illavan
	(q)	Kalal
	(r)	Malayali Billava
	(s)	Nadar
	(t)	Namadhari
	(u)	Thiyan
	(v)	Iliga
	(w)	Goondla
	(x)	Tiyan
4.	(a)	Kumbara
	(b)	Chakrasali
	(c)	Gunaga
	(d)	Ganagi
	(e)	Koyava

	(f)	Kula
	(g)	Kulala
	(h)	Kumbar
	(i)	Kumbard
	(j)	Kummara
	(k)	Kusavan
	(l)	Moolya
	(m)	Sajjan Kumbara
	(n)	Khumara
	(o)	Kumbhar
	(p)	Khumbhar
	(q)	Kulalar
5.	(a)	Kuruba
	(b)	Bharwad
	(c)	Dhanagar
	(d)	Goraya
	(e)	Halumatha
	(f)	Kurab
	(g)	Kuruban
	(h)	Kurumba
	(i)	Kurub
	(j)	Kurumban
6.	(a)	Nayinda
	(b)	Ambattan
	(c)	Bajanthri
	(d)	Bandari
	(e)	Chouriya
	(f)	Hadapada
	(g)	Hajama
	(h)	Kavutian
	(i)	Kelasi
	(j)	Kshaurika

	(k)	Kshowrad
	(l)	Mahale
	(m)	Mangala
	(n)	Melagara
	(o)	Nadiga
	(p)	Napitha
	(q)	Navalig
	(r)	Navi
	(s)	Nayanaja Kshatriya
	(t)	Nhavi
	(u)	Savitha
	(v)	Nayanaja Kshatri
	(w)	Nadig
	(x)	Kshowrik
	(y)	Kshowrika
7.	Buddhists	
8.	(a)	Tigala
	(b)	Agni Vamsha Kshatriya
	(c)	Agnivanni
	(d)	Agnikula Kshatriya
	(e)	Dharmaraja Kapu
	(f)	Palli
	(g)	Shambhukula Kshatriya
	(h)	Thigala
	(i)	Vanniar
	(j)	Vannikula Kshatriya
	(k)	Tigler
	(l)	Kurovan
9.	(a)	Viswakarma
	(b)	Achari
	(c)	Akkasale
	(d)	Ausala

(e) Badigar
(f) Badiwadla
(g) Bailapatar
(h) Bailu Akkasali
(i) Bailu Kammara
(j) Bogara
(k) Chaptegar
(l) Charodi
(m) Daivagnya Brahmin
(n) Gejjigara
(o) Kambar
(p) Kammalan
(q) Kammara
(r) Kamsala
(s) Kamsan
(t) Kanehagar
(u) Kanehora
(v) Kanehori
(w) Kanehugara
(x) Kansar
(y) Kasar
(z) Luhar
(aa) Mesta
(ab) Panchal
(ac) Pattar
(ad) Silpi
(ae) Sohagar
(af) Sonar
(ag) Sony
(ah) Sutar
(ai) Tacehan
(aj) Viswa Brahmin

(ak) Thattan
(al) Aksali
(am) Kamsal
(an) Badagi

10. (a) Aghori
(b) Karkarmunda

11. Agnani

12. Ambalavasi

13. Anduran

14. (a) Atari
(b) Athari

15. Bahurupi

16. Bakadra

17. (a) Bathal
(b) Battal
(c) Batter

18. Bawtar

19. (a) Bhaat
(b) Bohrot

20. Binapatta

21. Bingi

22. (a) Bagadi
(b) Bagaadi
(c) Bagdi

23. (a) Chaliyan
(b) Teruvan
(c) Challiya

24. Chamboti

25. Chambukutti

26. Mestha

27. Jingar

28. Ghadi

29. (a) Ghadsi
    (b) Ghadshi
30. (a) Pingle
31. (a) Gosavi
    (b) Gosain
32. (a) Gujar
    (b) Guzar
33. (a) Gurava
    (b) Gurou
34. (a) Gabbit
    (b) Gapit
    (c) Gaabit
    (d) Daalija
35. (a) Hanbar
    (b) Hanabaru
36. Handevazir
37. Handervut
38. Honniyar
39. (a) Hoovadiga
    (b) Hugar
    (c) Hoogar
    (d) Maalgar
    (e) Mali
    (f) Phool Mali
    (g) Phul Mali
    (h) Phulari
    (i) Phoolari
    (j) Jeer
40. Kadu Konkani
41. Karikudumbi
42. Karuva

43. (a) Khatik
(b) Katuka
(c) Katuga
44. Bogar
45. Kasbin
46. (a) Kolayiri
(b) Kolyiri
47. (a) Kanisan
(b) Kaniyar
(c) Kaniyaru
(d) Kaniya
(e) Kaniyan
(Other than Kollegal Tq. of Mysore District)
(f) Kanyan
48. (a) Kanbi
(b) Kulwadi
(c) Kunbi
49. Kutuma
50. Marta
51. (a) Marayan
(b) Maravan
52. Murrari
53. (a) Nadora
(b) Uppu Nadar
(c) Torke Nador
(d) Nador
(e) Nadavar
(f) Nadava
(g) Uppunador
54. Nalki
55. Osthan
56. (a) Pandaram

(b) Pandar
(c) Pandara

57. Panaba
58. Pannekara Konkani
59. Patra
60. Pichati
61. Pallavan
62. (a) Rajapuri
(b) Rajpur
(c) Balavalikar
63. Saniyaar
64. Shanan
65. (a) Sudir
(b) Sudra
66. Sutsali
67. Techayiri
68. Tilvi
69. (a) Gavandi
(b) Govandi
70. Vettuvan
71. (a) Yeklar
(b) Yaklar
(c) Egalika
72. (a) Gatti/Gattiyavaru
(b) Poledava/Poladavaru
73. Gudigara
74. (a) Darzi
(b) Bhavasar Kshatriya
(c) Chippi
(d) Chippiga
(e) Simpi
(f) Shimpi

	(g)	Sai
	(h)	Mirai
	(i)	Rangari
	(j)	Rangrez
	(k)	Nilari
	(l)	Namdev
	(m)	Namdev Simpi
	(n)	Rangare
	(o)	Neelagar
75.	(a)	Devanga
	(b)	Devang
	(c)	Koshti
	(d)	Hutgar/Hutkar
	(e)	Jed
	(f)	Winkar
	(g)	Julohi
	(h)	Hulkar
	(i)	Hatagar
76.	(a)	Neygi
	(b)	Kuruhina Setty
	(c)	Bill Magga
	(d)	Thogata
	(e)	Soniga
	(f)	Jam Khana
	(g)	Ayiri
	(h)	Avir
	(i)	Sale
	(j)	Padma Sale
	(k)	Saale
	(l)	Kaikolan
	(m)	Neikar
	(n)	Jadar

	(o)	Jandra
	(p)	Sakula Sale
77.	(a)	Pategar
	(b)	Pattekari
	(c)	Patiegar
	(d)	Somavamsha Sahasrarjuna Kshatriya
78.	(a)	Ganiga
	(b)	Teli
	(c)	Gandla
	(d)	Vaniyan
79.	Rajput	
80.	Amman Kodava	
81.	Anappan	
82.	(a)	Andi
	(b)	Andipandaram
83.	Baandhi	
84.	(a)	Bolaballala
	(b)	Baliala
85.	(a)	Bhatial
	(b)	Bhattia
86.	(a)	Chakkan
87.	Dogra	
88.	Gulli	
89.	Hindu Sardu/Sadaru	
90.	(a)	Jatti, Jetty
	(b)	Mallaru Malla Kshatriya
	(c)	Mushtiga
91.	(a)	Kalavanthi
	(b)	Bhogam/Teluga
92.	(a)	Kanakan
	(b)	Kanakar

93. (a) Kotegara
(b) Koteyar
(c) Kothati
(d) Kottegara
(e) Kotteyara
(f) Kumara Kshatriya
(g) Kumara Panth/Komarpant
(h) Rama Kshatriya
(i) Rama Raj Kshatriya
(j) Serugara (North Kanara)
(k) Servgar (South Kanara)
(l) Kote Kshatriya
94. (a) Kshatriya/Kshatri
95. Malawa
96. Maleya
97. Aryan
98. (a) Raju Kshatriya
(b) Raju-Raju
(c) Rajuwar/Rajavar/Rachevar
99. Somavamsha Kshatriya
100. Stanika
101. (a) Tulu
(b) Tuluva

Category - II (b)

1. Muslim

Category - III (a)

1. (a) Vokkaliga
(b) Vakkaliga
(c) Sarpa Vokkaliga
(d) Hallikar Vokkaliga
(e) Namdhari Vokkaliga

(f) Gangadkar Vokkaliga
(g) Das Vokkaliga
(h) Reddy Vokkaliga
(i) Marasu Vokkaliga
(j) Reddy
(k) Hallikar
(l) Kunchitiga
(m) Gouda
(n) Kapu
(o) Heggade
(p) Kamma
(q) Raddy
(r) Gownder

2. Kodagaru

3. (a) Balija
(b) Balajiga/Banajiga
(c) Naidu
(d) Bogam Teluga
(e) Telaga Balija
(f) Setty Balija
(g) Kasban
(h) Mannur-Munnar
(i) Mutrasi
(j) Maracha
(k) Janappan
(l) Balegara
(m) Banagara

Category - III (b)

1. (a) Veerashaiva Lingayath
(b) Lingayath Sub-Groups of Helava. Ambiga. Bhoyi. Gangamatha. Sunagara. Agasa. Madivala. Kumbara.

Kuruba, Bajanthri, Bandari, Hadapada, Kshaurika, Navalig, Navi, Akkasale, Badigar, Kammara, Kamsala, Panchal, Medara, Uppara, Gowli

2. (a) Maratha, Marata

(b) Are Kshatri, Are Maratha, Arya Maratha.

(c) Arya, Aryaru

(d) Konkan Maratha

(e) Kshatriaya Maratha

(f) Kulavadi

3. Christian

4. (a) Bunt/Bant

(b) Parivara Bant

5. Jains (Digambaras)

6. (a) Satani

(b) Chattada Srivaishnava

(c) Kadri Vaishnava

(d) Sameraya

(e) Sattandaval

(f) Sattadavan

(g) Vaishnava

Kerala

(1) **Throughout the State**

1. Agoan
2. Ambalakkaran
3. Anglo Indian
4. x x x x
5. x x x x
6. Aremahratl
7. Arya
8. Bandarl
9. Billava

10. Chakkala

11. x x x x

12. Chavalakkaran

13. Chattlos (Kottar Chottios, Parakko, Chottles, Elur Chattios, Attingal Chatiles, Pudukkada Chettlos Iranlal Chattlos, S Pondare Chattlos, Telugu Chottlas, Udnyamkulengara Chettles; Paroorkada Chattles, Sudhu Chettles, Manol Chottles, Wynadan Chottles and Kalavara Chettles).

14. Devadiga

15. Devenga

(15A. Dheevare (Areyan) (Valan) (Nulayan), (Mukkuvan Arayavathi) Valinjion (??) Panlakkal, Mekaya and Mukaveeran (??)

16. Ezhavas and Thiyyas

17. Ezhavathl

18. Ezhuthachan

19. Ganika

20. Gatti

21. Gowdn

22. Hegde

23. x x x x

24. Izhuvan (Liluvan or Ezhuvan)

25. Jogi

26. Kaduppattan

27. Kaikalan

28. Kolasi (Kalasi Panicker)

29. Kalari Kuiup or Kalari Panicker 30. Viswakar mas including Assari, Chaptegra, Kallasarl, Kalthachan, Kammala, Kamsele, Kannan Keruvan, Kitaren, Kollan, Malayalo Kammala, Moosari, Pandikammala, Pandithattan, Perumkollan, Thachan, Thattan, Vilkurup, Villasan, Viswabrahmanan or viswabrahmanai and Viswakarmala)

31. Kannadiyans

32. Kanisu or Koniyat Panicker. Kani or Kaniyan (Ganaka) or Kanisan or Kamnan

33. Kavuthiyan
34. Kavudiyaru
35. x x x x
36. Koteyar
37. Krishnanvaka
38. Kerala Mudalis
39. Kudumbis
40. Kusavan (Kulala, Kulals Nair or Andhra Nair or Anthuru Nair)
41. Kumbarans
42. Latin Catholics
43. Medivals
44. Mappila
45. Maravans
46. Maruthuvar
47. x x x x
48. Muslim
49. Nadars (Hindu Nadara and Nadars Included in S.I.U.C.)
50. Nalkkang
51 Odans
52. Scheduled Caste Converts to Christianity
53. Pandithars
54. Panniyar
55. Pattariyas
56. x x x x
57. Peruvannan (Varanavar)
58. Pulluvan
59. Rajapur
60. Chakravar Sacravar (Kavathi)
61. Sourashtras
62. Saliyas
63. Senai Thalavar (Elavaniar)

2. In Malabar District

11	1. x x x x	3. Ganjam Reddis
	2. Boyan	4. Vishavan

3. Throughout the State except Malabar District

	1. Kammara	3. Malayekandi
12	2. x x x x	4. Roddlars

4. Throughout the State except Kasargod Taluk of Malabar District Marati

Explanation - In this Schedule, Malabar District shall mean the Malabar District releted to in sub-section (2) of Section 5 of the States Reorganisation Act. 1956.

64. S.I.U.C. (excluding Nadars spacifiod in Item 49)

64 A. Thachar)

65. Tholkolans

66. Thottian

67. Vaduvans, Vadugans, Vadukars and Vadukas (Vadukans).

68. x x x x

69. Velaans (Valaan, Velaar)

70. Vanians (Vanika, Vanika Vaisya, Vanibha Chetty, Vania Chetty, Ayiravar, Nagarathar and Vanlyan).

71. Vaniyar

72. Vakkaliga

73. Veerasaivas (Yogis and Yogesware)

74. Veluthedathu Nair (Veluthedan and Vannathan)

75. Vilakkithala Nair (Vilakkithalavan)

76. Yadavas (Kolaya, Ayar, Mayar. Manlyanl and Iruman)

Madhaya Pradesh

क्रमांक नाम जाति/ उपजाति/वर्ग समूह

1. अहीर, गवली, गोली, जादव, (यादव) बरगाही, बरगाह, ठेठवार, राउत गोवारी, (ग्वारी) गोवरा, गवारी, ग्वारा, गोवरी, महाकुल (राउत) महकुल, गोप ग्वाली, लिंगायत,

2. असारा, असाड़ा

3. बैरागी (वैष्णव)

4. बंजारा, बंजारी, मथुर, नायक नायकड़ा, धरिया, सभाना, लबाना लामने.

5. बरई, तमोली, तम्बोली, कुमायट, कुमायत, यारई, बरई, (चौरसिया),

6. बढ़ई, सुतार, दवेज, कुन्देर (विश्वकर्मा),

7. यारी,

8. यसुदेव, यसुदेया, यासुदेव, यासुदेवा, हरबोला, कापडिया, कापड़ी, मैथिली, धारयार,

9. भड़भूजा, भुंजवा, भुर्जी, धुरी, या धूरी,

10. भाट, भारण, सुधिया, सारागी, पय, जनपालोंगी, जसोंगी, मरुसोनिया,

11. छीपा, भानसार, नीलगर, जीनगर, निराली, रंगारी, मनमाध,

12. ढीपर, भोई, कन्हार, धीवर/माखाह/नावड़ा/बुरहा, केवट,(कश्यप, निषाद्, रामकवार, बाधम), कीर (भोपाल, रायसेन, सीहोर जिलों को छोड़कर) ब्रिसिया (बृतिया) सिंघरहा, जालारी, (जालारनलु बस्तर जिले में) सोंधिया.

13. पंवार, गोवार, भोसर, भोसर

14. भुर्तिया, भुतिया

15. भोषा, मनभान्

16. भटिंयारा

17. बुनकर, चुनंधर, कुल्यांधिया, राजगिर

18. नितारी

19. दर्जी, छीपी, छिपी, माघी, (नामदेव)

20. धोबी (भोपाल, रायसेन, सिहोर जिलों को छोड़कर) बदली, बीठा, रजक

21. मीना (रावत) देशवाही, पंवासी. मीणा (विदिशा जिले की सिरोंज एवं लटेरी तहसील को छोड़कर)

22. किसार, किराई, भाकड़

23. गड़रिया, धनगर, कुरमार हटगर, हटकर, हाटकार गाड़री, धारिया, धोबी (गड़रिया) गारी, गायरी, गड़रिया (पाल बधेले).

24. कड़ेरे धुनकर, धुनिया, धनका, कोडार

25. कोष्टा, कोष्टी (देवागन) कोष्टा, माला, पदमशाली, साली, सुतसाली, सलेवार, सालवी, देवांग, जन्द्रा, कोस्काटी, कोश्काटी (लिंगायत) गढवाल, गढ़ेवाल, गरेवार, गरनार, हुकर, कोल्हाटी.

26. भोली/डमनली/डफली/ढोली, दमामी, गुरव

27. गुसाई, गोस्वामी

28. गूजर (गुर्जर)

29. लोहार, लुहार, लोहापीटा, मड़ोले, हुंगा लोहार, लोहपटा, गड़ोला, लोहार (विश्वकर्मा)

30. गारपगारी, नाष-जोगी, जोगीनाम, हरिदास

31. घोषी

32. सोनार, सुनार, झाणी, झाड़ी, (स्वर्णकार) अवधिया औधिया, सोनी (स्वर्णकार)

33. (अ) काछी, (कुशवाहा, शाक्य, मौर्य) कोयारी व कोड़री (कुशवाहा), पनारा, मुराई, सोनकर.

(ब) माली (सैनी), मसर

34. जोशी (भडडरी) डकोचा, डकोता.

35. लखेरा, लखेर, कधेरा, कधेर

36. ठठेरा, कंसार, कसेरा, तमेरा तग्बाटकर, ओटारी, ताम्रकार, तमेर, घड़वा, झारिया.

37. खातिया, खाटिया, खाती

38. कुम्हार (प्रजापति), कुंभार (छतरपुर, दतिया, पन्ना, टीकमगढ़, सतना, रीवा, सोधी व शहडोल जिलों को छोड़कर).

39. कुरमी, कुरमार, कुब्बी, कुर्मी, पाटीदार (कुलंगी, कुल्मी, कुलम्बी) कुर्मवंशी चन्द्राकर, चन्द्रनाह, कुंभी, मवैल, (मंगेल) सिरथी

40. कमरिया

41. कौरव, कांवरे

42. कलार (जायसवाल) कलाल, डडसेना

43. कलौता, कलौटा, कोलता, कोलटा

44. लोनियां, लुनियां, ओड़, ओड़े, ओड़िया नौनिया, मुरहा, मुराहा, मुड़ाहा, मुड़हा.

45. नाई (सेन, सविता, उसरेटे, शीवास) म्हाली, नाव्ही, उसरेटे.

46. नायटा, नायड़ा

47. मनका, मनिका, (छतरपुर, पन्ना, दतिया, टीकमगढ़, सतना, रीवा, सीधी, शहडोल जिलों को छोड़कर):

48. पटका, पटकी, पटना

49. लोधी, लोधा, लोध

50. सिकलीगर

51. तेली (ठाठ, साहू, राठौर)

52. तुरहा, तिरवाली, बङ्कर

53. तवायफ, किसडी, कसडी

54. वोवरिया

55. रोतिया, रीतिया

56. मानकर, नहाल

57. कोटवार, कोटयाल, (भिण्ड, धार, देवास, गुना ग्वालियर, इन्दौर, झामुआ, खरगौन, भंदसोर, मुरैना, राजगढ़, रतलाम, शाजापुर, शिवपुरी, उज्ञैन, एवं बिदिशा जिलों को छोड़कर)

58. खैरुवा

59. लोढ़ा (तवंर)

60. भोगार

61. रजनार

62. अभरिगा

63. तिउन, तूरी

64. भारूढ़

65. सुत सांरथी-सईस सहीस

66. तेलंगा, तिलया

67. रानवी

68. रजभर

69. खारोल

70. सरगरा

71. गोलान, गवलान, गौलान

72. रज़्ड़ रजझड़

73. जादम

74. दांगी

75. गयार/परधनिया

76. कुड़मी

77. मेर

78. बया गहरा/कौशल, बया

79. पिंजारा (हिन्दू)

80. विलोपित

81. अनुसूचित जातियाँ जिन्होंने ईसाई धर्म अथवा बौद्ध धर्म (नन बौद्ध) स्वीकार कर लिया है.

82. आंजना

83. धोरिया

84. गेहलोत मेवाड़ा

85. रेवांरी

86. रूआला/रूहेला

87. 1. रंगरेज
   2. भिश्ती
   3. छीपा
   4. हेला
   5. भटियारा
   6. धोबी
   7. मेवाती
   8. पिंजारा, नदद्दाफ, फकीर, बेहना, धुनिया, धुनकर
   9. कुजंड़ा, राईन
   10. मनिहार
   11. कसाई, करसाव
   12. मिरासी
   13. मिरधा
   14. बढ़ई (कारपन्टर) खरादी कमलीगर
   15. हज्ज़ाम (बारबर)
   16. हम्माल
   17. मोमिन जुलाहा (वे जुलाहे जो मोमिन हैं)
   18. लुहार, नागौरी
   19. राड़बी
   20. बंजारा
   21. मोची
   22. तेली, नागता, पिंडारी (पिंडारा) कांकर
   23. मेंगदी

24. कलईगर
25. नालबन्द
26. शीशगर
27. गोली
28. राजगीर
29. डफाली
30. धोबी व गवली गोली
31. सिवलीगर
32. संतरास
33. नट
34. शेख महतर

88. बैसवार

Maharashtra

विमुक्त जाति

जाति	तत्सम
1) बेरड	1) अ) **
	ब) नाईकवाडी
	क) तलवार
	ड) वाल्मिकी
2) बेस्तर	2) संचलू वड्डार
3) भामटा	3) अ) भमटी
	ब) गिरणी वड्डार
	क) कामाटी
	ड) पाथरूट
	इ) टकारी (मुस्लिम धर्मीयांसह)
	फ) उचले
4) कैकाडी	4) अ) धोंतले

(मुंबई, डाणे, कुलाबा, रत्नागिरी, नाशिक, धुळ, जळगाव, पुणे, अहमदनगर, सातारा, सांगली, कोल्हापूर, सोलापूर, औरंगाबाद, बीड, परभणी, उस्मानाबाद, नांदेड, जिल्हे व चंद्रपूर जिल्ह्यातील राजूरा तालुका यात)		ब) कोरवा क) माकडवाले किंवा कोंचीकोरवा ड) पामलोर इ) कोरवी
5) कंजारभाट	5)	अ) छारा ब) कंजार क) नात
6) कटाबू	6)	---
7) बंजारा	7)	अ) गोर बंजारा ब) लंबाडा/लंबारा क) लंभणी ड) चरण बंजारा इ) लभाण फ) मथुरा लभाण ग) कचकीवाले बंजारा ह) लमान बंजारा इ) लमाण/लमाणी ज) लबान क) ** ल) धाली/धालीया ग) धाडी/धारी न) सिंगारी व) नावी बंजारा प) जोगी बंजारा क्यु) ** र) ** स) बंजारी (शा. प. क्र.

	सीबीसी-1477/ 35512-का-5 दिनांक 18 ऑगस्ट, 1977.
8)	8) पाल पारधी
9) राज पारधी	9) अ) ** ब) गाव पारधी क) हरण शिकारी ड) **
10) राजपूत भागटा	10) अ) परदेशी भामटा ब) परदेशी भामटी
11) रामोशी	11) --
12) वडार	12) अ) गाडी वड्डर ब) जाती वड्डर क) माती वड्डार ड) पाथरवट इ) संगतराश/दगडफोडू
13) वाघरी	13) अ) सलात ब) सलात वाघरी
14) छप्परबंद (गुस्लीम धर्मीयासह)	

भटक्या जाति

जाति	तत्सम
1) गोसावी	1) बावा, 2) बैरागी, 3) भारती, 4) मिरी गोसावी, 5) भारती गोसावी, 6) सरस्वती पर्वत, 7) सागर, 8) बान किंवा वान, 9) तीर्थ आश्रम, 10) अरण्य घरभारी, 11) संन्यासी, 12) नाथपंथी गोसावी.

2) बेलदार	2) ओड
3) भराडी	3) अ) बाळ संतोशी ब) किंगरीवाले, क) नाथबावा, ड) नाथ जोगी, इ) नाथपंथी डवरी गोसावी
4) भुते	4) भोपे
5)	5) --
6) चित्रकथी	6) --
7) गारूडी	7) --
8) धिासाडी	8) घिसडी लोहार किंवा गाडी लोहार किंवा चितोडी लोहार, राजपूत लोहार
9) गोल्ला	9) गोल्लेवार, गोलेर, गोलकर
10) गोधळी	10) --
11) गोपाल	11) अ) गोपाल भोरपी, ब) खेळकरी
12) हेळवे	12) हिलव
13) जोशी	13) अ) बुडबुडकी ब) डमरूवाले क) कुडमुडे ड) मेंढगी इ) सरोदे फ) सहदेव जोशी म) सरवादे ह) सरोदा
14) काशी कापडी	14) --
15) कोल्हाटी	15) डोंबारी
16) मैराळ	16) अ) दांगट ब) वीर

17) मसनजोगी	17) 1) सुदगडसिप्द 2) गनजोशी
18) नंदीवाले	18) तिरमल,
19) पांगूळ	19) --
20) रावळ	20) राऊळ किंवा-रावळयोगी
21) सिक्कलगर	21) कटारी सेक्वलगर (गुस्लीम धर्मिय)
22) ठाकर (फक्त रत्नागिरी व सिंधुदुर्ग जिल्ह्यात	22) --
23) वेदू	23) **
24) वासुदेव	24) --
25) भोई शा.नि. स.क.सां.का.क्री. व प.वि. क्र.सीबीसी 1073/10615/ज-1, दिनांक 29-5-1974. शा. शुद्धिपत्र समक्रमांक: दिनांक 7 जून, 1974	25) 1) झिंगा भोई, 2) परदेशी भोइ 3) राजभोई, 4) भोई 5) कहार 6) गोडिया कहार, 7) धुरिया कहार 8) किरात 9) मछुआ 10) मांझी 11) जातिया 12) केवट 13) ढीवर 14) धीवर 15) धीमर 16) पालेवार 17) मछेंद्र 18) नावाडी 19) मल्हार 20) मल्हाव

	21) बोई
	22) गाढव भोई
	23) खाडी भोई
	24) खारे भोई
	25) ढेवरा
26) बहुरुपी	26) --
27) ठेलारी (धुळे, नासिक, लळगाव व औरंगाबाद जिल्ह्यात)	27) --
28) ओतारी	28) अ) ओतनकर ब) ओतकर क) बतारी ड) ओझारी
29) धनगर	29) 1) अहिर 2) डांगे 3) गटरी, 4) हंडे, 5) तेलवर, 6) हटकर 7) हाटकर, 8) शेगर 9) खुटेकर, 10) तेलंगी 11) तेल्लारी 12) कोकणी-धनगर, 13) कानडे, 14) वन्हाडे-धनगर 15) झाडे 16) झेंडे 17) कुरमार 18) माहुरे 19) लाडसे, 20) सनगर 21) धनवर
30) वंजारी	30) 1) बंजार, 2) वंजारा

1 अलितकार

2. बागडी

3. वगळले

4. बड़ीआ

5. बजानिआ
6. बाजीगर
7. बट्टाल
8. भांड
9. भवैया किंवा तारगल
10. भविण
11. भिस्ती किंवा पखाली
12. वगळले
13. बारी किंवा बारई
14. बेरीया
15. बेसदेवा
16. भडभुंजा
17. भांटा
18. भाट
19. चमथा
20. चांदलगडा
21. चरण किंवा गढवी
22. चारोडी
23. चिप्पा
24. दास किंवा दांगडीदास
25. दावगर
26. देपला
27. देवळी
28. देवदिग
29. बगळले
30. ढोली हश्मी/डफली
31. वग़ळले

32. वग़ळले
33. वगळले
34. वगळले
35. गंधारप
36. गुजराथ बावरी
37. गडारिया
38. गड्री
39. गढ़वी
40. गारपगारी
41. वग़ळले
42. गोचाकी
43. गुरव
44. गवळी
45. गवंडी
46. हलेपैक
47. वगळले
48. वगळले
49. जगीयासी
50. जजाक
51. जतिया
52. जातिगर
53. जव्हेरी
54. जोगी
55. जोगीण
56. जोहारी
57. जुलाहा, अन्सारी
58. जंगम

59. जिनगर
60. जाडी
61. वगळले
62. कम्मी
63. कापडी
64. वगळले
65. खाटी
66. वगळले
67. वगळले
68. वगळले
69. कोंगाडी
70. कोरचर
71. वगळले
72. कचोरा
73. कदैरा
74. कामाटी
75. कसबी
76. वगळले
77. वगळले
78. वगळले
79. वगळले
80. कुचबंध
81. कुछारिया
82. कुंभार किंवा कुम्हार
83. कुणवी (पोटजाती-लेवा कुणबी, लेवा पाटील, लेवा पटीदार)
84. वगळले
85. कामी

86. काठी
87. कासार (पोटजाती-कंचार, कचारी)
88. लाभा
89. लडीया, लढीया, लरिया
90. लडाफ किंवा लइडाफ, गसूरी
91. लखेरा
92. लोहार हडाड/मिस्त्री
93. माच्ची
94. मानभाव
95. वगळले
96. मारवार बांवरी
97. मे
98. मिना
99. महाली
100 मेदर
101. म्हाली
102. मिठा
103. वगळले
104. मथुरा
105. नामधारी
106. नामधारीपैक
107. निरशिकारी
108. नावी, न्हावी (सलगानी,हजाम)
109. नेथुरा
110. नोनीया
111. नक्काशी
112. नीली

113. नीलकांती
114. नेकार जाडा
115. पधारिया
116. पडीयार
117. पात्रदावरु
118. फासेचरी
119. फुडगी
120. पखाली
121. पांचाळ
122. पांका
123. पेरकी, पेरकेवाड, पेरीका, पेरीके, पेरका
124. पुतलीगर
125. परीट किंवा धोबी
126. पाटकर
127. फुलारी
128. रामेवर
129. राईकरी
130. बंडी
131. रचबंधिया
132. रंगारी
133. रॅंग्रडा
134. राओत, रावत, राऊतीया
135. रंग्रेज (भावसार, रंगारी)
136. वगळले
137. वगळले
138. वगळले
139. वगळले

140. संजोगी

141. सरानिया

142. वगळले

143. वगळले

144. वगळले

145. सुप्पालिंग

146. सुथारिया (सिंधमधील)

147. साहिस, साईस, शिस

148. सपेरा, नाथ

149. शिलावट

150. सिंगीवाला

151. स्वकुल साळी

152. वगळले

153. शिंपी इदिसी/दर्जी

154. सोनार

155. तांडेल

156. वगळले

157. तारगला

158. थेटयार

159. थोरीया

160. तांबट, त्वष्टा कासार, कासार

161. थोगती

162. बडी

163. वगळले

164. वंसफोड

165. बधाई (सुतार)

166. वर्थी

167. वगळले
168. येरकुला
169. आगरी, आगळे किंवा काळण
170. भावसार
171. कुरहीन शेट्टी
172. नीलगार, निली, निराळी
173. कोसकांती देवांग (क्र. सीबीसी-1468/83475/ज, दि. 19-1-68)
174. सुतार
175. फुतगुडी
176. वगळले
177. पिंजारा, पिंजारी, मन्सूरी
178. वगळले
179. भिलाला
180. डवरी
181. तेली
182. माळी (पोटजाती- फुलमाळी, फुले हळदे, काचा, कडू, बावने, आधप्रभू, अधशेटी, जिरे, उंडे, लिंगायत माळी इ.) बागवान (मुस्लिम धर्मीय)
183. लोणारी
184. वगळले
185. तलवार, कानडे
186. रघवी (विदर्भ जिल्ह्यातील)
187. भंडारी बावर्ची/भटीयारा (मुस्लिम धर्मीय)
188. गानली किंवा गांडली
189. पोवार किंवा पवार (पोवार किंवा पवार आडनावे असलेले इतर मागासवर्गीयांच्या यदीत समाविष्ट नाहीत)
190. काथार, काथार वाणी, कंठहार वाणी, वैश्य वाणी, कुलवंत वाणी, (लिंगायत वाणी किंवा लाड्वाडी सोडून)

191. मोमीन, अन्सारी
192. फकीर बंदरवाला
193. वगळले
194. घडशी
195. तांबोली, पान फरोश (मुस्लिम धर्मीय)
196. अनुसूचित जातीतून क्रिश्चन धर्म, स्विकारलेले
197. लंझाड
198. यादव
199. लाडसी
200. ठाकुर
201. गावित, गाबीव
202. अतार
203. औधिया
204. बादक, बारव
205. बगळू
206. मारवार बाओरी, मारबार बाघरी
207. गोसाई, उदासी
208. बालसंथनम
209. मथुरा बंजारा
210. शिंगाडे बंजारा
211. लबांडे
212. फानडे बंजारा
213. सुनार बंजारा
214. घालिया बंजारा
215. शिंगाड्या बंजारा
216. बाओंरीया
217. कोळी बारीया

218. बथिनी

219. बेगरी

220. भाम्पटा किंवा घंटीचोरे किंवा परदेशी

221. पोंग

222. दासर

223. उचिला

224. भांडदुरा, बिल्लवार

225. खारवी, धीवर भोई

226. भोयर

227. बिंदली

228. बुरबुक

229. चादर

230. चक्रवदय-दासर

231. चांडाळ

232. चेन्चू किंवा चेन्चवार

233. चिमूर

234. चिंताला

235. डाकालेरू

236. दर्जी

237. नाथपंथी

238. कुरबा, कुरुबार

239. हरकांत्रा, मांगेली, मांगेले, पागे, सुंदरी

240. वॅटस, भडवाल, रजाक

241. डोम्मारा

242. गाडाबा किंवा गोडबा

243. गंगाणी

244. गारोडी

245. गोल्लेर
246. गोदळा
247. हाबुरा
248. हरणी
249. हिल-रेडिडस
250. देवेरी
251. विनकर, वन्या, बनकर
252. काछिया
253. कोराच, पाडलोर
254. कलाल, कलार, लाड, लाडवक, गौड कलाल शिव्हारे.
255. कांदेल
256. कसेरा
257. कसाई, कसाब, कुरेशी
258. कटीपामुला
259. किरार
260. क्रिश्चन कोळी
261. कोराचार किंवा कोरवे
262. कोडकू सह कोरवा
263. कोमाकपु
264. कोंडू
265. लखारी
266. लोहार-गाडा, दोडी, खतवली, पांचाळ
267. चुनारी
268. माना
269. माहिल
270. मैदासी
271. माझवार

272. मतियारा, मतिहारा
273. मानकर खालु
274. मोंडीवार, मोंडीवारा
275. मुंडा
276. हजाम, कालसेरू, नावलिगा, कान्शी, नाभिक, नाई
277. पाचभोटला, पाचबोटला
278. पदमपारि
279. भिस्ती
280. पामूला
281. पंचमा
282. पंडा
283. फर
284. पिंजारी
285. पुरवाली
286. राचभोया
287. राउतिया
288. संगारी
289. संताल
290. साऊनता किंवा सोन्ता
291. सावतेली
292. सारे
293. भावगर, शिव शिंपी, नामदेव
294. शिंगडाव किंवा शिंगाड्या
295. सिंधूर
296. सोरें
297. सुन्रा
298. सुन्राई

299. भडाई

300. गंणिगा, गांची

301. थोटेवाडू

302. तिमाली

303. वालवाई

304. वडडेर (कालावडेर किंवा पाथरोड)

305. वनाडी

306. येनाडिवाड्स

307. येरगोलावाड किंवा थेल्ला पामालवाडस

विशेष गामारा प्रवर्ग

जातीचे नाव

1) गोवारी, गवारी

2) गाना

3) 1) कोष्टी, 2) हलवा कोष्टी, 3) वगळले 4) साळी, 5) लाडकोष्टी, 6) गढेवाल कोष्टी, 7) देशकर, 8) सालेवार, 9) पद्म शाली, 10) देवांग, 11) काची बंधे, 12) पटवीस, 13) सतसाले, 14) साडे, 15) जैनकोष्टी

4) 1) कोळी, तत्सम जाती 2) मच्छिमार कोळी, 3) अहीर कोळी, 4) खानदेशी कोळी, 5) पानकोळी 6) ख्रिश्चन कोळी, 7) चुंबळे कोळी, 8) पानभ्झरे कोळी, 9) कोळी सुर्यवंशी, 10) मांगेला, 11) सोनकोळी 12) वैती, 13) खारवा किंवा खारवी, 14) अनुसूचित जगातीमध्ये समावेश नसलेले कोळी

5) 1) मुन्नेरवार, 2) मुन्नुरवार, 3) मुन्नुर, 4) तेलगु मुन्नुर, 5) मुन्नुरवार तेलगु 6) मुन्नरकापू 7) कापेवार, 8) तेलगु कापेवार, 9) मुन्नरवारड, 10) तेलगु फुलमाळी, या जाती।

Orissa

1. Agharia, Agaria, Aghria
2. Aranedan
3. Asur
4. Badhal, Barhai, Bindhania, Sutradhar, Badhira and Badhria.
5. Badasuda
6. Baipari
7. Baira, Barai
8. Bairagi
9. Bariji or Barui
10. Barika, Bhandari, Napit and Nai
11. Bellara
12. Bentkar
13. Bhatua
14. Bania/Putulibandha Vaisya

    Sunari/Sunaree/Viswa Brahman/Putuli Bania/ Vashya Bania/ Vaishya Vaisya Bania/ Vashya/Bania/Vashya Banik/Vaishya Banik/Potali Bania/Gandha Banik/Vaishya Putuli Bania.

    Paudar Bania/Podar Bania.

    Kamila/Astalohi/ Astalohi Karmakar/Subarna Banik/Sunari Bania/Swarnakar/Subarna Bania/Sunari Banik.
15. Bhogta
16. Bhokta
17. Bhujan
18. Bhuliya
19. Birjhia
20. Bissoy-Barangi Jodia, Bennangi, Daduva, Frangi, Hollar, Jhoriya, Kollai, Konde, Paranga, Pengajodia, Sodojodia & Takoara.
21. Binedhanies
22. Bogada
23. Bolodhia

24. Buruashankar/Barna Suankar
25. Byagari
26. Chaupal
27. Chasa, *Pradhan/Padhan/Odapadhan/Odachasa*.
28. Chero
29. Cheruman
30. Chikbaraik
31. Chik
32. Chitra, Chitrakar, Chitrasilpi
33. Churia
34. Dahalia
35. Darji
36. Damal
37. Dangua
38. Dehuri
39. Dhakkada
40. Dhaner
41. Dumala, Dumal
42. Ghatwar
43. Girigiris
44. Godda
45. Gola, Golla, Gope, Sadgope, Ahir, Gour, Gouda, Goudo, Mekala Golla Puunu Golla, Yadav, Mathurapuria, Gouda, Gopapuria Gouda, Nanda Gouda, Jhadua Gouda. Dumala Gouda, Naria Gouda, Bashya Gopa, Maha Bhoi, Gandu, Nepalies, Gorkha.

    Gopal, Sholakhandia, Magadha Gouda Mahakul/Mahakud, Laxminarayan Gola, Goudia Gola.
46. Gudia or Guria, Gurja, Gunju
47. Gosangi
48. Gondu-Bato, Bhirthya, Dudho Kouriya, Hato, Jatako & Joria.
49. Habra

50. Hansi, Dera, Dewanga, Kosta, Vina, Tula bhina, Tanti, Patsalia, Buna. Rangani, Bunakara, Salia. Sukuli. *Saraka/ Saraka Tanti, Hativansa Tanti/Asina Tanti/Aswina Tanti/ Ashani Tanti/Aswinna Tanti/Bangali Tanti/Bangiya Tanti.*

Rangani Tanti/Rangani Tantes/Tanganee Tantee/Rangini Tanti/ Ranguni Tanti.

51. Holeya

52. Irula

53. Jadapus

54. Jaintrapans

55. Jogi or Yogi

56. Jyotish. Jyotisha Abadhan. Jyotish Nayak,

57. Jensan

58. Kalladi

59. Kammara, Kamara, Kamar, Kammaro, Muli, Loharu, Loharo, Astolohi Kamar

60. Kanakkan

61. Kandarpa

62. Kanjar

63. Kapudia

64. Karhara/Kachara/Kachera

65. Karimpalan

66. Karmali

67. Kattunayakan

68. Khaira

69. Khuria/*Thoria/Thodia/Thudia/Thura.*

70 Khandnals/Khandal, Khandual

71. Khatti-Khatti

72. Khatua

73. Khodra/Khadura/Kharuda.

74. Khetauri

75. Koda, Kuda

76. Koilar

77. Kolam
78. Kond (Kul)
79. Konda Kapu/Gagula Kapu, Kapu, Kampo
80. Kondareddy, Reddy dhakas & Reddy
81. Koraga
82. Kosalya, Goudus, Bosotheriya Goudus, Chiti Goudus, Dangayath Goudus, Doddu Kamariya, Dudu Kamaro, Ladiya Goudus & Pullo Soriya Goudus.
83. Kota
84. Kudiya
85. Kudubl
86. Kudumban
87. Kumbhar, Kulal, Kumhar, Kumbharo
88. Kundamatia
89. Kulta
90. Kurariar
91. Kuravan
92. Kurichchan
93. Kuruman (Kurumba)
94. Lakhra
95. Lambadi
96. Luhura
97. Machua
98. Maghi or Meghia
99. Magura
100. Mahunta
101. Magatha Goudus, Bermia Goudus, Boodo Magatha, Dongayath Goudh, Ladya Goudu, Poona Magatha and Sana Magatha.
102. Magadhi Goral
103. Maila
104. Maladasu

105. Malasar
106. Mali, Phulia, Sagbaris, Bhajemali, Muni
107. Malis-Korchia Malis, Paido Malis and Pedda Malis.
108. Mal Paharia
109. Manna Dhora
110. Maune
111. Marathi
112. Matangi
113. Mavilan
114. Minka
115. Moger
116. Mukhadora-Mokka Dhora
117. Muliya
118. Mundala
119. Muria
120. Nahaf
121. Nalakeyava
122. Nat
123. Nagavasam, Mahisya, and Saunties, Mahesh, Maheshya.
124. Nayadi
125. Nolia
126. Nuhura, Nuhuraj
127. Nuniya
128. Ojula or Metta, Kamasalie
129. Omeyita
130. Padaria, Pamaria, Pandara
131. Pagadia
132. Paigarapu
133. Paltan
134. Paky
135. Pal
136. Palasi

137. Paliyan
138. Paiko, Khandayat, Chasa Paiko, Paikali, Khandayat, Kalingi Sudra Khandayat, Alia, Mahanayak Sudra, and Baisya Karan
139. Palli
140. Pulayan
141. Pambada
142. Paniyan
143. Panjira
144. Panniandi
145. Paraiyan
146. Paravan
147. Parhaiya
148. Pathuria
149. Patara, Asini Patara/*Aswini Patara/Ashini Patara*, Goudia Patara.
150. Pogua
151. Pita
152. Raneyar
153. Ronas/Rana
154. Routia
155. Sagarpasha
156. Samban
157. Sankhari
158. Sanyasi, Moembram
159. Seerithi Goudu
160. Semman
161. Sholagar
162. Sauria Paharia
163. Sinke/Sinko
164. Suda
165. Sulia
166. Sunri/Sundi/Sundhi

167. Tana

168. Teli, Telli, Kubera, Talakar, Sahu, Bahaldia Ekadas Teli, Tailik Baishya

169. Telaga, Pamula/Teloga, Telugu, Telanga, Telenga & Telugu Kachara

170. Thanu

171. Thatari/Kansari

172. Thoti

173. Tiruvalluvar

174. Tivoro

175. Toda

176. Valluvan

177. Vannan

178. Vettuvan

179. Yandi

180. Yerna Golta

181. Yerukula

182. Kurmi, Kuruma Chasa, Kudumi, Kurma, Kurmi Mahto, Kurmi Khetriya, Kurumi & Kudumi Kshyatriya, Kurum.

183. Bhanja Puran

184. Bhopa & Raula

185. Mahla & Mahlar

186. Kalanji, *Khandayat* Kalanji, Odra Khandayat Kalanji, Kalinga, Kalingi, & Kaliji.

187. Shudra

188. Belama

189. Dalapati/Dalua

190. Rajasri Balasi/Balasi

191. Raju

192. Segidi, Srisayan

193. Dambo-Christian, Pano-Christian, Ganda-Christian.

194. *Kandha-Kumbhar.*

195. Dalakhandayat & Dalua-Paik.

196. Kapala Velama, Kapulu Elama, Koppala Velama, Koppala Elama, Kappula Elama, Kupala Velama, Kapala Elama & Kapala Elaga.

197. Banka.

198. Kshitibansa, Matibansa Ojha, Kshitibansa Naik, Ojhakaran, Kshitibansa Nayak, Matibansa, Matibansa Abadhan.

199. Arua.

200. Hatua.

201. Kalar.

202. Banayat Oriya, Benayat Oriya, Beneyit Odia, Banayat, Banayat Odia, Odia & Udia.

Punjab

1. Aheria, Aheri, Heri, Naik, Thori or Turi.
2. Barra.
3. Beta, Hensi or Hesi.
4. Changar.
5. Chirimar.
6. Daiya.
7. Gwaria, Gauria or Gwar.
8. Kanjar or Kanohan.
9. Kurmi.
10. Nar.
11. Rehar, Rahara or Re.
12. Ghirath including Chang and Bahti.
13. Kahar, Jhinwar or Dhinwar.
14. Ghasi, Ghasiara or Ghosi
15. Bagria.
16. Raigar.
17. Weaver (Jullaha).
18. Labana.

19. Gorkhas.
20. Kumhars.
21. Nais.
22. Dhobis.
23. Kamboj.
24. Rai Sikhs.
25. Barwar.
26. Barai, Tamoli.
27. Baragi, Bairagi.
28. Battera.
29. Bharbhunja, Bharbhuja.
30. Bhat, Bhatra, Darpi, Ramiya.
31. Bhuhalia Lohar.
32. Chahang.
33. Chimba, Chhippi, Chimba, Derzi Tonk
34. Dakaut.
35. Dhimar, Mallah, Kashyap Rajputs.
36. Faquir
37. Dhosali, Dosali.
38. Gawala, Gowala.
39. Gaddaria.
40. Jhangra Brahman.
41. Hajjam, Nari.
42. Jogi Nath.
43. Khati.
44. Rechhanad.
45. Khanghera.
46. Kucha band.
47. Thathera, Tamera.
48. Lakhera, Manihar.
49. Vanzara.
50. Madari.

51. Lohar.
52. Mochi
53. Mirasi.
54. Noongarh.
55. Nalband.
56. Shorgir.
57. Pinja, Penja.
58. Soi.
59. Singhikant, Singhiwala.
60. Teli.
61. Christians.
62. Daula or Soni.
63. Gujjar.
64. Arain.
65. Sanyasi Sadhu/Sanyasi Bawa.
66. Buzroos.
67. Mehra Rajputs.
68. Soni Rajputs.

Rajasthan

1. आहीर (यादव)
2. बढवा, जाचक, भाट, जागा, राव
3. चारण
4. बागरिया
5. बंजारा, वालदिया, लबाना
6. बढ़ई, जागिड़, खाती, सुथार, तरखान
7. भड़भूजा
8. छीपा (छीपी), भावसार, नाभा, खट्टी छीपा, रंगरेज, नीलगर
9. डाकोत, देशांतरी, रंगातामी
10. नगरचीन्दगामी, राणा, डायती (बारोट)

11. दरोगा, रावणा-राजपूत, हजूरी, वजीर
12. दर्जी
13. धाकड़
14. धीवर, कहार, भोई, सगरवंशी-माली, कीर, मेहरा, मल्लाह, षारी, निषाद, भिश्ती, मछुआरा
15. गडरिया (गाडरी), घोसी (ग्वाला), गायसी
16. गाड़िया-लोहार, गाडोलिया
17. घाची
18. तेली
19. गिरी, गोसाई (गुशांई)
20. गूजर, गुर्जर
21. हेला
22. जणवा, खारडिया (सीरवी)
23. जुलाहा
24. जोगी, नाथ, शिद्ध
25. काछी, कुशवाह, शाक्य
26. कलात, (टाक)
27. कन्डेरा, पिंजारा
28. कनवी, कलवी, पटेल, पात्रीदार, आजंणा, डांगी पटेल, कुलमी
29. खारोल, खारवाल
30. किरार (किराउ)
31. कुम्हार (प्रजापति, कुमावत, सुआरा
32. लखेरा (लखारा), कचेरा, मनिहार
33. लोधी (लोधा)
34. लोहार, पांचाल
35. महा-बाह्मण (अचारज), फकीर (कब्रिस्तान में कार्य करने वाले)
36. माली, सैनी, बागवान

37. मेर मेहरात-जठात, मेहरात-घोडात, चीता
38. गिरासी, हाडी, लंगा मगनियार
39. मोभिया (मोग्या)
40. नाई, सैन, वेदनाई
41. न्यारिया, न्यारगर
42. ओड
43. पटवा (फ्दाल)
44. रार्डका, रैघारी (देवासी)
45. रावत
46. साद, स्वामी, बैरागी, जंगम
47. सतिया-सिंधी
48. सिकलीगर, चन्दुलताप (उस्ता)
49. सिरकीवाल
50. स्वर्णकार, सुनार, सोनी, जड़िया
51. ठठेरा, कन्सारा, भरादा
52. तमोली (तम्बोली)
53. जागरी
54. जाट
55. रायसिख
56. हलाली, कसाई
57. दांगी
58. लोढे तवंर
59. सोंधिया
60. विश्नोई
61. मेव
62. गद्दी

63. फारूकी भटियारा
64. सिलावट (सोमपुरा, मूर्तिकार के अतिरिक्त)
65. खेरवा
66. धोली (मुस्लिम)
67. कायमखानी
68. कुंजड़ा राइन
69. सपेरा (गैर हिन्दू जाति)
70. मदारी, बाजीगर (गैर हिन्दू जाति)
71. नट (गैर हिन्दू जाति)
72. गाड़ित नागीरी
73. सिन्धी मुसलमान
74. खेलदार

Sikkim

1. Bhujel.
2. Gurung.
3. Limboo.
4. Rai.
5. Manger.
6. Sunuwar.
7. Tamang.

Explanation I - The expression 'Limboo' includes Tsong, Subba and Yakthungba.

Explanation II - The expression 'Sunuwar' includes Koincha/ Mukhia.

Tamil Nadu

Backward Classes (Other than Most Backward Classes and Denotified Communities)

1. Agamudayar including Thozhu or Thuluva Vollala.
2. Agaram Vellan Chottiar.
3. Alwar, Azhavar and Alavar (in Kanniyakumari District and Shencottah Taluk of Tirunelveli-Kattabomman District).

4. Servai (except Tiruchirapalli and Pudukkottai Distrct).

5. Ansar.

6. Arayar, Nulayar (in Kanniyakumari District and Shencottah taluk of Tirunelveli-Kattabomman District).

7. Archakarai Vellala.

8. Aryavathi (in Kanniyakumari District and Shencottah Taluk of Tirunelveli-Kattabomman District).

9. Ayira Vaisyar.

10. Baoagar.

11. Billava.

12. Bondil.

13. Boyas (except Tiruchirapalli, Pudukottai, The Nilgiris, Salem and Dharmapuri Districts).

Pedda Boyar (except Tiruchirapalli and Pudukottai District) Oddars (except Thanjavur, Nagapattinam Quaid-e-Milleth, Tiruchirapalli, Pudukottai and Madurai, Dindigul-Anna Districts).

Kaloddars (except Chengalpattu-MGR, Ramanathapuram, Pasumpon Muthuramalinga Thavar, Kamarajar, Madurai, Dindigul Anna, Puddukottai, Tiruchirappalli, Tirunelveli-Kattabomman, Chidambaranar and Salem Districts).

Nellorapet Oddars (except North Arcot Ambedkar and Tiruvannamalai Sambuvarayar Districts).

Sooramari Oddar's (except North Arcot Ambedkar and Tiruvannamalai Sambuvarayar Districts).

14. Chakkala (except Pasumpon Muthuramalinga Thevar, Kamarajar, Ramanathapuram, Thanjavur, Nagapattinam Quaid-e-Millath, Pudukkottai, Tiruchirappalli, Madurai, Dindigul Anna and The Nilgiris Districts).

15. Chavalakarar (in Kanniyakumari District and Shencottah Taluk of Tirunelveli-Kattabomman District).

16. Chettu or Chetty (including Kottar Chetty, Elur Chetty, Pathira Chetty, Vadayalchetty, Padukkdai Chetty) (in Kanniyakumari District and Shencottah Taluk of Tirunelveli-Kattabomman Districts).

17. Chowdhry.

18. Converts to Christianity from Scheduled Castes irrespective of the generation of conversion for the purpose of reservation of seats in Educational Institutions and for seats in Public Services.

19. C.S.I. formerly S.I.U.C. (in Kanniyakumari District and Shencottah Taluk of Tirunelveli Kattabomman District).

20. Donga Dasaris (except Chengalpattu-MGR, Tiruchirapalli, Pudukottai, Madras and Salem Districts).

21. Dakkani Muslims.

22. Devangar, Sedar.

Sooramani Oddar (except North Arcot Ambedkar and Tiruvannamalai Sombuvaryar Districts

23. Domos' (except Puduckottai and Tiruchirapalli Districts)

Dommars (except Thanjavur, Nagapactinam Quaid-a-Milleth, Pudukkottai, North Arcot Ambedkar and Tiruvannamalai Sambuvarayar Districts).

24. Dudekula.

25. Enadi.

26. Ezhavathy (in Kanniyakumari District and Shencottah Taluk of Tirunalveli-Kattabomman District).

27. Ezhuthachar (in Kanniyakumari District and Shencottah Taluk of Tirunelveli-Kattabomman District).

28. Ezhuva (in Kanniyakumari District and Shencottah Taluk of Tirunelveli-Kattabomman District).

29. Gangavar.

30. Gavara, Gavarai and Vadugar (Vaduvar) (other than Kamma, Kapu Balija and Reddi).

31. Gounde.

32. Gowda (including Gammala, Kalali and Anuppa Gounder).

33. Hegde.

34. Idiga.

35. Itlathu Pillaimar, Illuvar, Ezhuvar and Illathar.

36. Jhetty.

37. Jogis (except Chengalpattu-MGR, Madurai, Dindigul Anna, South Arcot Vallalar, Villupuram Ramasami Padayachiyar, North Arcot Ambedkar and Tiruvannamalai Sambuvarayar Districts).

38. Kabbera.

39. Kaikolar, Sengunthar.

40. Kaladi (except Pasumpon Muthuramalinga Thevar, Kamarajar, Ramanathapuram, Madurai, Dindigul Anna, Thanjavur, Nagapattinam Quaid-e-Milleth, Pudukkottai and Tiruchirappalli District).

41. Kalari Kurup including Kazlari Panicker (in Kanniyakumari District and Shencottah Taluk of Tirunelveli-Kattabomman District).

42. Kalingi.

43. Kallar (including Easanattu Kallar, Gandarvakottai Kallars (except Thanjavur, Nagapattinam Quaid-e-Milleth and Pudukkottai Districts).

Koottappal Kallars (except Pudukkottai and Tiruchirappalli Districts) Piramalai Kallars (except Pasumpon Muthuramalinga Thevar, Ramarajar, Ramanathapuram, Madurai, Dindigul Anna, Puddukkottai and Thanjavur, Nagapattinam Quaid-e-Milleth Districts).

Periyasooriyur Kallars (except Tiruchirappalli and Pudukuottai Districts).

44. Kallar Kula Thondaman.

45. Kalveli Gounder.

46. Kambar.

47. Kammalar or Viswakarma, Viswakarmala (including Thattar, Porkolla Kannar, Karamar, Kollar, Thacher, Kal Thacher, Kamsala and Viswabrahmin).

48. Kani, Kanisu, Kaulyar Panikkar.

49. Kaniyala Vellalar.

50. Kannada Saineegar, Kannadiyar (Throughout the State) and Dasapalanjika (Coimbatore, Periyar and the Nilgiris Districts).

51. Kannadiya Naidu.
52. Karpoorachattiar.
53. Karuneegar (Seer Karuneegar, Sri Karuneegar, Sarattu Karuneegar, Kaikatti, Karuneegar, Machuvazhi Kanakkar, Sozhi Kanakkar and Sunnambu Karuneegar).
54. Kasuakara Chettiar.
55. Katesar, Pattamkatti.
56. Kavuthiyar.
57. Kerala Mudali.
58. Kharvi.
59. Khatri.
60. Kongu Vaishnava.
61. Kongu Vellalars (including Vellala Gounder, Nattu Gounder, Narambukkatoi Gounder, Tirumudi Vellalar, Thondu Vellalar Pala Gounder, Poosari Gounder, Anuppa Vellala Gounder, Kurumba Gounder, Padaithalai Gounder, Chendalai Gounder, Pavalankatti Vellala Gounder, Pala Vellala Gounder, Sanku Vellala Gounder and Rachinagiri Gounder).
62. Koppala Valama.
63. Koteyar.
64. Krishnauvaka (in Kanniyakumari District and Shencottah Taluk of Tirunelveli - Kattabomman District).
65. Kudikara Vellalar.
66. Kudumbi (in Kanniyakumari District and Shencottah Taluk of Tirunelveli - Kattabomman District).
67. Kuga Vellalar.
68. Kunchidigar.
69. Labbais including Rowthar and Marakayar (whether their spoken language is Tamil or Urdu.)
70. Lambadi.
71. Latin Catholics (in Kanniyakumari District and Shencottah Taluk of Tirunelveli - Kattabomman Distict).
72. Lingayat (Jangama).

73. Mahratta (non-Brahmni) (including Namdev Mahratta).
74. Malayar.
75. Male.
76. Maniagar.
77. Mapilla.
78. Maravars (except Thanjavur, Nagapattinam Quaid-e-Milleth, Pudukkottai, Ramanathapuram, Pasumpon Muthuramalinga Thevar, Kamarajar, Tirunelveli Kattabomman and Chidambaranar Districts) including Karumaravars, Appanad Kondayamkottai Maravar (except Pasumpon Mathuramalinga Thevar, Kamarajar, Ramanathapuram, Madurai and Dindigul-Anna Districts) and Sembanad Maravars (except Pasumpon Muthuramalinga Thevar, Kamarajar and Ramanathapuram Districts).
79. Moondrumandai Enbathunalu (84) Ur. Sozhia Vellalar.
80. Mooppan.
81. Muthuraja, Muthuracha, Muttiriyar, Muthiriyar, Mutharaiyar.
82. Nadar, Shanar and Gramani (including Christian Nadar, Christian Shanar and Christian Gramani).
83. Nagaram.
84. Naikkar (in Kanniyakumari District and Shencottah Taluk of Tirunelveli-Kattabomman District).
85. Nangudi Vellalar.
86. Nanjil Mudali (in Kanniyakumari District and Shencottah Taluk of Tirunelveli-Kattabomman District).
87. Odar (in Kanniyakumari District and Shencottah Taluk of Tirunelveli - Kattabomman District).
88. Odiya.
89. Oottruvalanattu Vellalar.
90. O.P.S. Vellalar.
91. Ovachar.
92. Paiyur Kotta Vellalar.
93. Pamulu.

94. Panar (except in Kanniyakumari District and Shencottah Taluk of Tirunelveli - Kattabomman District where the community is a scheduled-caste).

95. Panisaivan (including Virakodi Vellala).

96. Kathikarar in Kanniyakumari District.

97. Pannirandam Chettiar or Uthama Chettiar.

98. Parkavakulam (including Surithimar, Nathamar, Malayamar, Moopanar and Nainar).

99. Perike (including Perike Balija).

100. Perumkollar (in Kanniyakumari District and Shencottah Taluk of Tirunelveli Kattabomman District).

101. Podikara Vellalar.

102. Pooluva Gounder.

103. Poraya.

104. Pulavar (in Coimbatore and Periyar Districts).

105. Pulluvar or Pooluvar.

106. Pusala.

107. Reddy (Ganjam).

108. Sadhu Chetty (including Telugu Chetty, Twenty four Manai Telugu Chetty).

109. Sakkaravar or Kavathi (in Kanniyakumari District and Shencottah taluk of Tirunelveli Kattabomman District).

110. Salivagana.

111. Saliyar, Padmasaliyan, Pattusaliyar, Pattariyar and Adhaviyar.

112. Savalakkarar.

113. Senaithalaivar, Senaikudiyar and Illaivaniar

114. Sheik.

115. Sourashtra (Patnulkarar).

116. Sozhia Vellalar (including Sozha Vellalar, Vetrilaikarar, Kodikalkarar and Keeraikarar)

117. Srisayar

118. Sundaram Chetty

119. Syed

120. Thogatta Veerakshatriya

121. Tholkollar (in Kanniyakumari District and Shencottah Taluk at Tirunelveli - Kattabomman District)

122. Tholuva Naicker and Vetalakara Naicker

123. Thoraiyar

124. Thoriyar

125. Ukkirakula Kshatriya Naicker

126. Uppara, Uppillia and Sagara

127. Urali Gounder (except Tiruchirapalli and Pudukottai Districts) and Orudaya Gounder or Oorudaya Gounder (in Madurai, Dindigul-Anna. Coimbatore, Periyar, Tiruchirapalli, Pudukottai and Salem District).

128. Urikkara Nayakkar

129. Vallambar

130. Valmiki

131. Vaniyar, Vania Chettiar including Gandla, Gandvad, Telikula and Chekkalar)

132. Veduvar and Vedar (except in Kanniyakumari District and Shencottah Taluk of Tirunelveli-Kattabomman District where the community is a Scheduled Caste).

133. Veerasaiva (in Kanniyakumari District and Shencottah Taluk of Tirunelveli - Kattabomman District).

134. Velar.

135. Vellan Chettiar

136. Veluthodathu Nair (in Kanniyakumari District and Shencottah Taluk of Tirunelveli - Kattabomman

137. Vokkaligar (including Vakkaligar, Okkaligar, Kappillgar/ Kappaliya, Okkaliga Gowda, Okkaliya, Gowda, Okkaliya Gowder, Okkaliya Gowda).

138. Wynad Chetty (The Nilgiris District).

139. Yadhava (including Idaiyar, Telugu Speaking Idaiyar known as Vaduga Ayar or Vaduga Idaiyar or Golla and Asthanthra Golla).

140. Yavana.

141. Yerukula.

142. Converts to Christianity from any Hindu Backward Classes Community or Most Backward Classes Community of Denotified Communities except the Converts to Christianity from Meenavar, Parvatharajukulam, Pattanavar, Sembadavar, Mukkuvar or Mukayar and Paravar.

143. Orphans and destitute children who have lost their parents before reaching the age of ten and are destitutes; and who have nobody else to take care of them either by law or custom; and also who are admitted into any of the schoolsor orphanages runpy the Government of recognised by the Government.

Part - B **Most Backward Classes**

1. Ambalakarar.
2. Andipandaram.
3. Bestha, Siviar
4. Bhatraju (Other than Kshatriya Raju).
5. Boyar, Oddar.
6. Dasari.
7. Dommara.
8. Eravallar (except in Kanniyakumari district and Shencottah Taluk of Tirunelveli Kattabomman District where the Community is a Scheduled Tribe).
9. Isaivellalar.
10. Jambuvanodai.
11. Jangam.
12. Jogi.
13. Kongu Chettiar (in Coimbatore and Periyar Districts only).
14. Koracha.
15. Kulala (including Kuyavar and Kumbarar).
16. Kunnuvar Mannadi.
17. Kurumba.
18. Kuruhini Chetty.

19. Maruthuvar, Navithar, Mangala, Velakattalavar, Velakatalanair and Pronopakari.
20. Mond Golla.
21. Moundadan chetty.
22. Mahendra, Medara.
23. Mutlakampatti.
24. Narikoravar.
25. Nokkar.
26. Vanniakula Kshatriya (including Vanniya, Vanniya, Vannia-Gounder, Gounder of Kander, Padayachi, Palli and Agnikula-Kshatriya).
27. Paravar (except in Kanniyakumari District and Shencottah Taluk of Tirunelveli Kattabomman district where the community is Scheduled Caste) (including Converts to Christianity).
28. Meenavar (Parvatharajakulam, Pattanavar, Sembadavar) (including Converts to Christianity).
29. Mukkuvar or Mukayar (including Converts to Christianity).
30. Punnan Vettuva Gounder.
31. Pannayar (other than Kathikarar in Kanniyakumari District).
32. Sathatha Sri Vaishanava (including Sathani, Chattadi and Chattada Srivaishnava).
33. Sezhia Chetty.
34. Telugupatty Chetty.
35. Thottja Naicker (including Rajakambalam Gollavar, Sillavar, Thockalavar and Thozhuva Naicker).
36. Thondaman.
37. Valaiyar (including Chettinad Valayars).
38. Vannar (Salaivai Thozhilalar) (including Agasa, Madivala, Ekali, Rajakula, Veluthadar and Rajaka) (except in Kanniyakumari District and Shencottah Taluk of Tirunelveli Kattabomman District where the community is a Scheduled Caste).
39. Vettaikarar.

40. Vettuva Gounder.
41. Yogeeswarar.

Tripura

1. Acharji (Ganak).
2. Badyakar, Dhuli, Nagarchi, Sabdakar.
3. Baishnab.
4. Barui, Barujibi.
5. Bauri.
6. Bhar, Rajbhar.
7. Bhumij, Bumij.
8. Bin
9. Bind.
10. Chouhan.
11. Dosadh, Dosad.
12. Gara.
13. Gareri.
14. Goala, Gope, Yadav, Aheer.
15. Haledas, Halladas; Haloadas.
16. Jhara.
17. Kandh.
18. Kapali.
19. Karmakar, Kamar.
20. Kairi.
21. Kumbhakar, Kumar, Rudrapal
22. Kuri.
23. Kurmi
24. Lohar.
25. Manipuri, Bishnupriya, Manipuri.
26. Marai.
27. Modak.

28. Mat, Natta.
29. Napit, Shil.
30. Nayak.
31. Nepali (Limbo, Matwali, Rai).
32. Punjya, Nunia.
33. Pan.
34. Pankli, Painak.
35. Pasi
36. Rai (Orlya)
37. Raily
38. Sutradhar.
39. Telenga.
40. Tanti, Tati.
41. Teli (Oriya).
42. Yogi, Jogi, Nath.

Uttar Pradesh

01. अहीर, यादव, यदुवंशीय, ग्वाला
02. अरख, अर्कवंशीय
03. काछी, काछी-कुशवाहा, शाक्य
04. कहार, कश्यप
05. केवट या मल्लाह, निषाद
06. किसान
07. कोडरी
08. कुम्हार, प्रजापति
09. कुर्मी, चेनऊ, पटेल, पटनवार, कुर्मी-मल्ल, कुर्मी-शेयवार
10. कम्बोज
11. कसगर
12. कुंजड़ा या राइन
13. गोसाई

14. गूजर
15. गड़ेरिया, पाल और बघेल
16. गद्दी, घोषी
17. गिरि
18. चिकवा, कस्साव, करेशी, चक
19. छीपी, छीपा
20. जोगी
21. झोला
22. डफाली
23. तमोली, बरई, धौरसिया
24. तेली, सामानी, रोगनगर, साहू, रोनियार, गन्धी, अर्राक
25. दर्जी, इदरीसी, काकुस्य
26. धीवर
27. नवकात
28. नट (जो अनुसूचित जाति की श्रेणी में न सम्मिलित हों)
29. नायक
30. फकीर
31. बंजारा, रंकी, मुकेरी, मुकेरानी
32. बढ़ई, बढ़ई-शेफी, विश्वकर्मा, पांचाल, भागदिया, जांगिड़, धीमान
33. बारी
34. बैरागी
35. बिन्द
36. बियार
37. भर, राजभर
38. भुर्जी या भड़भूंजा, भूज, कांटू, कसोधन
39. भठियारा
40. माली, शैनी

41. मनिहार, कचेर, लखेरा
42. मुराय या मुराई, मौर्य
43. मोमिन, अंसार
44. मिरासी
45. मुस्लिम कायस्थ
46. नद्दाफ (पुनिया)मन्सूरी, कन्डेरे, वडेरे, करण (कर्ण)
47. मारछा
48. रंगरेज, रंगपा
49. लोध, लोधा, लोधी, लोट, लोधी-राजपूत
50. लोहार, लोहार-शफी
51. लोनिया, नोनिया, गोले-ठाकुर, लोनिया-चौहान
52. सोनार, सुनार, स्वर्णकार
53. स्वीपर (जो अनुसूचित जाति की सूची में सम्मिलित न हो) हलालखोर
54. हलवाई, मोंदनवाल
55. हज्ज़ाम, नाई सलमानी, सविता, श्रीवास
56. राय शिकख
57. राबंका-भिश्ती, गिश्ती-अब्बासी
58. धोबी (जो अनुसूचित जाति की श्रेणी में न सम्मिलित हो)
59. कसेरा, ठठेरा, ताम्रकार
60. नानबाई
61. मीर शिकार
62. शेख सरवरी (पिराई) पीराही
63. मेव, मेवाती
64. कोष्टा/कोष्टी
65. रोड़
66. खुगरा, संगतराश, हंसीरी
67. मोची

68. खागी

69. तंवर सिंघाड़िया

70. कतुआ

71. माहीगीर

72. दांगी

73. धाकड़

74. गाड़ा

75. तंतवा

76. जोरिया

77. पटवा, पटहारा, पटेहरा, देववंशी

78. जाट

79. कलार, कलवार, कलाल

West Bengal

1. Kapali.
2. Baishya Kapali.
3. Kurmi
4. Sutradhar.
5. Karmakar.
6. Kumbhakar, Kumar.
7. Swarnakar
8. Teli, Kolu.
9. Napit.
10. Yogi-Nath.
11. Goala-Gope (Pallav Gope, Ballav Gope, Yadav Gope, Gope Ahir, Yadav).
12. Moira-Modak (Halwai).
13. Barujibi, Barui.
14. Satchasi.
15. Malakar.

16. Tanti.
17. Kansari.
18. Shankhakar.
19. Koori/Koiri.
20. Raju.
21. Tamboli/Tamli.
22. Nagar.
23. Karani.
24. Dhanuk.
25. Sarak.
26. Jolah (Ansari-Momin).
27. Roniwar.
28. Kosta/Kostha.
29. Christians.
    Converted from Scheduled Castes.
30. Bhujel.
31. Newar.
32. Mangar (Thapa, Rana).
33. Nembang.
34. Sampang.
35. Bunchheng.
36. Thami.
37. Yogi.
38. Dhimal.
39. Lakhera/Lahera
40. Fakir, Sain.
41. Kahar.
42. Tamang.
43. Betkar (Bentkar).
44. Chitrakar.
45. Hawari.
46. Tuhra.

47. Bhar.
48. Dhunia.
49. Khandait.
50. Patidar.
51. Gangot.
52. Kasai.
53. Hele-Helia-Chasi Kaibarta.
54. Banshi-Barman.
55. Nashya-Sekh.
56. Pahadia Muslim.
57. Khen.
58. Sukli.
59. Sunuwar.
60. Bharbhuja.

Chandigarh

1. Ahoria, Aheri, Hori, Naik, Thori or Turi.
2. Borrer/Barra.
3. Bota/Tota, Hansi/Hensi or Hesi.
4. Chamgar/Changar.
5. Chirimar/Chrimar.
6. Daiya.
7. Gwaria, Gauria or Gwar.
8. Kanjur or Kanchan / Kunchan.
9. Kummi / Kurmi.
10. Nar.
11. Rohar, Rehare/Rohard or Ree/Re.
12. Ghirath including Chahng and Bahti.
13. Kahar, Jhinwar or Dhinwar/Dhinear.
14. Ghani/Ghazi, Goasiara/Ghasiara or Ghosi/Ghosia.
15. Bagria.
16. Weavers (Jullaha).

17. Labana.
18. Kumhar/Kumahars.
19. Nais.
20. Dhobis.
21. Kamboj.
22. Rai Sikh.
23. Barwar.
24. Barai, Tarboli/Tomboji.
25. Batera/Battera.
26. Bairagi, Baregi/Baragi.
27. Bharbunja, Bharbhuja/Bharbhuria.
28. Bhat, Bhatra, Darpi, Amiya.
29. Bhuhalia-Lohar.
30. Chahang/Chang.
31. Chimba/Chiba/Chhimba, Chipi, Chhippi/Chimpa/Darji/ Darj, Tank.
32. Dahakaut/Dakuat.
33. Dhimar, Mallah/Mallah, Kashyap Rajput/Kasya Rajputs.
34. Faquir.
35. Dhosali/Bhosali, Dosali.
36. Gawla/Gawala, Gowala/Gowala.
37. Gadderia/Gadaria.
38. Jhangara Brahaman/Jhangra Brahman/Jangra Brabman.
39. Hazam Nai/Hajjam Nai.
40. Jogi Nath.
41. Khati.
42. Rachban/Rechhand.
43. Khanghera.
44. Kuchband/Kuch Band.
45. Ththera/Thethera, Tamera.
46. Lakhora, Kamhar/Maninar.
47. Vanzara.
48. Madari.

49. Lohar.
50. Mochi.
51. Mhasi.
52. Noonga.
53. Nalband.
54. Shorgie.
55. Pinja, Pomja/Ponja.
56. Soi.
57. Singhliar/Singhikant, Singhwala/Singhiwala.
58. Toll.
59. Christian converted from Scheduled Castes.
60. Dauln, Soni Barderi/Soni.

Daman & Diu

1. Bhandari.
1A. Banjara, Lambadi, Lamani, Sugali.
2. Christian Chamar.
3. Christian Mahar.
4. Dhangar.
5. Dhobi.
6. Dhor.
7. Gauda.
8. Goggi.
9. Gosavi.
10. Kasar.
11. Koli.
12. Kumbi.
13. Mitna.
14. Naidu.
15. Nath, Jogi.
16. Rhavi, Nai.
17. Sagar.
18. Yadav, Gavli.

Pondicherry

[Notified vide Gazette of the UT dated 19th Feburary, 2001]

1. Agamudiyas (including Thuluva Vellalas).
2. Ayeeravaisiar - confined to Acharapakkam Chettiar, Beri Chettiar, Manjapudoor Chettiar, Vadambar Chettiar.
3. Converts to Christianity from and Hindu Backward Classes Community irrespective of the Generation of Conversion.
4. Converts to Christianity from Scheduled Castes irrespective of the Generation of Conversion.
5. Dekkani Muslims (Pondicherry and Karaikal Regions only).
6. Gramani/Sanar / Nadar / Ezhava / Tiyya.
7. Irular/ Vettaikarar/ Kattunaicker.
8. Isai Vellalar.
9. Jangam/ Jangamar.
10. Kalavanthula.
11. Kamsali.
12. Kannada Devanga / Telugu Devanga.
13. Karuneegar / Kannakkupillai.
14. Khatriyas.
15. Konda Reddiar.
16. Kongu Vellalar.
17. Kuyavar / Kulalar / Kumbarar / Kummari - including Mannudayar, Pathar, Poonul Kuyavar, Velaar.
18. Latin Catholics.
19. Mahratta (Non-Brahmin) including Khatik.
20. Mappila.
21. Marudha Naidu.
22. Maruthuvar / Nayee Brahmin / Mangali - including Ambattan, Navithar, Pandithar, Pariyari, Pronopakari.
23. Meenavar/ Agnikulakshatriya / Mukkuvan - including Chettiar, Chinna Pattinavar, Meenava Chettiar, Nattar, Paravar, Parvatharajakulam, Pattinavar, Pattinava Chettiar, Periya Pattinavar, Sembadavar.

24. Lubbai including Maricar, Ravuthar, Saibu, Shaik, Syed.
25. Mukkulathor / Devar - including Agamudaya Devar, Kallar, Maravar.
26. Nainar.
27. Ottar.
28. Padmasaliar/ Padmasali/ Saliar / Salian / Pattu Saliar / Saliars.
29. Palayapattu Naidu.
30. Parkavakulam - including Malayaman, Nathaman, Parkavakula Pillai, Parakavakula Udayar, Suruthiman.
31. Pattu Chettiar.
32. Reddy (Ganjam).
33. Sadhu Chetty / 24 Manai Telugu Chetty / Telugupatty Chetty.
34. Salia Chettiar.
35. Senai Thalaivar.
36. Sengunthar / Kaikolar.
37. Settibalija.
38. Sozhia Vellalar.
39. Vadamalai Chettiar.
40. Valayal Naidu / Balija Naidu / Cavara Naidu / Gavaralu
41. Vandayar.
42. Vaniar / Vaniya Chetty.
43. Vannan / Vannar / Ekali / Mannan / Rajaka / Chakkali.
44. Vanniakula Kshatriya - including Gounder, Naicker, Padayatchi, Palli, Vanniar.
45. Vellala Chettiar.
46. Viswakarma / Kammalar / Thatchar / Porkollar / Karumar / Kannar / Kalthatchar / Thattar / Viswakarmala / Pathar.
47. Yadava/Gollalu - including Idayar, Konar, Sambar Yadava, Yadava Pillai.
48. Yadava Naidu.
49. Yerukula.

Appendix - II

Central List of Other Backward Classes

Sl. No.	Name of the Caste/sub-caste/ synonym/community	State/Union Territory
1.	Abbasi, Bhishti, Sakka	Delhi
2.	Abdal	Bihar
3.	Achukatiavandlu	A.P.
4.	Achukatlavandlu	Pondicherry
5.	Agamudayar including Thozhu or Thuluva Vellala	TN
6.	Agamukdiyas (including Thuluva Vellalas)	Pondicherry
7.	Agariya	Bihar
8.	Agaru	A.P., Pondi.
9.	Agasa	Kerala, Pondi.
10.	Agasa, Lingayat Agasa, Sakala, Madivala/Madivalaru, Lingayat Madivala, Sakalavadu, Tsakala, Chakala, Vannan, Dhobi, Parit, Rajaka	Karnataka
11.	Agharia	MP
12.	Agharia, Agaria, Aghria	Orissa

13.	Aghori	Bihar
14.	Aghori, Karkarmunda	Karnataka
15.	Agnani	Karnataka
16.	Agnikula Kshatriya (Pallekapu, Palloreddi, Vannekapu Vannereddi)	Pondicherry
17.	Agnikulakshatriya, Pallireddi, Vadabalija, Bestha,Jalari, Gangavar, Gangaputra, Goondla, Vanyakulakshatriya, Vannekapu, Vannereddi,Pallikapu, Pallireedi, Nayyala, Pattapu	A.P.
18.	Agri	Gujarat, D&NH
19.	Agri, Agale or Kalan	Maharashtra
20.	Agri, Kharwal	Delhi
21.	Aheri or Ahori, Heri, Naik, Thori, Turi	H.P., Chandi.
22.	Aheria, Aheri, Heri, Naik, Theri or Turi or Thori	Haryana, Pnb.
23.	Aheria/Aheriya	UP
24.	Ahir, Ayar Bericha	Gujarat
25.	Ahir, Bharvad, Yadav	D&NH
26.	Ahir, Brajwasi, Gasli, Gawali, Goli, Lingayat-Gaoli, Gowari, (Gwari), Gawari, Gowra, Gwara, Jadav, Yadav, Raut, Thethwar, Gop/Gopal	MP
27.	Ahir, Yadav	Raj., UP
28.	Ahir, Yadav, Gwala	Delhi
29.	Ahirgoala	Assam
30.	Ahom	Assam
31.	Alia	Orissa
32.	Alitkar	Maharashtra

33.	Alwar	Pondi.
34.	Alwar, Azhavar and Alavar (in Kanniyakumari District and Sheon-cottah Taluk of Tirunelveli Distt.)	TN
35.	Amaat	Bihar
36.	Ambalakaran	Pondi.
37.	Ambalakarar, Ambalakaran	TN
38.	Ambalakkaran	Kerala
39.	Ambalavasi, Ambalakarma, Ambalakaran	Karnataka
40.	Ambattan	Karnataka
41.	Ambika	Pondi.
42.	Anandan	Pondi.
43.	Andi Pandaram	TN, Pondi.
44.	Anduran	Karnataka
45.	Anglo Indian	Kerala, Pondi.
46.	Arayan (Nulayan) Araya	Pondi.
47.	Arain	Pnb.
48.	Arain, Rayee, Kunjra	Delhi
49.	Arak, Arakvanshiya	Delhi, UP
50.	Aranedan	Orissa
51.	Arayar, Arayan, Nulayar (in Kanniyakumari Dist. and Sheon-cottah Taluk of Tirunelveli District)	TN
52.	Archakari Vallala	TN
53.	Archakatalavandu	Pondi.
54.	Ard Pop	H.P.
55.	Are Mahrati	Pondi.
56.	Arekatika, Katika	A.P.
57.	Aremahrati	Kerala
58.	Arya	Kerala, Pondi.
59.	Aryakshatriya, Chittari, Giniyar, Chitrakara, Nakhas	A.P.

60.	Arya Mala	Assam
61.	Aryavathi (in Kanniyakumari District and Sheoncottah Taluk of Tirunelveli District)	TN
62.	Aryavathi (Nairuseri)	Pondi.
63.	Asara	MP
64.	Ashtralohi/Ashtalohi Karmakar, Kamila, Sunari, Sunaree, Viswa Brahman (Sunari), Swarnakar/ Swaransilpi	Orissa
65.	Asur	Assam, Orissa
66.	Atagara	A.P.
67.	Atagara, Atagora	Pondi.
68.	Atari, Athari	Karnataka
69.	Atirasa (of Polavaram, Gopalapuram, Koyyalagudem, Buttayagudem, Chagallu	A.P. Mandals of West Godavari Distt. & Devipattanam, Korukonda and Gokavaram Mandals of East Godavari Distt.
70.	Atishbaz, Darugar	UP
71.	Attur Kilnad Koravar (in Salem, South Arcot, Ramanathanpuram, Kamarajar and Psumpon Muthuramadigam District)	TN
72.	Attur Melnad Korvar (in Salem district)	TN
73.	Ayyaraka	A.P.
74.	Bad/Baddon	Haryana
75.	Badaga	Pondi.
76.	Badagar	TN
77.	Badasuda	Orissa
78.	Badhai, Barhai, Khati, Tarkhan,	

	Jangra-Brahmin, Vishwakarma, Ramgarhis, Panchal, Dheeman	Delhi
79.	Badhbhunja, Bhunjwa, Bhurji, Dhuri or Dhoori	MP
80.	Badhai, Barhai, Bindhania, Suradhar, Badhira, Badharia	Orissa
81.	Badhai, Jangid, Khati, Kharadi, Suthar, Tarkhan	Raj.
82.	Badi	Delhi
83.	Badi/Baddon	Haryana
84.	Badi (Nepali), Damai (Nepali), Gainay (Nepali), Kami (Nepali), and Sarki (Nepali)	Manipur
85.	Badia	Maharashtra
86.	Badwa, Bhat, Rao, Jachak, Jaga	Raj.
87.	Badyakar, Dhuli, Nagarchi, Sabdkar	Tripura
88.	Bafan (Muslim)	Gujarat
89.	Bagaria	Raj.
90.	Bagdi	Bihar, Maharashtra
91.	Bagria or Bagaria H.P., Pnb.,	Haryana, Chandi.
92.	Bahach Hanjie and Shikara Wallas house-boat owners)	(excluding J&K
93.	Bahti	H.P.
94.	Bahurupi Maha.	Karnataka,
95.	Baiga	Assam
96.	Baijara	Assam
97.	Bailapatar, Bailpatar, Bilapatar	Karnataka
98.	Baipari	Orissa
99.	Baira	Orissa

100.	Bairagi Orissa, UP	Delhi, MP,
101.	Bairagi, Baragi H.P., Pnb.	Haryana,
102.	Bairagi, Baragi/Baregi	Chandi.
103.	Bairagi, Bava, Bavaji, Byaragi, Bavani	Karnataka
104.	Bairwa, Berwa	Delhi
105.	Baishnab	Tripura
106.	Baishya Kapali	WB
107.	Bajania	Maha.
108.	Bajania, Bajenia	Karnataka
109.	Bajigar	Maha.
110.	Bajadra	Karnataka
111.	Balasanthu, Bahurupi	A.P.
112.	Balasanthoshi	Karnataka
113.	Balija, Balajiga, Banajiga, Bale Balajiga, Dasa Banajiga, Naidu, Bogam Teluga, Telaga Balija,Teluga Banajiga,Setty Balija, Setty Banajiga, Kasban,Mannur/Munnar, Mutrasi, Matracha,Janappan, Balegara, Lingayat Balegala/Baleshettaru	Karnataka
114.	Balolika	Pondi.
115.	Bandara	A.P.
116.	Bandari	Kerala
117.	Bandi	Maha.
118.	Bangi, Bhangi, Khakrob (Sweepers) those in the list of SCs)	(excluding J&K
119.	Bangshi	Tripura
120.	Banjara, Mukeri, Makrani (all Muslim)	MP.
121.	Banjara, Baladia, Labana	Raj.

122.	Banjara, Banjari, Goar Bangara, Lambada/Lambara/ Lambade, Lambahni, Charan Banjara, Labhan Mathura Labhani, Mathura Banjara, Kachikiwale Banjara, Laman Banjara, Laman/Lamani, Laban, Dhali/Dhalia, Dhalia Banjara, Dhadi/ Dhari, Singari, Navi Banjara	Maharashtra
123.	Banjara, Kachiriwala Banjara, Laman Banjara, Bamania Banjara, Laman/ Lambani, Bajari, Mathura, Mathura Labhan, Mathura Banjari,Navi Banjara, Jogi Banjara, Nayak, Nayakada, Lambana/Lambara, Lambhani, Labhana	MP
124.	Banjara, Mukeri, Ranki, Mekrani Laban, Labana, Lamne, Dhiriya	UP
125.	Banjara, Lambadi, Lamani, Sugali	Daman & Diu
126.	Banpar	Bihar
127.	Baral, Waaral, Wari (Chaurasia), Tamoli, Tamboli, Kumavatt, Kumavat	MP
128.	Barbars (Rural only)	J&K
129.	Barhai	Assam
130.	Barhai, Badhai, Vishwakarma, Ramgarhia	UP
131.	Barhai (Carpenter)	MP
132.	Barhai, Sutar, Suthar, Kunder, Vishwakarma	MP
133.	Barhai (Vishwakarma)	Bihar
134.	Barai	Bihar
135.	Barai, Bari, Tamboli	Delhi
136.	Barai, Tamboli	Haryana, Chandi
137.	Barai, Waari, Wari (Chaurasia), Tamoli, Tamboli, Kumavatt, Kumavat	MP
138.	Bari	Bihar, Raj.,

		UP
139.	Bari or Barai	Maha.
140.	Baria	Assam
141.	Baria or Koli Baria	Maha.
142.	Bariji, Barui, Tambuli, Tamali	Orissa
143.	Barika, Bhandari, Napit, Nai	Orissa
144.	Barjubi	Assam
145.	Baroi	Assam
146.	Barot, Vahivancha, Charan, Gadhvi, Gadhavi (where they are not STs)	Gujarat
147.	Barra	Haryana, Pnb., Chandigarh
148.	Barui	Assam, Tripura
149.	Barujibi	W. B.
150.	Barwar	Haryana, Pnb., Chandi.
151.	Basdeva/Vasudeva	Maha.
152.	Basor	Assam
153.	Basphor	Assam
154.	Bata, Hensi or Hesi	H.P.
155.	Bathal, Battal, Batter, Battar	Karnataka
156.	Batoerha	H.P.
157.	Battera	Haryana, Pnb., Chandi.
158.	Battu Turkas	TN
159.	Bauri	Assam
160.	Bauria/Bawria (excluding those in SCs)	Delhi
161.	Bavri or Baori	Gujarat
162.	Bawa, Atit Bawa, Goswami, Vairagi Bawa, Gosai, Ramanandi,	

	Puri, Bharti, Kapdi Nath Bawa, Bharathari, Margi, Gangajalia, Dashnami Bawa, Giri, Deshnam Goswami	Gujarat
163.	Bawtar	Karnataka
164.	Bazigar	Karnataka
165.	Bazigar, Nat Kalandar (excluding those in SCs)	Delhi
166.	Beda	H.P.
167.	Bedaru, Valimiki, Barki, Parivara, Bendar, Berad, Boya, Naikamakkalu, Naikwadi, Palegar, Ramoshi, Talwar, Valmikimakkalu, Vedan, Parivara Nayaka	Karnataka
168.	Beddi	Assam
169.	Bedia	Assam
170.	Beldal, Od	Maha.
171.	Beldar	Assam, Bihar
172.	Bellara	Orissa
173.	Bentkar	Orissa
174.	Berad/bedar, Naikwadi, Talwar, Valmiki	Maha.
175.	Beria	Karnataka
176.	Beshtar, Bunde-Bestar	Karnataka
177.	Bester, Sanchaluwaddar	Maha.
178.	Bestha, Beztha (Jalarula Nagavadaity)	Pondi.
179.	Bestha, Siviar	TN
180.	Beta, Hensi or Hesi	Haryana, Pnb., Chandi.
181.	Betkar (Bentkar)	WB
182.	Bhaat	Maha.
183.	Bhaat, Bhatraj, Bohrot, Bhatraju	Karnataka

184.	Bhadbhuja	MP
185.	Bhadbhunja	Gujarat, Maha.Raj.
186.	Bhalia	Gujarat
187.	Bamta, Bhamti, Girni Waddar, Kamati, Pathrut,Takari, Uchale	Maha.
188.	Bhampta, Bhompta, Paradeshi Bhampta, Bhomtra, Takari,Uchillian	Karnataka
189	Bhamta, Pardeshi Bhamta	Gujarat
190.	Bhand	J&K, Maha., UP
191.	Bhandari	Gujarat, Karnataka, Maha. Daman & Diu
192.	Bhanja Puran	Orissa
193.	Bhanta	Maha.
194.	Bhar	Bihar, UP, WB
195.	Bharbhunja, Bharbhuja	Haryana, Pnb.
196.	Bharbhuja or Bharbhunga, Bharbunha	H.P.
197.	Bhar, Rajbhar	Pnb., Chandi.
198.	Bhar, Rajonar	Tripura
199.	Bharadi, Balasantoshi, Kinggriwale, Nath Bava, Nath Jogi, Nath Pandhi, Davari Gosavi	Maha.
200.	Bharaik	Assam
201.	Bharbhooja, Kanu	Delhi
202.	Bharbhunja, Bharbhuja	Chandi.
203.	Bhardi, Bhargi	Karnataka
204.	Bharood	MP
205.	Bharwad (except where they are STs) Motabhai Bharwad, Nanabhai Bharwad, Gadaria	Gujarat
206.	Bhaskar	Bihar

207.	Bhat	Delhi
208.	Bhat, Bhatt	Bihar
209.	Bhat, Bhatta, Darpi	H.P.
210.	Bhat, Bhatra, Darpi, Ramiya	Haryana, Pnb., Chandi.
211.	Bhat, Charan (Charahm), Sawli, Sutiya, Rav, Jasondhi, Maru-Sonia	MP
212.	Bhataraja	A.P.
213.	Bhatiara	Delhi
214.	Bhatiara (Muslim)	Bihar, Raj., UP
215.	Bhatiyara	MP
216.	Bhatiyara (Muslim)	MP
217.	Bhatraju	Pondi.
218.	Bhatraju (other than Kshatriya Raju)	TN
219.	Bhatta	Assam
220.	Bhattu/Chattu	Haryana
221.	Bhatua	Orissa
222.	Bhavaiya, Targala	Maha.
223.	Bhavassar Kshatriya, Bangarajulu, Rongare, Darji, Simpi	Pondi.
224.	Bhavin	Karna., Maha.
225.	Bhawasar	Maha.
226.	Bhil	Assam
227.	Bhishti, Bhishti-Abbasi (Muslim)	MP
228.	Bhisti or Pakhali	Maha.
229.	Bhogta	Orissa
230.	Bhoi, Bhoiraj, Dhimar, Zinga Bhoi, Kevat Bhoj, Bhanara Bhoi, Machhindra Bhoi, Palwar Bhoi, Kirat Bhoi, Kahar Bhoi, Pardeshi, Bhoi, Shrimali Bhoi	Gujarat
231.	Bhoi/Boi, Zinga Bhoi, Pardeshi Bhoi, Raj Bhoi, Kahar, Gadia Kahare, Dhuria Kahar, Kirat, Machwa, Manzi,	

	Jatia, Kewat, Dhiwar, Dhiwar Bhoi, Dheewar, Dhimar, Palewar, Machhendra, Navadi, Malhar, Madhav, Gadhav Bhoi, Khadi Bhoi, Khare Bhoi, Dhevra	Maharashtra
232.	Bhokta	Assam
233.	Bhottodas, Bodo Battadu, Muria Bhottada, Sano Bhottada	Pondi.
234.	Bhrhmi	D&NH
235.	Bhuhalia	H.P.
236.	Bhuhalia Lohar	Haryana,Pnb.
237.	Bhuhalia-Lohar, Bhubalia-Lohar	Chandi.
238.	Bhuihar, Bhuiyar	Bihar
239.	Bhujan	Orissa
240.	Bhujel	Sikkim, WB
241.	Bhuliya	Orissa
242.	Bhumias, Bado Bhumias, Bhuri Bhumia	Pondi.
243.	Bhumji	Assam
244.	Bhumji, Bumjo	Tripura
245.	Bhundari	Pondi.
246.	Bhunjva, Bhurji, Dhuri or Dhoori	MP
247.	Bhurji, Bharbhuja, Bharbhunga, Bhooj, Kandu	UP
248.	Bhurtia, Bhutiya	MP
249.	Bhute, Bhope	Maha.
250.	Bhuyan	Assam
251.	Billala	Maha.
252.	Billava	Kerala, TN, Pondi.
253.	Bin	Tripura
254.	Binapatta	Karnataka
255.	Bind	Bihar, Tripura, UP

256.	Binedhanies	Orissa
257.	Bingi	Karnataka
258.	Binjia	Assam
259.	Birhar	Assam
260.	Birjhia	Orissa
261.	Birjia	Assam
262.	Birjhia	Orissa
263.	Bishnupriya Manipuri	Tripura
264.	Bissoy	Pondi.
265.	Bissoy-Barangi Jodia, Bennangi, Daduva, Frangi, Hollar, Jhoriya, Kollari, Konde, Paranga, Pengajodia, Sodojodia, Takoara	Orissa
266.	Biyar	UP
267.	Bogad, Bogadi, Bagadi, Bogodi, Bagaadi, Bagdi, Bagodi	Karnataka
268.	Bogada	Orissa
269.	Bolodhia	Orissa
270.	Bondil	TN
271.	Bondili	Pondi.
272.	Bondo	Assam
273.	Bony	Pondi.
274.	Bot	UP
275.	Bowri	Assam
276.	Boyar	TN, Pondi.
277.	Budabukkala	A.P.
278.	Budbudki, Budbudkala, Devari, Joshi	Karnataka
279.	Bungchheng	WB
280.	Buruashankar, Bama Suankar	Orissa
281.	Buttal	Maha
282.	Byagari	Orissa, Pondi.
283.	Chahang	Pnb

284.	Chain, Chayeen	Bihar
285.	Chak	Delhi
286.	Chakkala	Kerala, TN, Pondi.
287 .	Chakravar, Sakravar (Kavathi)	Kerala
288.	Chaliyan, Teruvan, Challiya	Karnataka
289.	Chamling	WB
290.	Chamar	Assam
291.	Chambodi	Karnataka
292.	Chambukutti	Karnataka
293.	Chamtha	Maha.
294.	Chandalgada/Chandalagade	Maha.
295.	Chandrabanshi (Kahar)	Bihar
296.	Chang	Haryana, Chandi.
297.	Chang or Chahang	H.P.
298.	Changar	Haryana, H.P., Pnb.
299.	Changayampadi Koravar (in North Arcot dist.)	TN
300.	Chanou	Bihar, Chandi.
301.	Chapota	Bihar
302.	Chaptegar, Chaptegara	Karnataka
303.	Chaptpgra	Pondi.
304.	Chara, Chhar, Chhara	Karnataka
305.	Charan	Haryana, Raj.
306.	Charan or Gadhavi	Maha.
307.	Charan Gadhvi	Gujarat
308.	Charodi	Maha.
309.	Charodi, Mestha	Karnataka
310.	Chasa, Odachasa, Banayat Oriya	Orissa

311.	Chatadi (Chattada or Srivaishnava)	Pondi.
312.	Chaupal	Orissa.
313.	Chavalakaranas	Pondi.
314.	Chavalakarar (in Kanniyakumari district and Sheoncottah taluk of Tirunelveli dist.)	TN
315.	Chavalakkaran	Kerala
316.	Chekkalas whose normal occupation is oil Crushing like, Cap Vaniyans	Pondi.
317.	Chere	Assam
318.	Chero	Orissa
319.	Cheruman	Orissa
320.	Chettadara	Pondi.
321.	Chetties (Kottar Chetties), Parakka Chetties, Elur Chetties, Atingal Chetties, Padukkada Chetties, Iraniel Chetties, Sri Pandara Chetties, Telugu Chetties, Udayamkulangara Chetties, Wanadan Cehtties, Kalavara Chetties, Sadhu Chetties and 24 Manai Telugu Chetties)	Kerala
322.	Chettu or Chetty (including Kottar Chetty, Elur Chetty, Pathira Chetty, Valayal Chetty) (in Kanniyakumari district and Sheoncottah taluk of Tirunelveli district)	TN
323.	Chhaparband, Chapparbanada (Muslim)	Karnataka
324.	Chhapparband (including Muslim)	Maha.
325.	Chhara, Kanjar/Kanjar Bhat, Nat	Maha.
326.	Chhara, Adodia, Sansi	Gujarat
327.	Chhimba/Chimba	Chandi.
328.	Chhipa	Gujarat, Maha.
329.	Chhipa, Chhipe	UP

330.	Chhipa (Chhipi), Nama, Bhavsar	Raj.
331.	Chick Banik	Assam, Orissa
332.	Chik (Muslim)	Bihar, Orissa
333.	Chikwa, Qassab (Qureshi), Kasai/Qassai, Chak	UP
334.	Chimba or Chhimba, Chhipi, Chimpa, Darzi	Haryana
335.	Chimba or Chimbe, Chippi or Faqir, Chhipi, Darzi, Tonk	Pnb.
336.	Chippa/Chhipa (Muslim)	MP
337.	Chippa, Chhipa, Bhavasar, Nilgar, Jingar, Nirali, Ramgari, Rangari, Rangrez, Rangarej, Rangraz, Rangredh, Chippa-Sindhi-Khatri	MP
338.	Chippi, Tonk, Darzi	Delhi
339.	Chippolu (Mera)	A.P.
340.	Chirimar	Haryana, H.P., Pnb.
341.	Chirimar/Chrimar	Chandi.
342.	Chitara	Karnataka
343.	Chitari	MP
344.	Chitra, Chitrakar	Orissa
345.	Chitrakar	WB
346.	Chitrakathi	Maha.
347.	Chitrakathijoshi	Karnataka
348.	C.K. Koravar (in south Arcot district)	TN
349.	Chopemari	A.P.
350.	Choudang	Assam
351.	Chouhan	Tripura
352.	Chowdhari	Assam
353.	Christian Chamar	Daman & Diu
354.	Christian converts from OBCs	Bihar, TN

355.	Christian Mahar	Daman & Diu
356.	Chunara	Gujarat
357.	Chunchar	Karnataka
358.	Chungar	Raj.
359.	Chunkar, Chungar/Choongar, Kulbandhiya, Rajgir	MP
360.	Churia	Orissa
361.	Churihar (Muslim)	Bihar, WB
362.	Chutia, Chutiya	Assam
363.	Chuvalia Koli	Gujarat
364.	C.S.I. formerly S.I.U.C. in Kanniyakumari district and Sheoncottah Taluk of Tirunelveli dist.	TN
365.	Dabgar	Maha.
366.	Dabi Koravar in Thanjavur, Trichirapally, Pudkukottai and North Arcot dist.)	TN
367.	Dafali (Muslim)	Bihar, UP
368.	Dafer (Hindu & Muslim)	Gujarat
369.	Dahalia	Orissa
370.	Daiya	Haryana, H.P., Pnb. Chandi.
371.	Dakaut	Haryana, Pnb.,
372.	Dakaut/Dahakaut	Chandi.
373.	Dakaut, Deshantri	Raj.
374.	Dakaut, Prade	Delhi
375.	Damal	Orissa
376.	Damami, Nagarchi	Raj.
377.	Dambali Faqir	J&K
378.	Dandari	Assam
379.	Dandasi	Assam
380.	Dang-Dasar	Karnataka
381.	Dangi	Bihar, MP

382.	Dangua	Orissa
383.	Darji	Orissa
384.	Daroga, Daroga-Rajor, Ravana-Rajput, Hazuri, Wazir	Raj.
385.	Darvesu	Karnataka
386.	Darzi	Raj., UP
387.	Darzi, Cheepi/Chhipi/Chipi, Shipi, Mavi (Namdev)	MP
388.	Darzi, Bhavasar Kshatriya, Chippi, Chgippiga, Simpi, Shimpi, Lingayat Simpy, Sivasimpy, Sai, Mirai, Rangari, Rangrez, Nilari, Namdev, Namdev Simpy, Rangare, Neelagar, Lingayat Neelagar	Karnataka
389.	Das or Dangdidas	Maha.
390.	Dasari	Pondi.
391.	Dasari (formerly engaged in Bhikshatana)	A.P.
392.	Dasari (including Donga Dasari and Gudu Dasari)	TN
393.	Davadiga, Devadigar, Moili, Moyili, Devadig, Devali, Sappaliga, Sheregar, Servegar, Suplig	Karnataka
394.	Dawala, Soni (Dawala), Nyaria	Haryana
395.	Dawari/Davari	Maha.
396.	Debgar	Gujarat
397.	Dehuri	Orissa
398.	Dekkani Muslim	TN
399.	Depala	Maha.
400.	Deshwali, Mewati (excluding Sironj Tehsil of Vidisha District)	MP
401.	Devadiga	Pondi.
402.	Devadigi	Kerala
403.	Devagudi Talayari	TN

404.	Devanga	A.P., Kerala, Maha.
405.	Devanga, Devangan	Pondi.
406.	Devanga, Devang, Koshti, Hutgar/ Hutkar, Jed, Lingayat Bilijedaru/Jeda, Winker, Juloha,Hutkar, Hatgar, Lingayat Hatgar	Karnataka
407.	Devangar, Sedar	TN
408.	Devdig	Maha.
409.	Devhar	Bihar
410.	Devli	Maha.
411.	Dhakad	Raj.
412.	Dhakhada	Orissa, Pondi.
413.	Dhamin	Bihar
414.	Dhaner	Orissa
415.	Dhangar	Goa, Daman & Diu
416.	Dhangar/Dhanwar, Ahir, Telwar, Hatkar, Tellari, Kannade, Kurmar, Sangar, Kokni-Dhangar	Maha.
417.	Dhanuk	Bihar, WB
418.	Dhanwar	Assam, Bihar
419.	Dhaukar	Bihar
420.	Dhaula or Soni, Sunar/Swarnkar	Pnb.
421.	Dheevara (Arya, Arayavathi, Mukkuvan, or Kukaya, Mogaveera, Valan, Bovi Mukayar, Nulayan, Valinijiar and Paniakkal)	Kerala
422.	Dhekaru	Bihar
423.	Dhemar or Dhimar or Dhiwar	H.P.
424.	Dhimal	WB
425.	Dhimar	Bihar
426.	Dhimar, Mallah, Kashyap-Rajpoot, Kahar, Jhinwar or Jhimar, Dhiwar, Khewar, Mehra, Nishad	Haryana,Pnb.

427.	Dhimar/Dhimer, Bhoi, Kahar, Kahra,Dhiwar, Mallah, Nawda, Navda, Turaha, Kewat (Rackwar, Raikwar), Kir (excluding Bhopal, Raisen and Sehor districts, Britiya/ Vritiya, Sondhiya	MP
428.	Dhimar, Dhinwar, Jhinwar, Kahar, Mallah	Chandi.
429.	Dhinwar or Jhinwar, Jheewar	H.P.
430.	Dhinwar, Jhinwar, Nishad, Kewat/ Mallah (excluding those in SCs), Kahar, Kashyap (non-Brahmin)	Delhi
431.	Dhivar, Kahar, Bhoi, Sagarvanshi-Mali, Keer, Kallah, Mehra	Raj.
432.	Dhivar, Dhiver	UP
433.	Dhobi	Gujarat, Haryana, Pnb., Chandi., D&NH,Daman &Diu,
434.	Dhobi (Muslim)	Bihar, MP
435.	Dhobi (other than those in SCs list)	Raj., UP
436.	Dhobi (other than those in SCs), Qassar	Delhi
437.	Dhobi (excluding Bhopal, Raisen and Sehore Districts) i.e. excluding the area where they are listed as SCs.	MP
438.	Dhobi, Rajak, Madval (excluding Christian Dhobi)	Goa
439.	Dholi	Karnataka, Maha.
440.	Dholi, Dafaali/Dufali, Gurav/Guraw	MP
441.	Dhor	Daman & Diu
442.	Dhosali, Dosal	H.P.

443.	Dhosali, Dosali	Haryana, Pnb., Chandi.
444.	Dhunia (Muslim)	Bihar, WB
445.	Dhunia, Pinjara, Kandera-Karan, Dhunnewala	Delhi
446.	Digwan, Jingar	Karnataka
447.	Divecha Koli	Gujarat
448.	Dobba Koravar (in Salem dist.)	TN
449.	Dobbai Koracha (in Tiruchirappally and Pudukottai dist.)	TN
450.	Dode Gujar, Dore Gujar	Maha.
451.	Dohar	UP
452.	Dombidasa	Karnataka
453.	Dommara	A.P., Pondi.
454.	Dommara (including Domb & Dommar)	TN
455.	Donga ur. Koracha	TN
456.	Doom (excluding those in SCs list)	J&K
457.	Dosadh, Dasad	Tripura
458.	Dovalkar	Pondi.
459.	Dudekula	TN
460.	Dudekula, Laddaf, Pinjari or Noorbash	A.P.
461.	Dudokula Pinjari	Pondi.
462.	Dudubi	Pondi.
463.	Dumala, dumal	Orissa
464.	Durgamurga, Burburcha	Karnataka
465.	Dusad	Assam
466.	Ediga, Gowda (Gammalla, Kalalee), Goundla, Settibalija (of Visakhapatnam, East Godavari, West Godavari and Krishna District)	A.P.
467.	Enadi	TN, Pondi.

468.	Eravaliar	Pondi.
469.	Eravallar (except Kanniyakumari dist. and Shencottah taluk of Tirunelveli dist. where the community is a ST)	TN
470.	Exhava (Exhuva, Ezhava illuvan)	Pondi.
471.	Exhuthachan	Pondi.
472.	Ezhava, Izhavan, Ishavan, Ezhavan, Ezhuva, Izhuva, Ishuva, Izhuvan, Ishuvan, Ezhuvan, Izhava, Izhavan, Ishavan, Illuva, Illuvan, Irava, Iruva, Thiyyan, Thiyya	Kerala
473.	Ezhavathi	Kerala
474.	Ezhavathy (in Kanniyakumari dist. and Sheoncottah taluk of Tirunelveli dist.)	TN
475.	Ezhuthachan	Kerala
476.	Ezhuthachar (in Kanniyakumari dist. and Sheoncottah taluk of Tirunelveli dist.)	TN
477.	Ezhuva (in Kanniyakumari dist. and Sheoncottah taluk of Tirunelveli dist.)	TN
478.	Fakir	Delhi
479.	Fakir/Faquir	Haryana. H.P., Chandi., Raj., UP
480.	Fakir/Faquir (Muslim)	Guj.
481.	Fakir Bhandarwala	Maha.
482.	Fakir, Sain	WB
483.	Fishermen including Gada Hanz	J&K
484.	Full-Mali, Baghban, Bagban, Bagwan	Karnataka
485.	Gaadla/Gandavars	Pondi.
486.	Gaalda Konkani	Pondi.
487.	Gabit, Gabbit, Gapit, Gaabit,	

	Daalija, Daavat	Karnataka
488.	Gadalia or Gadi-Luharia	Gujarat
489.	Gadaria	H.P., Maha., UP
490.	Gadaria, Pal	Haryana
491.	Gadaria/Gaddaria	Chandi.
492.	Gadaria, Gadheri, Gaddi, Garri	Delhi
493.	Gadaria (Gadri), Ghosi (Gvala), Gaddi	Raj.
494.	Gadariya, Dhangar, Kurmar, Hatgar, Hatkar, Haatkaar, Gaadri, Gadaria, Gari, Gayari	MP
495.	Gaddaria	Pnb.
496.	Gaddi	Bihar, H.P.
497.	Gaddi (Muslim)	MP
498.	Gaddi, Ghosi	UP
499.	Gadhai (Muslim)	Gujarat
500.	Gadhavi	Maha.
501.	Gadia-Lohar, Gadola	Raj.
502.	Gadri	Maha.
503.	Gajula Balija (who are traditionally associated with bangles)	A.P.
504.	Galiara (Muslim)	Gujarat
505.	Gamika	Kerala
506.	Ganagavar	TN
507.	Ganak in Districts of Cachar, Karimganj and Hailakandi	Assam
508.	Ganali or Gandali	Maha.
509.	Gonda	Assam
510.	Gandrab or Gandharb	Bihar
511.	Gandarvakottai Koravar (in Thanjavur, Tiruchira-Pally Pudukottai	

	and South Arcot dist.)	TN
512.	Gandharap	Maha.
513.	Gandla	Pondi.
514.	Gandla, Telikula, Devathilakula	A.P.
515.	Gangai (Ganesh)	Bihar
516.	Gangakula, Gangemakkalu, Ganga-matha, Gangaputra, Gowrimatha, Ambig, Ambiga, Bestha, Kabbaliga, Kabbili, Kabber, Kabbera, Kharvi, Bhoi, Bhoyi, Boyi, Thoreya, Harakanthra, Hariakanthra, Kahar, Meenagar, Mogaveera, Kharia, Sunnagar, Siviyar, Parivara, Galadakonkani	Karnataka
517.	Gangavars	Pondi.
518.	Gangiredlavaru	A.P.
519.	Gangota, Ganghth	Bihar
520.	Ganiga, Lingayat Ganiga/Ganigar, Lingayat Sajjan/Sajjanaganigar, Teli, Gandla	Karnataka
521.	Ganika (including Nagavamasam)	Pondi.
522.	Ganjam Reddi (in Malabar district referred to in sub-section (2) of section (5) of the Stated Reorganisation Act, 1956)	Kerala
523.	Gara	Tripura
524.	Gareri	Tripura
525.	Garhi-Lohar	Haryana
526.	Garpagari, Joginath, Nathjogi	MP
527.	Garpagri	Maha.
528.	Garudi/Gavadi, Ghisadi	Maha.
529.	Gatti	Kerala, Pondi.
530.	Gatti/Gattiyavaru	Karnataka
531.	Gavandi	Maha.

532.	Gavara	A.P., Pondi.
533.	Gavara, Gavarai (Kavarai) and Vadugar (Vaduvar) (other than Kamma, Kapu, Balija and Reddi)	TN
534.	Gawala, Gowala	Pnb.
535.	Gawala, Gowala, Ahir/Yadav	Haryana
536.	Gawala/Gwala/Gowala/Gowale/ Gawla	Chandi.
537.	Gawaria, Gauria, Gwar	H.P., Pnb.
538.	Gawda	Goa
539.	Gazula balija, Gazulasetti (Gajula)	Pondi.
540.	Geudus Bato, Bhirithya, Dodho-kouria, Hato, Jatako and Joria	Pondi.
541.	Ghadi	Karnataka
542.	Ghadshi, Ghadsi	Karnataka
543.	Ghadshi	Maha.
544.	Ghai	H.P.
545.	Ghanchi	Raj.
546.	Ghanchi (Muslim), Teli, Modh Ghanchi, Teli Sahu, Teli Rathod	Gujarat
547.	Ghansi	Assam
548.	Ghasi, Ghasiara or Ghosi	Haryana,Pnb.
549.	Ghasi, Ghasiara or Ghosia	H.P.
550.	Ghasiara, Ghosi	Delhi, Chandi.
551.	Ghatowar	Assam
552.	Ghatwar	Bihar, Orissa
553.	Ghedia Koli	Gujarat
554.	Ghirath or Ghidath	Haryana
555.	Ghirath including Chang and Hhati	H.P., Pnb. Chandi.
556.	Ghisadi	Karnataka
557.	Ghisadi Lohar, Gadi Lohar, Ghitodi Lohar, Rajput Lohar	Maha.

558.	Ghosh, Gop, Gowala, Gawala, Goal, Goala	Assam
559.	Ghoshi	MP
560.	Giddidki, Pingle, Pingale	Karnataka
561.	Girgiris	Orissa
562.	Giri	Tripura, UP
563.	Giri, Gosain (Gushain)	Raj.
564.	Goala, Gope (Pallav Gope, Ballav Gope, Gope, Ahir and Yadav)	WB
565.	Goala, Gope, Yadav, Aheer	Tripura
566.	Gobba	Pondi.
567.	Gochaki	Maha.
568.	Godaba	A.P., Pondi.
569.	Godda	Orissa
570.	Goddi	Daman & Diu
571.	Godi (Chhava)	Bihar
572.	Gola, golla, Gope/Gop, Sadgope/ Sadgop, Ahir, Gour, Gouda, Goudo, Mekala Golla, Punnu Golla, Yadav, Gopal/Gopala, Sholakhandia, Magadha Goudia, Laxminarayan Gola and Gouda Gola	Orissa
573.	Gola Rana	Gujarat
574.	Golla, Gollewar, Goler, Golkar	Maha.
575.	Golla, Gouli, Lingayat Gowli/ Gauli/Kawadiga, Gopal, Yadav, Asthana Golla, Yadava, Adavi Golla, Gopala, Gopali	Karnataka
576.	Gond	Assam
577.	Gonda	Assam
578.	Gondali, Ghondali, Gondaliga, Gondhali, Gondhalli	Karnataka
579.	Gondhali	Maha.

580.	Gondi, Modya Gond and Rajo Gonda	Pondi.
581.	Gondu-Bato, Bhirthya, Budho Kouriya, Hato, Jatako, Joria	Orissa
582.	Goniga, Sadu Setty, Sadhu Chetty, Sadhu Setty, Sadhu Chetty, Sadhu Shetty, Teluga Chetty, Teluga Chettiar, Telugu Shetty, Sadhu Setty, Sadhu Chetty, Sadhu Shetty, Telugu Chetty, Telugu Chettiar, Telungupati Chetty, Telungu Chettiar, 24 Mane Telugu Shetty, 24 Mane Telugu Chetty, 24 Mane Telugu Chettiar, 24 Manai Telugu Chetty, 24 Manai Telugu Chettiar, Salaparu, Sanaparu, Snapar, Salapar, Janapar, Janapan, Janapachetty, Janapashetty, Janapasetty, Gonichetty, Gonigamane	Karnataka
583.	Goojar/Gurjar	MP
584.	Gopal, Gopal Bhorpi, Khelkari	Maha.
585.	Gorait	Assam
586.	Gorh, Gourh (onlu in the district of Saran & Rohtas)	Bihar
587.	Gorkha	Haryana, H.P., Pnb.
588.	Gosangi	Orissa
589.	Gosavi	Goa, Daman & Diu
590.	Gosavi, Bava, Bairagi, Bharati, Girigosavi, Bharati Gosavi, Saraswati Parbat, Sagar, Ban cr Van, Teerth Ashram	Maha.
591.	Gosavi, Gosayi, Gosain. Atit	Karnataka
592.	Gossain	UP
593.	Goud	Bihar

594.	Gound or Gowdi, Machhus, Pal, Paiko Patra or Patara, Sundi or Telli, Tanti, Yeranagollas, Oriya Or Veddy Samantho, Oriya Backward Classes Badhai, Bhokta, Darji, Gour	Pondi.
595.	Gounder	TN
596.	Gowala, Gwala	H.P.
597.	Gowda	Kerala
598.	Gowda, Gouda (including Gamalla or Kalali)	Pondi.
599.	Gowda (including Gammala, Kalali and Anuppa Gounder)	TN
600.	Gowli	Maha.
601.	Gramini	Haryana
602.	Grammani, Shanan, Nadar	Pondi.
603.	Grati (Rural only)	J&K
604.	Guada	Daman & Diu
605.	Gudala	A.P.
606.	Gudia, or Guria, Gurja, Gunju	Orissa
607.	Gudigara	Karnataka, Pondi.
608.	Gujar	UP
609.	Gujar, Gurjar	Delhi, Raj.
610.	Gujar, Guzar	Karnataka
611.	Gujjar	Haryana, Pnb., Chandi.
612.	Gujjar or Gujar (in merged areas only)	H.P.
613.	Gujrath Baori	Maha.
614.	Gulgaliya	Bihar
615.	Gurav, Lingayat Gurav, Gurov, Tambli,Tamballa, Gurava, Gurou	Karnataka
616.	Gurung	Sikkim

617.	Guruv/Gurav	Maha.
618.	Gusai/Gosai/Gosan, Gosaib	MP
619.	Gutgudi	Maha.
620.	Gutgudi	Maha.
621.	Gwaria, Gauria or Gwar	Haryana, Chandi.
622.	Habra	Orissa
623.	Hajam	H.P.
624.	Hajjam, Nai, Sain, Salmani	Haryana
625.	Hajjam/Hazam, Nai	Chandi.
626.	Hajjam (Barber), Nai (Barber), Salmani (all Muslim)	MP
627.	Hajjam, Naik	Pnb.
628.	Hajjam (Nai), Salmani, Nai, Sain (Nai)	UP
629.	Halalkhor, Hela, Lalbegi (other than those in SCs list)	UP
630.	Halapaik	Maha.
631.	Halawakki-Wakkal, Vakkal, Gram Vakkal, Gam Gowda, Gam Gawada, Gavada, Karevakkal, Kunchavakkal, Attevakkal, Shilwakkal, Halakkivakkal	Karnataka
632.	Hawari, dhobi (other than those included in SCs List)	WB
633.	Halwai	UP
634.	Hanabaru, Krishna Golla, Anubaru, Atanabaru, Hanbar, Hanabar	Karnataka
635.	Handervut	Karnataka
636.	Handevazir	Karnataka
637.	Hansi, Tanti, Sukuli, Vina, Tulabhina, Rangani, Dera, Dewanga, Kosta, Salia, Patsalia, Buna, Bunkar/Bunkara, Bangali Tanti/Bangiya Tanti, Matibansa	

	Tanti, Asina Tanti, Aswina Tanti, Ashani Tanti, Aswinna Tanti	Orissa
638.	Haranshikari, Chigaribetegar, Vaghri, Wagiri, Nirshikari, Bagri, Baori, Phasachari, Vagri	Karnataka
639.	Hari	Assam
640.	Hatkar	A.P.
641.	Hatkar/Hatker	Maha.
642.	Hatua	Orissa
643.	Hdiga (including Settibalijas of East and West Godavari dists.)	Pondi.
644.	Hegde	Kerala, TN, Pondi.
645.	Hela (Muslim)	MP
646.	Hela/Halia/Chasi-Kiaibartta, Das Kaibartta	W.B.
647.	Hela, Janwa, Sirvi	Raj.
648.	Helava, Holeva	Karnataka
649.	Helva	Pondi.
650.	Helve, Hilav	Maha.
651.	Hingora (Muslim)	Gujarat
652.	Holeya	Orissa
653.	Holra	Assam
654.	Honniyarq	Karnataka
655.	Hoovadiga, Hugar, Hoogar, Lingayat Hugar/ Hoogara, Hoogaran Maalgar, Lingayat Malgar, Mali, Phoolmali, Phulmali, Phulari, Phoolari, Jeer, Lingayat Jeer	Karnataka
656.	Howgar, Hawgar, Hawadiga	Karnataka
657.	Idaisi or Darzi (Muslim)	Bihar
658.	Idiga	TN

659.	Idiga (including Sett Balija)	Pondi.
660.	Idiga, Ediga, Eliga, Higa, Halepaik, Billava, Devar, Malayali Billava, Deevar, Devaramakkalu, Namdhari, Kalal Goundla, Goondla, Thiyan Tiyan, Ezhava, Thiyya	Karnataka
661.	Illathu Pillaimar, Illuvar, Ezhuvar and Illathar	TN
662.	Illuvan (Ezhvan)	Pondi.
663.	Inji Koravar (in Thanjavur, Tiruchirapally and Pudukottai dist.)	TN
664.	Irula	Orissa
665.	Irulas	Pondi.
666.	Isai Vellalar or Melakarar	Pondi.
667.	Isaivellalar	TN
668.	Izhuvan (Illuvan or Ezhuvan)	Kerala
669.	Jadapus	Orissa, Pondi.
670.	Jagiasi	Maha.
671.	Jaintrapans	Orissa
672.	Jaiswar	Haryana
673.	Jajak	Maha.
674.	Jakkala	A.P.
675.	Jakkulas	Pondi.
676.	Jalarlu	Pondi.
677.	Jambuvandondai	Pondi.
678.	Jambuvanodai, Vankodai	TN
679.	Jandara	Pondi.
680.	Jangam	Maha., TN, Pondi.
681.	Jangam (whose traditional occupation is begging)	AP
682.	Jangama	TN
683.	Jangam whose traditional occupation is begging	A.P.

684.	Jansali, Sivania, Myangar, Jingar, Dasania, Chamadia, Bharatbhara, Chandlia, Sonari, Aaribharatbhara	Gujarat
685.	Jat (Muslim)	Gujarat
686.	Jat (except in Bharatpur and Dhaulpaur Dists.)	Rajasthan
687.	Jatigar	Maha.
688.	Jatiya	Maha.
689.	Javeri	Maha.
690.	Javeri, Jawari	Karnataka
691.	Jetty	Pondi.
692.	Jhadi	Maha.
693.	Jhangra Brhaman, Khati, Lohar, Ramgharia, Turkhan	Punjab
694.	Jhangra-Brahman or Jangra-Brahman or Jangid Brahman, Khati, Ramgarhia, Suthar, Dhiman, Tarkhan, Barhai, Baddi	Haryana
695.	Jhangra-Brahman/Jhangara-Brahman/Jangra-Brahman, Khati	Chandi
696.	Jhara	Tripura
697.	Jheewar	J&K
698.	Jhetty	TN
699.	Jhoja	UP
700.	Jingar	A.P., Maha.
701.	Jogi	A.P., Kerala, Maha. Sikkim, UP, WB, Pondi.
702.	Jogi (including Jogis)	TN
703.	Jogi, Goswami	Delhi
704.	Jogi, Joger, Sanjogi, Jogar	Karnataka
705.	Jogi (Jugi)	Bihar
706.	Jogi, or Yogi	Orissa

707.	Jogi, Nath, Jangam-Jogi	Haryana, Pnb., Chandi., Raj.
708.	Jogin	Maha.
709.	Johari	Karnataka, Maha.
710.	Jolah (Ansari Momin)	WB
711.	Jolha	Assam
712.	Joshi, Budbudki, Damruwale, Sahedev Joshi, Sarvade, Saroda	Maha.
713.	Joshinandiwala, Odde, Oddilu, Vaddi, Vaddelu	A.P.
714.	Julaha (excluding those in SCs)	Delhi
715.	Julaha (Hindu & Muslim), Kachhi, Kachhi Kushwaha, Kachhi-Shakya	Rajasthan
716.	Julaha, Momin, Julaha-Ansari, Momin-Ansari	Maha.
717.	Julaha-Momin, Julaha-Ansari, Momin-Ansari	MP
718.	Julaha, Ansari (other than those in SC list)	H.P.
719.	Julaya, Garana, Taria, Tari and Ansari (All Muslim)	Gujarat
720.	Jullaha/Julaha (Weavers) (excluding those in SCs)	Chandi
721.	Jullaha including Kabir Panthi Julaha (excluding those in SCs)	H.P., Pnb.
722.	Jyotish	Orissa
723.	Kabbara	Pondi.
724.	Kabbera	TN
725.	Kachhi (Kushwaha/Koshwaha Maurya), Koyari/ Koiri (Kushwaha), Shakya, Murai, Panara/Panahara, Sonkar	MP

726.	Kachhi, Kachhi-Kushwaha, Shakya	UP
727.	Kachhi, Kachhi Shakya, Kachhi Maurya, Kachhi Kushawaha	Pnb.
728.	Kachhi, Koeri, Murai, Murao Kadar	Delhi
729.	Kachhia, Kachhi, Kachhi-Kushwaha, Koiri	Maurya-Gujarat
730.	Kachi	A.P.
731.	Kachi, Kachhi, Kachhia	Maha.
732.	Kachora	Maha.
733.	Kadaiyan	Pondi.
734.	Kadan	Orissa, Pondi.
735.	Kadar	Bihar
736.	Kadera	Maha.
737.	Kadere/Kadore, Dhunkar, Dhuniya, Dhanka Kodar	MP
738.	Kadu Konkani	Karnataka
739.	Kaduppattan	Kerala, Pondi.
740.	Kagzi	Bihar
741.	Kahar	H.P., WB
742.	Kahar, Tanwar Singhariya	UP
743.	Kahari, Kumbhar,	D&NH
744.	Kaikadi	A.P., Gujarat
745.	Kaikadi (in Mumbai, Thana, Kolaba, Ratnagiri, Nashik, Dhule, Jalgaon, Pune, Ahmednagar, Satara, Sangli, Kolhapur, Sholapur, Aurangabad, Nanded Districts and Rajura (Tehsil of ChandrapurDistrict) Dhontle, Korva, Makadwale or Kochi Korva, Pamlor, Korvi) (throughout the State)	Maharashtra
746.	Kaikolan	Kerala
747.	Kaikolan or Kaikola (Sengunthar. Sengundar)	Pondi.

748.	Kaikolan, Kaikolar, Sengunthar	TN
749.	Kaivartta/Kaibartta	Bihar
750.	Kala Koravar (in Thanjavur, Tiruchirapally and Pudukottai dist.)	TN
751.	Kaladi	TN
752.	Kalahandi	Assam
753.	Kalaigar (Muslim)	MP
754.	Kalaikar	Goa
755.	Kalal	Gujarat
756.	Kalal (Tak)	Raj.
757.	Kalal, Kalar, Sav Kalar	Maha.
758.	Kalandi Baishanaba/Kalandi Vaishnab	Orissa
759.	Kalal, Kalar, Kalwar	UP
760.	Kalari Kurup or Kalari Panicker	Kerala
761.	Kalari Kurup including Kalari Panicker (in Kanniyakumari Dist. and Sheoncottah taluk of Tirunelveli dist.)	TN
762.	Kalandar	Bihar
763.	Kalanga	Orissa
764.	Kalanji/Kalinji/Kalingi	Orissa
765.	Kalar, Kalal	MP
766.	Kalarikurups (Kairal Panicker)	Pondi.
767.	Kalavanthula	Pondi.
768.	Kalbi	Raj.
769.	Kalihandi	Assam
770.	Kalingi	TN, Pondi.
771.	Kalinji Dabikoravar (in Thanjavur and Pudukottai dist.)	TN
772.	Kalkari, Kelkari, Khelkari	Karnataka
773.	Kalladi	Orissa
774.	Kallan	Pondi.

775.	Kallan Mooppan or Kallan Mooppar	Kerala
776.	Kallar	Pondi.
777.	Kallar (including Esanattu Kallar, Gandarvakottai Kallar, Koottappal Kallar, Pirampati Kallar and Periasooriyar Kallar)	TN
778.	Kallar Kula Thondaman	TN
779.	Kalota/Kolta/Koltta	MP
780.	Kalveli Gounder	TN
781.	Kalwar	Delhi, Orissa, West Bengal
782.	Kalwar, Kalal, Eraqui	Bihar
783.	Kamalas (Viswakarmula)	Pondicherry
784.	Kamali	Assam
785.	Kamabhakthula	A.P.
786.	Kamar (Lohar, Karmakar, Visvakarma)	Bihar
787.	Kamati	Maharashtra
788.	Kamati, Kaman	Karnataka
789.	Kambedia Bhagat	Gujarat
790.	Kambar	TN
791.	Kamboj	Haryana, Pnb., Chandi.
792.	Kammalan (Kamsala, Viswabrahmin and Viswakarma, Thattar, Por Kollar, Thachar,Kalthachar, Kollar, Karumar, Karuvan)	Pondicherry
793.	Kammalar or, Viswakarama, (including Thattar, Porkollar, Kannar Karumar Kollar, Thacher, Kalthacher Kamsala and Viswabrahmin	TN
794.	Kammara (excluding Malabar dist. as referred to in sub-section (2) of	

	section 5 of the State Reorganisation Act, 1956)	Kerala
795.	Kammara, Kamara, Kamar, Kammaro, Muli, Lohuru, Loharo	Orissa
796.	Kammi	Maharashtra
797.	Kanakkan	Orissa
798.	Kanate	Karnataka
799.	Kanbi	Rajasthan
800.	Kanbi, Kulwadi, Kunbi	Karnataka
801.	Kandarpa	Orissa
802.	Kandera, Pinjara, Mansoori	Rajasthan
803.	Kandh	Tripura
804.	Kandra	A.P., Pondi.
805.	Kangasia	Gujarat
806.	Kanghera	H.P.
807.	Kani, Kanian or Kaniyan, and, Kanisu or Kaniyar Panikkar, Ganka, Kanisy	Pondicherry
808.	Kani, Kanisu, Kaniyar Panikkar	TN
809.	Kanisan, Kaniyar, Kaniyaur, Kaniya, Kaniyan, (other than Kollegal Taluqa of Mysore District), Kanyan, Balyaya	Karnataka
810.	Kanisu or Kaniyar Panicker, Kani or Kaniyan (Ganaka) or Kanisan or Kamnan	Kerala
811.	Kanjar	Orissa
812.	Kanjar or Kanchan	Haryana, H.P., Pnb. Chandi.
813.	Kanjara-Bhata	A.P.
814.	Kanjari, Kanjar, Kanjir	Karnataka
815.	Kanjirbhat, Khanjarbhat, Kanjirbhaat	Karnataka

816.	Kannada Saineegar, Kannadiyar and Dasapalanjika (Coimbatore, Periyar and Nilgiris Dist.)	TN
817.	Kannadiyan	Kerala
818.	Kansari	WB
819.	Kanu	Bihar
820.	Kapadi	D&NH
821.	Kapadia	Bihar
822.	Kapali	Tripura, WB
823.	Kapdi	Maharashtra
824.	Kapudia	Orissa
825.	Karani	WB
826.	Karhara/Kachara/Kachera	Orissa
827.	Karikalabhakthulu, Kaikolan or Kaikola (Sengundam or Sengunther)	A.P.
828.	Karikudumbi	Karnataka
829.	Karimpalan	Orissa
830.	Karmakar	WB
831.	Karmakar, Kamar	Tripura
832.	Karmali	Assam, Orissa
833.	Karmariya	MP
834.	Karuneegar (Seer Karuneegur, Sri Karuneegar, Sarattu Karunageer, Kekatti Karunageer, Nathu	TN
835.	Vijhi Kankar, Sozhi Kankar and Sunnanbbhu Karuneegar)	
836.	Karuva	Karnataka
837.	Kasab (Kasai) (Muslim)	Bihar
838.	Kasabi/Kisbi	MP
839.	Kasgar	UP
840.	Kasai	Raj.
841.	Kasai-Quraishi	WB

842.	Kasai, Katik, Khatik, Katuka, Katuga, Kasab, Aray	Karnataka
843.	Kasai, Qassab, Quraishi	Delhi
844.	Kasai, Kasab, Kassab, Quasab, Qassab, Qassab-Qureshi (all Muslim)	MP
845.	Kasar	Daman & Diu
846.	Kasar (sub-castes Kanchar, Kanchari)	Maharashtra
847.	Kasar, Kansar, Kanchori, Kanchera, Kanchugara, Bogar	Karnataka
848.	Kasbi	Maharashtra
849.	Kasbin	Karnataka
850.	Kasera, Tamera, Thathiar	Delhi
851.	Kasera, Thathera, Tamrakar, Kalaikar	UP
852.	Kashan	Assam
853.	Kashikapdi, Kashikapadi, Tirumali	Karnataka
854.	Kasikapadi	Maharashtra
855.	Kasikapadi	A.P.
856.	Katabu	Maharashtra
857.	Katabu, Katabar	Karnataka
858.	Katesar, Pattamkatti	TN
859.	Kathar (Kathar Wani, Kanthahar Wani) (Lingayat Wani or Ladwani excluded)	Maharashtra
860.	Kathi	Gujarat, Maha.
861.	Katipapala	A.P.
862.	Kattunayakan	Orissa
863.	Kaumbhakar, Kumar	Tripura
864.	Kaura	Bihar
865.	Kavadi	Karnataka
866.	Kavudiyaru	Kerala

867.	Kavuthiyan	Pondi.
868.	Kavuthiyan, Authon	Kerala
869.	Kavutiyan	Karnataka
870.	Kawar	Assam, Bihar
871.	Kelasi	Pondi.
872.	Keori/Koiri	WB
873.	Keot	Assam
874.	Kepmari or Reddika	AP
875.	Kepmari (in Chengalpattu, Pudukottai and Tiruchirapally dists.)	TN
876.	Kerala Mudali	Kerala, TN
877.	Kerala Mudali, Kerala Muthali	Pondi.
878.	Kewat, Keot	Bihar
879.	Kewat or Mallah	UP
880.	Kepmare or Reddika	A.P.
881.	Keshap Rajput	H.P.
882.	Khadwar (only in the district of Sivan and Rohtas)	Bihar
883.	Khaira	Orissa
884.	Khandnals	Orissa
885.	Khangar	Bihar
886.	Khanghera	Haryana, Pnb., Chandi.
887.	Khant	Gujarat
888.	Kharia	Assam
889.	Kharol	MP, Raj.
890.	Kharvi	TN, Pondi.
891.	Kharwa-Bhadela	Gujarat
892.	Khati	Maharashtra
893.	Khati-Khatti	Orissa
894.	Khatiya, Khati	MP

895.	Khatbune	Delhi
896.	Khatik	Bihar, Gujarat
897.	Khatik (other than those in SCs list)	Delhi
898	Khatik (other than those in SC list) Kasai, Kasab, Kasai-Qureshi	
899.	Khatki or Kasai, Chamadia Khatki, Halari Khatki (all Muslim)	Gujarat
900.	Khatri	TN
901.	Khattis-Khatti, Kammarao, Lohara	Pondi.
902.	Khatua	Orissa
903.	Khatwa	Bihar
904.	Khatwe	Bihar
905.	Khelta	Bihar
906.	Kherwar	Assam
907.	Khetauri	Orissa
908.	Khetauri Khataur	Bihar
909.	Khodal	Assam
910.	Khodra, Khadura, Kharuda	Orissa
911.	Khond	Assam
912.	Khonyor	Assam
913.	Khristi, Gujarati-Christian (converts from SCs only)	Gujarat
914.	Khumra, Sangtarash, Hansiri	UP
915.	Kichagara	Karnataka
916.	Kinthala Kalinga, Buragam (Kalinga, Buragam Kalinga, Pandiri Kalinga)	A.P.
917.	Kirar, Kirad	Raj.
918.	Kirar, Kirad, Dhakar/Dhakad	MP
919.	Kisan	UP
920.	Kitara	Pondi.
921.	Kochh	Bihar
922.	Koda, Kuda	Orissa

923.	Kodu	Pondi.
924.	Koeri, Koiri	UP
925.	Kohdala	Pondi.
926.	Kohli (this does not cover members of the Khatri caste/community who originally belong to the Punjab and use Kohli as a title/surname)	Maharashtra
927.	Kohor	Assam
928.	Koilar	Orissa
929.	Koiri	Assam, Tripura
930.	Kol	Assam
931.	Kolaga (Misal)	D&NH
932.	Kolam	Orissa
933.	Kolarios or Munivanies	Pondi.
934.	Kolasi (Kalasi Panicker)	Kerala
935.	Kolayan Urali	Karnataka
936.	Kolhati, Dombari	Maharashtra
937.	Kolhati, Kolhatigi	Karnataka
938.	Koli Daman & Diu	D&NH,
939.	Koli, Kharvi (including Christian Kharvi)	Goa
940.	Koli, Christian Koli, Chumble, Gabit, Kharwa or Kharwi, Machhimar Koli, Mangela/Mangala, Panbhare (Panbhari), Son Koli, Koli Suryavamshi, Vaiti, Ahir Koli, Pan Koli, bari	Maha.
941.	Koli, Idaria Koli, Kharwa-Koli, Rathwa-Koli, Bariat-Koli, Bhebaria-Koli	Gujarat
942.	Kolla, Kollala	Karnataka
943.	Kolyiri, Koleri, Kolari	Karnataka
944.	Kommar	Pondi.
945.	Kond (Kul)	Orissa

946.	Konda Kapu	Orissa
947.	Kondareddy, Reddy Dhakas	Orissa
948.	Kondpan	Assam
949.	Kongari	Maharashtra
950.	Kongu Navithan	Kerala
951.	Kongu Vallalar (including Vallala Gounder &	TN
952.	Kopplavalam	Pondi.
953.	Koppulavelama	A.P., TN
954.	Koppula Vellama	Orissa
955.	Koracha	TN, Pondi.
956.	Koraga	Orissa
957.	Koravar (in Chengalpattu, Ramanathapuram, Kamarajar, Pasumpen, Mutouramalingam,Pudukottai, Thanjavur, Tiruchirappalli, Tirunelveli, Madras, Madurai and the Nilgiris districts)	TN
958.	Korcha, Koracha	A.P.
959.	Korchar	Maharashtra
960.	Korku	Bihar
961.	Kormakar	Assam
962.	Korwa	Assam
963.	Korwar, Korwari, Kaikadi, Koragar, Yerkala, Erakala, Kunchi, Korva, Koramasetty, Yerykala	Karnataka
964.	Kosalya Goudus, Bosotheriya Goudus, Chiti Goudus, Dangayath Goudus, Doddu Kamariya, Dudu Kamaro, Ladiya Goudus, Pullo Soriya Goudus	Orissa, Pondi.
965.	Kosavans, Kuyayar	Pondi.
966.	Kosta, Koshta	Bihar
967.	Koshta/Kosta, Kosti/Koshti, Devaugan, Dewang, Salwidewang, Mala, Padamhali,	

	Pademsali, Sali,Sutsali, Salwar/Salewar, Jendra/Jandra, Koskati, Garhwal, Garhewal, Garewar, Garwal	MP
968.	Koshta/Koshti	UP
969.	Koshti	A.P., Gujarat, Maharashtra
970.	Koskanti Devanga	Maha.
971.	Kota	Orissa
972.	Kotari, Kottari, Kotary, Kottary	Karnataka
973.	Kotayar(Shoragit a Kshatriya)	Pondi.
974.	Kotekshatriya, Rama Kshatriya, Ramaraja Kshatriya, Servagara (South Serugara (North Kanara),	Karnataka Kanara),
	Koteyar, Kotegara, Kotegar(other than those in SCs list), Kotekar	MP
975.	Koteyar	Kerala, TN
976.	Kotwal	Assam
977.	Kotwar/Kutwar, Kotwar (excluding Bhind, Dhar, Dewas, Guna, Gwalior, Indore, Jhabua, Khargone,Mandsaur, Morena, Raigarh, Ratlam, Shajapur, Shivpuri, Ujjain, and Vidisha districts)	MP
978.	Koya	Assam
979.	Koyava	Karnataka
980.	Krishnabalija (Dasari, Bukka, Bukka Ayavar)	A.P.
981.	Krishnanvaka	Kerala, Pondi.
982.	Krishnavaka (in Kanniyakumari district and Shencottah taluk of Tirunelveli dist.)	TN
983.	Kurba (except in Coorg district), Kurub, Kurab, Kuraban, Kurumban, Kurumba, Lingayat Kuruba/Kurubaru, Halumatha, Dhangar, Bharwad, Gorava	Karnataka
984.	Kuchband	Haryana, Pnb.

985.	Kuchbandh	Maharashtra, Chandi.
986.	Kuchhria	Maha.
987.	Kudiya	Orissa
988.	Kudubi	Karnataka, Orissa
989.	Kudumban	Orissa
990.	Kudumbi	Kerala, Pondi.
981.	Kudumbi (in Kanniyakumari district and Shencottah taluk of Tirunelveli dist.)	TN
992.	Kuga Vallalar	TN
993.	Kulahia	Bihar
994.	Kulala (including Kuyavar, Kumbarar and Velar)	TN
995.	Kulavadi (Sudra) Marati (belonging to Uttar Kannada District)	Karnataka
996.	Kulela, Kulala, Kummari	Pondi.
997.	Kulfaqir	J&K
998.	Kulta	Orissa
999.	Kumar, Rudra Paul of district of Cachar, Karimganj and Hailakandi)	Assam
1000.	Kumar/Kurami/Kurmi, Kunbi, Kurmi (Patidar, Kulami, Kulmi, Kulambi, Gavel/Gabhel)	MP
1001.	Kumara Panth, Komarpant, Komarpaik	Karnataka
1002.	Kumbaran	Pondi.
1003.	Kumbhakar	WB
1004.	Kumbri Maratha (belonging to Uttra Kannada District)	Karnataka
1005.	Kumhar/Kumahar	Chandi.
1006.	Kumarbhag Pahadia	Bihar
1007.	Kumbaran	Kerala

1008.	Kumbhar	Goa
1009.	Kumbhar/Kumar	Maharashtra
1010.	Kumbhar Kulal, Kumhar, Kumbharo, Kandha-Kumbhar	Orissa
1011.	Kumbhar (Prajapati), Kumawat	Raj.
1012.	Kumbhar (Prajapati, Varia)	Gujarat
1013.	Kumhar, Prajapati	Delhi, Pnb., UP
1014.	Kumhar (Prajapati), Kumbhar (excluding Chhatarpur Datia, Panna, Tikamgarh, Satna, Rewa, Sidhi, and Shahdol districts)	MP
1015.	Kumbara, Kummara, Khummara, Kumbhar, Khumbhar, Lingayat Kumbar/Kumbara, Kusavan, Kulala, Kulalar, Moolya	Karnataka
1016.	Kumhar	Assam
1017.	Kumhar, Kumahar (village potters)	J&K
1018.	Kummara or Kulala or Salivahana	A.P.
1019.	Kunapuli	A.P.
1020.	Kunbi	Goa, Daman & Diu
1021.	Kunbi (sub-castes; Lewa Kunbi, Lewa-Patil, Lewa Patidar)	Maharashtra
1022.	Kunchidigar	TN
1023.	Kundamatia	Orissa
1024.	Kunjara, Raine (Muslim)	MP
1025.	Kunjra or Rayeen	UP
1026.	Kunnuvar Mannadi	TN, Pondi.
1027.	Kupadhar, Kushiari, Parh	Assam
1028.	Kuraiar	Orissa
1029.	Kurakula	A.P.
1030.	Kuravan	Orissa

1031.	Kurhini Chetty	TN
1032.	Kurhinshetty	Maharashtra
1033.	Kuri	Tripura
1034.	Kurichchan	Orissa
1035.	Kurma, Kurmi	Karnataka
1036.	Kurmar	Maharashtra
1037.	Kurmi	Assam, Delhi, Haryana, H.P. Chandi., Tripura, UP, WB
1038.	Kurmi, Kahar, Jhidwar or Jhinwar, Dhinwar, Dhiwar	Pnb.
1039.	Kurmi, Kurma Chasa, Kudumi, Kuduma, Kurma, Kurmi Mahto, Kurmi Khetriya, Kurumi, Kudumi Kshyatriya	Orissa
1040.	Kurmi (Mahto) Kurmi (Mahto) (in Chhotanagpur Division only)	Bihar
1041.	Kuruba or Kuruma	A.P.
1042.	Kuruman (Kurumba)	Orissa
1043.	Kurumba (where they are not STs)	TN
1044.	Kurumba, Kuruba, Kurubar, Kuruva	Pondi.
1045.	Kusavan	Pondi.
1046.	Kushwaha (Koeri)	Bihar
1047.	Kusivan (Kulala, Kulala Nair or Andhra Nair or Anthura Nair)	Kerala
1048.	Kuthaliya Bora (belonging to Almora, Pithoragarh, Bageswar and Nainital dists.)	UP
1049.	Kutuna	Karnataka
1050.	Labana	H.P.
1051.	Labana or Lobana	Haryana

1052.	Labana or Lavana	Pnb.
1053.	Labana, Mehravat, Goti, Hadkashi, Zod, Dhinga	Gujarat
1054.	Labana, Vanzara	Chandi.
1055.	Labbai	Pondi.
1056.	Labbai, Rowthar and Marakayar (where their spoken language is Tamil or Urdu)	TN
1057.	Labha	Maharashtra
1058.	Ladaff, Laddaf	Maharashtra
1059.	Ladar, Lad, Ladaru Yelagar	Karnataka
1060.	Ladia, Ladhia, Lari/Laria	Maharashtra
1061.	Lakhra	Orissa
1062.	Lambadi	Orissa, Pondi.
1063.	Lingayat Banagar Pelya, Shathai, Baman	Karnataka
1064.	Lahar	Assam
1065.	Laheri	Bihar
1066.	Lakhara/Lakhwara/Laxkar	Gujarat
1067.	Lakhera/Lakher, Kachera/Kacher	MP
1068.	Lakhera	Maharashtra
1069.	Lakhera/Laahera	W.B.
1070.	Lakhera, Manihar	Delhi, Haryana, Chandi.
1071.	Lakhera (Lakhara), Manihar	Raj.
1072.	Lambadi	TN
1073.	Lanzad	Maharashtra
1074.	Latin Catholic	Kerala
1075.	Latin Catholic (Kanniyakumari dist. and Shencottah taluk of Tirunelveli dist.)	TN

1076.	Limboo (including Tsong, Subbha, and Yakthungba	Sikkim
1077.	Lodh, Lodha	Haryana
1078.	Lodh, Lodha, Lodhi	A.P., MP, Raj.
1079.	Lodh, Lodha, Lodhi, Lodhi-Rajput	UP
1080.	Lodha	Assam, Gujarat
1081.	Lodhi	Assam
1082.	Lodhi, Lodha, Lodh, Maha-Lodh	Delhi
1083.	Lohar	Maharashtra, Tripura
1084.	Lohar or Luhar, Saifi, Panchal	Haryana, UP
1085.	Lohar, Luhar, Lohpita, Gadoley, Gadela, Lohpata, Lohpeta, Vishwakarma	MP
1086.	Lohar, Panchal	Raj.
1087	Lohar, Tarkhan	J & K
1088.	Lonari	Karnataka, Maharashtra
1089.	Loniya/Luniya/Lonia/Lunia, Odh, Odhe, Odhiya, Ode, Odiya, Naaniya, Muraha, Muraaha,Mudaha, Mudaaha, Nunia, Nonia	MP
1090.	Lonia, Noniya, Luniya, Gole Thakur, Nunere	UP
1091.	Luhar, Bhubhalis, Saifi	Delhi
1092.	Luhar/Lohar/Panchal	Gujarat
1093.	Luhar, Saifi, Nagauri Luhar, Multani Luhar (all Muslim)	MP
1094.	Luhura	Orissa
1095.	Machi, Machhera	Delhi
1096.	Machhi	Maharashtra
1097.	Machhi (Hindu), Kharwa, Khalas, Dhimar, Dhivar, Bitna, Tandel, Mangela, Khalasi, Sarang, Kahar	Gujarat

1098.	Machua	Orissa
1099.	Madar	Bihar
1100.	Madari (Muslim in Bihar)	Assam, Bihar, Haryana, H.P., Pnb., Chandi., UP
1101.	Madari, Bazigar	J&K
1102.	Madari, Nath, Bharathari	Gujarat
1103.	Madivala	Kerala
1104.	Madugar or Modavar or Venthakkara	Pondi.
1105.	Magadhi Goral	Orissa
1106.	Magatha Goudus, Bermia Goudus, Boodo Magatha, Dongayath Goudu, Ladya Goudu, Poona Magatha, Sana Magatha	Orissa
1107.	Maghi, or Meghia	Orissa
1108.	Magura	Orissa
1109.	Maha-Brahman (Acharaj)	Raj.
1110.	Mahaedra, Mahadra, Medara	Pondi.
1111.	Mahali	Maha.
1112.	Mahar (excluding those in SCs)	Goa
1113.	Mahatam	H.P.
1114.	Mahato	Assam
1115.	Mahendra, Medara	TN
1116.	Mahia (Maiya)	Gujarat
1117.	Mahishya Das, Mahisya	Assam
1118.	Mahla/Mahlar	Orissa
1119.	Mahli	Assam, Maha.
1120.	Mahratta (non-Brahmin) (including Namdev Mahratta)	TN
1121.	Mahtar, Lalberi, Halalkhor, Bhangi (all Muslim)	Bihar

1122.	Mahunta	Orissa
1123.	Maila	Orissa
1124.	Maimal (Muslim Fisherman)	Assam
1125.	Mairal, Dangar, Vir	Maharashtra
1126.	Majhwar	Bihar
1127.	Majothi Kumbhar, Darbar or Daban, Majothi (all Muslim)	Gujarat
1128.	Majwar	Assam
1129.	Makrana (Muslim)	D&NH
1130.	Makrani (Muslim)	Gujarat
1131.	Mal Paharia	Orissa
1132.	Maladasu	Orissa
1133.	Malakar	WB
1134.	Malar (Malhar)	Bihar
1135.	Malasar	Orissa
1136.	Malayan, Malayar	TN
1137.	Malayekandi (excluding Malabar distict as referred to in sub-section (2) of section 5 of the States Reorganisation Act 1956)	Kerala
1138.	Malc	TN
1139.	Male	Pondi.
1140.	Mali (where they are not Scheduled Tribe)	A.P.
1141.	Mali, Phulia, Sabhbaria, Bhajemali, Muni, Raula (Raula of Ganjam District only), Malis, Korchia Malis, Paido Malis, Pooda Malis	Orissa
1142.	Mali, Fool Mali, Marathi Mali, Kach Mali, Jire Mali, Bagban, Rayeen	Gujarat
1143.	Mali (sub-castes: Phulmali, Phule, Halade, Kacha, Kadu, Bawane, Adhprabhu, Adhshethi, Jire, Unde,	

	Lingayat Mali, Banka Mali, Marar, Maral, Savta Mali, Van Mali, Bagban/Rayeen	Maharashtra
1144.	Mali (Malakar)	Bihar
1145.	Mali, Saini	UP
1146.	Mali (Saini), Marar	MP
1147.	Mali, Saini, Bagwan, Rayee/Rayeen, Kunjra	Raj.
1148.	Mali, Saini, Southia, Sagarwanshi-Mali, Nayak	Delhi
1149.	Mallah	H.P.
1150.	Mallah (Surhiya, Kewat Murawari)	Bihar
1151.	Malpatharia	Assam
1152.	Manbhav	Maharashtra
1153.	Mandula	A.P.
1154.	Mangala (Nayee-Brahman)	Pondi.
1155.	Mangar (Magar)	Bihar
1156.	Manger	Sikkim
1157.	Maniagar	TN
1158.	Manihar, Kacher, Lakher, Lakhera (including Lakhera sub-caste of Brahmins in Tehri Garhwal Region), Churihar	UP
1159.	Manihar (Muslim)	MP
1160.	Manipuri	Tripura
1161.	Manipuri Muslim	Assam
1162.	Mankar	MP
1163.	Manki	Assam
1164.	Manna Dhora	Orissa
1165.	Mannan	Karnataka
1166.	Mannus	Pondi.
1167.	Mappila	Kerala, TN, Pondi.

1168.	Marar	Tripura
1169.	Marati (excluding Kasargod Taluk of Malabar District in Kerala)	Kerala, Orissa
1170.	Marathi	Pondi.
1171.	Maravan	Kerala
1172.	Maravar	Karnataka
1173.	Maravar (including Karumaravar, Appanad Kondayamkottai Maravar and Sembanad Maravar)	TN
1174.	Maravar, Maravaw	Pondi.
1175.	Marayan, Maravan	Karnataka
1176.	Marchha	UP
1177.	Maria	Assam
1178.	Markande	Bihar
1179.	Marta	Karnataka
1180.	Maruthuvar	Kerala
1181.	Maruthuvar, Navithar	Pondi.
1182.	Maruthuvar, Navithar, Mangala, Velakkattalavar, Velakkattalanair and Pronopakari	TN
1183.	Marwar Baori	Maharashtra
1184.	Masanjogi, Sudgadsiddha, Mapanjogi	Maharashtra
1185.	Masaniayogi	Karnataka
1986.	Matangi	Orissa
1187.	Mathura	A.P., Maha
1188.	Matwa or Matwe-Kureshi (Muslim) Gavli (Hindu)	Gujarat
1189.	Maulik	Bihar
1190.	Maune	Orissa
1191.	Mauriaro, Mauriara	Bihar
1192.	Mavilan	Orissa
1193.	Mdivla, Madivala	Pondi.

1194.	Me	Maharashtra
1195.	Me or Meta	Gujarat
1196.	Medar	Maharashtra
1197.	Medari or Mahendra	A.P.
1198.	Medari, Lingayat Medhar, Burud, Gauriga, Medara	Karnataka
1199.	Meenavar	Pondi.
1200.	Meenavar, Parvatharajakulam, Pattanavar, Sembadavar (including converts to Christianity)	TN
1201.	Mehra	H.P.
1202.	Meite, Meetei (including Meitei Brahmin, Meitei/ Meetei Sanamahi Meitei Rajkumar)	Manipur
1203.	Meitei Pangal	Manipur
1204.	Melakudi or Kudiyan	Pondi.
1205.	Memar, Raj	Delhi
1206.	Mena (Bhil)	Gujarat
1207.	Meo	Haryana
1208.	Mer	Gujarat
1209.	Mer (Mehrat-Kathat, Mehrat-Ghodat, Cheeta)	Raj.
1210.	Merasi, Mirasi	Delhi
1211.	Meru, Mer	MP
1212.	Methar (Muslim)	A.P.
1213.	Mewati, Meo (Muslim)	MP, UP
1214.	Mina	Maharashtra
1215.	Mina/Meena	Delhi, Haryana
1216.	Minka	Orissa
1217.	Mir, Dhadhi, Langha, Mirasi (all Muslim)	Gujarat
1218.	Mirasi	Haryana, H.P., J&K, Pnb. Chandi., UP

1219.	Mirasi (Muslim)	MP
1220.	Mirasi, Dhadi	Raj.
1221.	Mirdha (Muslim) (excluding Jat Muslim)	MP
1222.	Mirdhar	Assam
1223.	Mirisin (Muslim)	Bihar
1224.	Mirshikar (Muslim)	Bihar
1225.	Mistri (Suthar/Sutar)	Gujarat
1226.	Mitha	Maharashtra
1227.	Mitna	Daman & Diu
1228.	Miyana, Miana (Muslim)	Gujarat
1229.	Mochi (excluding those in SCs)	Delhi, Haryana, Chandi., Raj. UP
1230.	Mochi (Muslim in MP) (Other than SCs in PNB)	MP. Pnb.
1231.	Modi	Assam
1232.	Modi Bans	Pondi.
1233.	Modiga, Modikara, Modikar	Karnataka
1234.	Mogaveera	Pondi.
1235.	Mogia (Mogya)	Raj.
1236.	Mohali	Assam
1237.	Moili, Moli	Pondi.
1238.	Moira (Halwai), Modak (Halwai)	WB
1239.	Momin (Muslim)	Bihar
1240.	Momin (Ansar, Ansari), Julah	UP
1241.	Monda Koravar	TN
1242.	Mondepatta	A.P.
1243.	Mondgolla	Pondi.
1244.	Mondivaru, Mondibanda, Banda	A.P.
1245.	Monger	Orissa

1246.	Mongola	Pondi.
1247.	Moniagar	Pondi.
1248.	Moopan	TN
1249.	Moran, Mathak	Assam
1250.	Moundadan	Pondi.
1251.	Moundadan Chetty	TN
1252.	Mudava/Muduga	Pondi.
1253.	Mudhar	Karnataka
1254.	Mudiraj, Mutrasi, Punugollu	A.P.
1255.	Mukhadora-Mokka Dhora	Orissa
1256.	Mukhani alias Moovari	Kerala
1257.	Mukhari	Pondi.
1258.	Mukhi	Assam
1259.	Mukkavan	Karnataka
1260.	Mukkuvan or Kukayan, Mogayan, Logavan (including Bovis)	Pondi.
1261.	Mukkuvan, Mukkuvar or Mukayar (including converts to Christianity)	TN
1262.	Mukri (Mukeri) (Muslim)	Bihar
1263.	Muliya	Orissa
1264.	Munda	Assam
1265.	Mundala	Orissa
1266.	Munnurukapu (Telengana)	A.P.
1267.	Murao or Murai, Maurya	UP
1268.	Muria	Orissa, Pondi.
1269.	Murrari	Karnataka
1270.	Muslim Kayastha	UP
1271.	Muthuraja, Muthuracha, Muttiriyar, Muthiriyar, Mutharaiyar	TN
1272.	Muthuraja	Pondi.
1273.	Mutiakampatti	Pondi.
1274.	Muttiriyan/Muthiriyar	Pondi.

1275.	Nadar (including Christian Nadar)	Pondi.
1276.	Nadar (Hindu Nadar, Nadar included in the SIUC and Nadar belonging to Christian religious denominations other that the SIUC)	Kerala
1277.	Nadar, Shanar and Gramani, including Christian Nadar Christian Shanar and Christian Gramani	TN
1278.	Naddaf (Dhunia), Mansoori, Behna, Kandere, Kadere, Pinjara	UP
1279.	Nadora, Uppunador, Torke Nador, Nador/Nadavar/ Nadava	Karnataka
1280.	Nagar (this does not include Maithili Brahmins and immigrant Nagars from other Stated who are Brahmins and Baniyas)	Bihar, WB
1281.	Nagaralu	A.P., Pondi.
1282.	Nagaram	TN
1283.	Nagararam	Pondi.
1284.	Nagasia	Assam
1285.	Nagatha Goudus, Bernia Goudub, Boodo Magatha, Dengoyath Goudo, Ladya Goudu, Poona Magatha and Sana Magatha	Pondi.
1286.	Nagavaddilu	A.P.
1287.	Nagavaddily	Pondi.
1288.	Nagavamsa (Nagavamsa)	A.P.
1289.	Nagbansi	Assam
1290.	Nahar	Orissa
1291.	Nai	Bihar
1292.	Nai (Valand)	D&NH
1293.	Nai (Kuleen Brahman)	H.P.
1294.	Nai, Sain	Pnb.
1295.	Nai, Sain, Baid Nai	Raj.

1296.	Nai (Sain, Savita, Shriva), Mhali, Navhi/ Navi	M.P.
1297.	Nai, Hajjam, Nai (Sabita)	Delhi
1298.	Naidu Gavara	Pondi.
1299.	Naiker, Vanniya	Pondi.
1300.	Naikkan	Kerala
1301.	Naikkans Naicken	Pondi.
1302.	Naikkar (in Kanniyakumari dist. and Shencottah Taluk of Tirunelveli dist.)	TN
1303.	Nairy	Karnataka
1304.	Naiya	Bihar
1305.	Nakkala	A.P., Pondi.
1306.	Nalakeyava	Orissa
1307.	Nalakodaya	Pondi.
1308.	Nalband	Delhi, Haryana, H.P., Pnb. Chandi.
1309.	Nalband (Muslim)	Bihar, MP
1310.	Nalband, Sais	UP
1311.	Nalki	Karnataka
1312.	Namdev Simpi	Pondi.
1313.	Namdhari	Maharashtra
1314.	Namdhari Paik	Maharashtra
1315.	Namshudra	Bihar
1316.	Nandiwala	Karnataka
1317.	Nandiwale, Tirmal	Maharashtra
1318.	Nangudi Vellalar	TN
1319.	Naniar	Pondi.
1320.	Nanjil Mudali (in Kanniyakumari dist. and Shencottah taluk of Tirunelveli dist.	TN
1321.	Napit	Assam, WB
1322.	Napit, Shil	Tripura

1323.	Naqashi/Naqqashi	Maharashtra
1324.	Naqqal	Delhi, UP
1325.	Nar	Haryana, H.P., Pnb., Chandi.
1326.	Narikoravan	Pondi.
1327.	Narikoravar	TN
1328.	Nat	Orissa
1329.	Nat (Muslim)	Bihar
1330.	Nat (other than those in SCs list)	Haryana, M.P.
1331.	Nat, Natta	Tripura
1332.	Nat, Natuva	Karnataka
1333.	Nat, Nat-Bajania, Bajigar, Natada	Gujarat
1334.	Nath	Assam
1335.	Nathjogi	Goa, Daman & Diu
1336.	Nathpanthi, Daurigosayi	Karnataka
1337.	Navi, Nhavi/Nai/Nabhik	Maharashtra
1338.	Navundian	Pondi.
1339.	Nayadi	Orissa
1340.	Nayak	Tripura, UP
1341.	Nayata, Nayada	MP
1342.	Nayi-Brahmin (Mangali, Mangala, Bhajanthri)	A.P.
1343.	Nayinda, Lingayat Nayinda, Nayanaja Kshatriya, Nayanaja Kshtri, Hajjam/ Hajam, Nhavi, Nadig, Ambattan, Mangala, Kelasi, Kshowrad, Kshowrik/ Kshaurika/Kshowrika, Chouriya, Navalinga/ Navaligara/Navi, Napitha, Savitha, Bandari/Bhandari, Lingayat Bandari, Bajanthri/ Bhajanthri, Lingayat Bajantri, Mahale, Hadapada, Lingayat Hadapada,Melagara, Pariyala	Karnataka
1344.	Neelakanthi	A.P.

1345.	Neelakanthi	A.P.
1346.	Neeli (Nelli)	A.P.,
1347.	Neeli	Maharashtra
1348.	Neelkanti	Maharashtra
1349.	Nekar, Jada	Maharashtra
1350.	Nembang	WB
1351.	Nepali (Limbo, Matwali, Rai)	Tripura
1352.	Nepali (i.e. Thapa, Guruna, Lama, Gaine, Rai, Chetri, Chatri, Chhetri, Lihu, Magar, Lohar, Dami, Sarki i.e. Cobbler)	Assam
1353.	Nessi or Kurni	A.P.
1354.	Nethura	Maharashtra
1355.	Neygi, Pattasale, Lingayat Neygi/Nekar /Neygi, Kurushinasetty, Lingayat Kuruhinashetty, Bilimagga, Lingayat Bilimagga, Thogata, Soniga, Jamkhana, Ayiri, Avir, Sale, Padmasale, Saale, Kaikolan, Neikar, Jadar, Lingayat Jadaru, Sakulasale	Karnataka
1356.	Nhavi, Nai	Daman & Diu
1357.	Nhavi, Nai, Nabhik, Napit, Mahalo	Goa
1358.	Nilgar, Neela, Nirali	Maharashtra
1359.	Nirshikari	Maharashtra
1360.	Niyargar, Niyargar-Multani,. Niyaria (all Muslim)	MP
1361.	Nokka	Pondi.
1362.	Nokkar	AP, TN
1363.	Nolia	Orissa
1364.	Nonia, Nunia	Assam, Bihar
1365.	Nonia, Loniya, Luniya, Nuniya,	Maharashtra
1366.	Noongar	Haryana, Pnb., Chandi.

1367.	Nuhura, Nuhuraj	Orissa
1368.	Nuniya	Orissa
1369.	Nuniya, Nunia	Tripura
1370.	Nut (other that those is SCs list)	UP
1371.	Nyaria	Raj.
1372.	Od	Gujarat
1373.	Odan	Kerala
1374.	Odans, Odde, Voddoo or Vadda or Veddai Odon (Donga), Odiya	Pondi.
1375.	Odar (in Kanniyakumari dist. and Shencottah Taluk of Tirunelveli dist.)	TN
1376.	Odd	Raj.
1377.	Oddar (including Boya, Donga Boya, Gorrela Dodda Boya, Kalvathila Boya, Pedda Boya, Oddar, Kaloddar, Nellorepet Oddar and Sooramari Oddar)	TN
1378.	Odde, Boyan (in Malabar district as referred to in sub-section (2) of section 5 of the State Reorganisation Act, 1956)	Kerala
1379.	Odiya	TN
1380.	Oiulu	Pondi.
1381.	Ojulu, or Metta, Kamasalie	Orissa
1382.	Omanaito	Pondi.
1383.	Omeyita	Orissa
1384.	Oraon	Assam
1385.	Osthan	Karnataka
1386.	Otari	Karnataka
1387.	Otari, Otankar, Otkar, Vatari Ojhari	Maharashtra
1388.	Other Muslims excluding (i) Bohra, (ii) Cutchi Menmon (iii) Navayat (iv) Turukkan (v) Dakhani Muslim	Kerala
1389.	Other Muslims excluding (i) Cutchi	

	Memon (ii) Navayat (iii) Bohra or Bhora or Borah (iv) Sayyid (v) Sheik (vi) Pathan (vii) Mughal (viii) Mahdivia/ Mahdavi (ix) Konkani or Jamayati Muslims	Karnataka
1390.	Ottanaickan	Pondi.
1391.	Ovachar	TN
1392.	Padaria, Pamaria, Pandara	Orissa
1393.	Padayachi	Pondi.
1394.	Padharia	Maharashtra
1395.	Padiar	Maharashtra
1396.	Padit	Karnataka
1397.	Padmasali	Pondi.
1398.	Padmashali-Pattushali	Gujarat
1399.	Padmasali (Sali, Saliyan, Pattusali, Senapathrulu, Thogata Sali)	A.P.
1400.	Pagadai	Orissa
1401.	Pagui	Goa
1402.	Pahad, Pahadi	Maharashtra
1403.	Pahira	Bihar
1404.	Paidi	Assam
1405.	Paigarapu	Orissa, Pondi.
1406.	Paiko	Orissa
1407.	Painda	Pondi.
1408.	Pakhali Maha.	Gujarat,
1409.	Pakhiwara	Delhi
1410.	Paky	Orissa
1411.	Pal	Orissa
1412.	Pal (Bherihar-Gaderi), Gadaria	Bihar
1413.	Pal Pardhi	Maharashtra
1414.	Pala-Ekari	A.P.

1415.	Palackari	Pondi.
1416.	Palasi	Orissa, Pondi.
1417.	Paliyan	Orissa
1418.	Palli	Orissa, Pondi.
1419.	Pamaria (Muslim)	Bihar
1420.	Pambada	Orissa
1421.	Pambala	A.P.
1422.	Pamlor	Karnataka
1423.	Pamula	A.P.
1424.	Pamulu	TN, Pondi.
1425.	Pan	Assam, Tripura
1426.	Panaba	Karnataka
1427.	Panar (except in Kanniyakumari dist. and Shencottah taluk of Tirunelveli dist where the community is SC)	TN
1428.	Panasa, Pansa	Karnataka
1429.	Panchal	Maharashtra
1430.	Pandara, Pandar, Pendara, Pendari, Pindari	Karnataka
1431.	Pandaram, Pandar, Pandare	Karnataka
1432.	Pandi	Bihar
1433.	Pandi Thattan	Pondi.
1434.	Pandithar	Kerala
1435.	Pandithar (Anpattn, Pranopkari and Nasivan)	Pondi.
1436.	Pangal	Tripura
1437.	Pangul	Maharashtra
1438.	Panika Karnataka	Assam,
1439.	Panika (except in districts of Chhattarpur, Datia, Panna, Rewa, Satna, Shahdol,	

	Sidhi and Tikamgarh where it is included in STs list)	MP
1440.	Paniyan	Orissa
1441.	Panjira	Orissa
1442.	Panka	Maharashtra
1443.	Panki, Painak	Tripura
1444.	Panna Vettuva Goundor	Pondi.
1445.	Pannagadikara	Pondi.
1446.	Pannaiyar or Pannayar	Pondi.
1447.	Pannayar (including Kathikarar in Kanniyakumari Dist.)	TN
1448.	Pannekara-Konkani	Karnataka
1449.	Pannirandam Chettiar or Uthama Chettiar	TN
1450.	Panniyandi	Orissa
1451.	Panniyar	Kerala
1452.	Paraiyan	Orissa
1453.	Paramban	Pondi.
1454.	Paravan	Orissa
1455.	Paravan (Christians)	Pondi.
1456.	Paravar including converts to Christianity (except in Kanniyakumari dist and Shenocottah taluk of Tirunelveli dist where the community is a SC)	TN
1457.	Pardhi (Mirshikari Nirshikari)	A.P.
1458.	Pareet or Dhobi (including Gujarati Dhobi)	Maharashtra
1459.	Parhaiya	Orissa
1460.	Pariki Muggula	A.P.
1461.	Parja	Assam
1462.	Parkavakulam (Suruthimar including those Suruthimar who call themselves as Moopanar, Nathamar including those	

	Nathamar who call themselves as Nainar, Malayamar)	TN
1463.	Parol Madivala	Pondi.
1464.	Parrakavakulam (Surithinaman), Malayanan, Nathaman, Moopanar, Nainar	Pondi.
1465.	Parya	Bihar
1466.	Pasi	Assam, Tripura
1467.	Passi	A.P.
1468.	Patara/Patra, Goudia Patara	Orissa
1469.	Pategar, Patvekari, Patregar	Karnataka
1470.	Pathar Chera, Sangtarash	Delhi
1471.	Pathukudi	Pondi.
1472.	Pathuria	Orissa
1473.	Patka, Patki, Patwa	MP
1474.	Patkar	Maharashtra
1475.	Patkar (Khatri)	A.P.
1476.	Patnulkaran	Pondi.
1477.	Patra	Karnataka
1478.	Patradavaru/Patradaveru	Maharashtra
1479.	Patramela	Karnataka
1480.	Patratanti	Assam
1481.	Patrikulam, Patrakulam	Pondi.
1482.	Pattanavan, Paravatharajakulam	Pondi.
1483.	Pattariya	Kerala
1484.	Pattariyas or Pattarias	Pondi.
1485.	Pattulakaran	Pondi.
1486.	Patwa	Delhi
1487.	Patwa (Phadal)	Raj.
1488.	Patwa, Patua, Pathar (excluding Agarwala, Deobansi, Kharewal or Khandelwal who are Sub-castes of	

	Baniya or Kharwar who claim to The rank of Rajpur), Tatwa	UP
1489.	Peddammavandlu	A.P.
1490.	Pemdi (Muslim)	MP
1491.	Pengua	Orissa
1492.	Pentias	Pondi.
1493.	Perika (Perike Balija, Puragiri Kshatriya)	A.P.
1494.	Perike (including Perike Balija)	TN
1495.	Perike, Perike Balija, Piragiri Kshatriya	Pondi.
1496.	Perki/Perkewad	Maharashtra
1497.	Perumbadlan	Pondi.
1498.	Perumkollans	Pondi.
1499.	Perumkollar (in Kanniyakumari dist. and Shencottah taluk of Tirunelveli dist.)	TN
1500.	Peruvannan	Pondi.
1501.	Peruvannan (Varanavar)	Kerala
1502.	Phasechari	Maharashtra
1503.	Phudgi	Maharashtra
1504.	Phulari	Maharashtra
1505.	Picchigunta	Pondi
1506.	Pichati	Karnataka
1507.	Pichgutala, Pichigunta, Pichuguntala	Karnataka
1508.	Pielai	Pondi.
1509.	Pillava	Pondi.
1510.	Pinganiya	Bihar
1511.	Pinja, Penja	Haryana, Pnb., Chandi
1512.	Pina or Penja, Panja	H.P.
1513.	Pinjara (Hindu)	MP

1514.	Pinjara, Naddaf, Fakir/Faquir, Behna, Dhuniya, Dhunkar, Mansoori (all Muslim)	MP
1515.	Pinjara/Pinjari	Maharashtra
1516.	Pinjara, Ganchi-Pinjara, Mansuri-Pinjara (all Muslim)	Gujarat
1517.	Pinjara, Pinjari, Nadaf, Ladaf, Mansoori	Karnataka
1518.	Pita	Orissa
1519.	Podikara Vellalar	TN
1520.	Polinativalivelama (of Srikakulam & Vishakhapatanam District)	A.P.
1521.	Polinativalma of Srikakulam and Visakhapatnam dists.	Pondi.
1522.	Pomnala	Pondi.
1523.	Pondara	A.P.
1524.	Ponnai Koravar (in North Arcot dist.)	TN
1525.	Poosala	A.P.
1526.	Poraya	TN, Pondi.
1527.	Powar, Bhoyar/Bhoyaar	MP, Maha.
1528.	Pradhan	Assam, Bihar
1529.	Prajapati, Kumbhar	Bihar, Delhi, Haryana, H.P.
1530.	Pulavar or Poolavar, Pooluva Gounder	TN
1531.	Pulayan	Orissa
1532.	Pullavan	Karnataka, Kerala, Pondi.
1533.	Pusala	TN
1534.	Pusala, Pusalavaan, Pusalvandlu	Pondi.
1535.	Putligar	Maharashtra
1536.	Rabari (where they are not STs), Sorathia Rabari	Gujarat

1537.	Rachhbandhia	Maharashtra
1538.	Rachevar	Maharashtra
1539.	Raghavi (in Vidarbha district)	Maharashtra
1540.	Raghwi/Raghvi	MP
1541.	Rahabari	Haryana, Pnb.
1542.	Rai	Sikkim
1543.	Rai (Oriya)	Tripura
1544.	Rai Sikh Chandi., Raj.	Haryana, Pnb.,
1545.	Rai Sikh (Mahatam)	U.P.
1546.	Raigar (other than those in SCs list)	Haryana
1547.	Raika, Rebari (Debasi)	Raj.
1548.	Raikari	Maharashtra
1549.	Raily	Tripura
1550.	Raj (Memar)	UP
1551.	Raj Pardhi, Gaon Pardhi, Haran Shikari	Maharashtra
1552.	Rajaka	A.P., Pondi.
1553.	Rajapur	Kerala
1554.	Rajapuri, Rajpur, Balavalikar	Karnataka
1555.	Rajapuri, Raju	Pondi.
1556.	Rajbanshi (Risiya and Poliya)	Bihar
1557.	Rajbhar	Bihar
1558.	Rajbhar, Bhar	Gujarat
1559.	Rajdhobi	Bihar
1560.	Rajpur Bhamta, Pardeshi Bhamta, Pardeshi Bhamta	Maharashtra
1561.	Rajput	Karnataka
1562.	Raju	WB
1563.	Rajwar	Assam, MP
1564.	Ramgarhia	Chandi.

1565.	Ramoshi	Maharashtra
1566.	Raneyar	Orissa
1567.	Rangari	Maharashtra
1568.	Rangrej (Muslim)	MP
1569.	Rangrej (Bahawsar or Rangari)	Maharashtra
1570.	Rangrez	Delhi
1571.	Rangrez, Nilgar	Raj.
1572.	Rangarez or Bhavasara Kshtriya	A.P.
1573.	Rangrez (Muslim)	Bihar, Delhi, Maha.
1574.	Rangrez, Nilgar, Leelgar, Lallari	Haryana
1575.	Rangrez, Rangwa	UP
1576.	Rangwa	Bihar, WB
1577.	Raot, Rawt, Rautia, Raval, Raual or Raval-Yogi	Maharashtra
1578.	Rathodia	Gujarat
1579.	Rauther	Pondi.
1580.	Rautiya, Rotiya	MP
1581.	Rauttiya	Bihar
1582.	Raval-Ravalia, Jati or Raval Yogi, Raval Jati, Jagaria	Gujarat
1583.	Rawat	Raj.
1584.	Rayeen (Kunjra)	W.B.
1585.	Rayeen or Kunjra (Muslim)	Bihar
1586.	Rechband	Haryana, H.P., Pnb., Chandi.
1587.	Raddiar/Reddian (excluding Malabar district as referred to in sub-section (2) of section 5 of the States Reorganisation Act, 1956)	Kerala
1588.	Rehar, Rehara	Pnb.
1589.	Rehar, Rehare/Rehara, Rer/Re	Chandi.

1590.	Rehar or Rihar, Rehara or Ro	Haryana
1591.	Reinudas	Karnataka
1592.	Riaigar	Pnb.
1593.	Rona	Pondi.
1594.	Ronas	Orissa
1595.	Routia	Orissa
1596.	Sad Swami	Raj.
1597.	Sadajoshi	Karnataka
1598.	Sadan, Dedan	Pondi.
1599.	Sadhuchetty	A.P.
1600.	Sadhu Chetty (including Telugu Chetty, Telugupatty Chetty, Twenty four Manai Telugu Chetty)	TN, Pondi.
1601.	Sagalis	Pondi.
1602.	Sagar	Daman & Diu
1603.	Sagarpasha	Orissa
1604.	Sahis, Sahis, Shis	Maharashtra
1605.	Sahora	Assam
1606.	Saiees, Sahees, Sayees	MP
1607.	Saifi	Pnb.
1608.	Saini	Haryana, Pnb., Chandi.
1609.	Saiva Vellalan	Pondi.
1610.	Sakka-Bhishti, Saqqa-Bhishti, Bhishti-Abbasi	Raj.
1611.	Sakkaraithamadai Koravar (in North Arcot dist.)	TN
1612.	Sakkaravar or Kavathi (in Kanniyakumari dist. and Shencottah taluk of Tirunelveli dist.)	TN
1613.	Sakravar (Kavathi)	Pondi.
1614.	Salat (excluding Sompura Salat)	Gujarat

1615.	Salem Melnad Koravar (in Madurai, Coimbator Periyar, Pudukottai, Tiruchirapalli, Salem andNorth Arcot dists.)	TN
1616.	Salem uppu Koravar (in Salem dist.)	TN
1617.	Salian (Pattaraya), Saliyas, Saliyan, Pattusali, Senapathulu, Kamithoktulu, Sale, Jhogata Sali	Pondi.
1618.	Salivagana, Sahivahana	TN
1619.	Saliya	Kerala
1620.	Saliyar, Padmasaliyar, Pattusaliyar, Pattariya and Adhaviyar	TN
1621.	Saloi	Assam
1622.	Samban	Orissa
1623.	Sampang WB	
1624.	Sanaithalaivar (Senaikudiyan)	Pondi.
1625.	Sandhi (Muslim)	Gujarat
1626.	Sangar	Maharashtra
1627.	Sangatrash (only in the district of Nawadah)	Bihar
1628.	Saniyar	Karnataka
1629.	Sanjogi	Maha.
1630.	Sankhari	Orissa
1631.	Sansi	J&K
1632.	Sansia	Karnataka
1633.	Santhal, Santal	Assam
1634.	Sanyasi	Karnataka, Sikkim
1635.	Sanyasi, Membram	Orissa
1636.	Sapera, Nath	Maharashtra
1637.	Saqqa-Bhishti, Bhishti-Abbasi	UP
1638.	Sarak	WB
1639.	Saraka/Sarska Tanti	Orissa

1640.	Saranga Palli Koravar	TN
1641.	Sarania Karnataka, Maharashtra	Gujarat,
1642.	Saraswat: Non-Brahmin	Kerala
1643.	Sargara	Gujarat
1644.	Sarodi, Saroda	Karnataka
1645.	Sarollu	A.P.
1646.	Sarvera	Assam
1647.	Satani (Chattadasrivaishnava, Chatadi)	A.P.
1648.	Satari, Chattada-Shri Vaishnava, Vaishnava	Karnataka
1649.	Satarkar	Karnataka
1650.	Satchasi	WB
1651.	Sathatha Srivaishnava (including Sathanai, Chattadi and Chattada Srivaishnava)	TN
1652.	Sathwara	Gujarat
1653.	Satiya-Sindhi	Raj.
1654.	Sauria Paharia	Orissa
1655.	Sauta (Sota)	Bihar
1656.	Savalakkarar	TN
1657.	Sayee (Muslim)	Bihar
1658.	Scheduled Castes converts to Christianity and their Progeny	A.P., Assam, Bihar, Karna., Kerala, MP, Maharashtra, Orissa, Pnb., Chandi. WB, TN, Pondi.
1659.	Seerithi Goudu	Orissa
1660.	Semman	Orissa

1661.	Senai Thalavar (Elavaniar)	Kerala
1662.	Senaithalaviar, Senaikudiyar and Illaivaniar Pair	TN
1663.	Senai Thalvivar (Elavabanias)	Pondi.
1664.	Setti Balija	Pondi.
1665.	Shaksaz	J &K
1666.	Shanan	Karnataka
1667.	Shankhakar	WB
1668.	Sheikh Sarvari (Pirai), Peerahi	UP
1669.	Shekhra	Bihar
1670.	Shershahbadi	Bihar
1671.	Shikkaligar, Shikalgar, Sikkaligar	Karnataka
1672.	Shikligar	Gujarat
1673.	Shilavat	Maharashtra
1674.	Shimpi	Goa, Maha.
1675.	Shivhari	Bihar
1676.	Sikkalgar, Katari	Maharashtra
1677.	Shoes repairers (working without the aid of machines)	J &K
1678.	Sholagar	Orissa
1679.	Shorgir	Pnb., Chandi.
1680.	Shorgir or Shergir	Haryana
1681.	Shrawan, Sarwan	Gujarat
1682.	Shudra (in Puri dist. only)	Orissa
1683.	Shupri attal (excluding those in SCs list)	J &K
1684.	Siddi	Karnataka
1685.	Siddi (where they áre not STs)	Gujarat
1686.	Sikligar	J&K, MP, Raj.
1687.	Singiwala	Maharashtra
1688.	Sirkiwal	Raj.
1689.	Sistakkaranm	Pondi.

1690.	Singhikant, Singhiwala	Pnb.,
1691.	Singhikant/Singiwala/Singhiwala	Chandi.
1692.	Singlikant or Singikant, Singiwala	Haryana
1693.	Sinke	Orissa
1694.	Sipai, Patni Jamat or Turk Jamat (all Muslim)	Gujarat
1695.	SIUC (excluding Nadar specified in item No.42 which is item No. 49 of the State List)	Kerala
1696.	Sodhi, Sodi, Sundi, Sondi	MP
1697.	Soi	Haryana, H.P., Pnb., Chandi.
1698.	Sollar	Pondi.
1699.	Somavamsha Arya Kshatriya, Tambat, Nalbund, Chitragar, Chitara, Chittari	Karnataka
1700.	Sonar	Maharashtra
1701.	Sonar, Sunar	Bihar, UP
1702.	Sonar, Sunar, Swarnakar, Jhhari, Jhhadi, Awedhiya, Audhiya	MP
1703.	Sourashtra	Kerala
1704.	Sourashtra (Patnulkarar)	TN
1705.	Sozha Vellar (including Sozha Vallar, Vetrilaikaar, Kodikalkarara and Keeralkarar	TN
1706.	Sozhia Chetty	TN
1707.	Srisayana	Pondi.
1708.	Srisayana (Segidi)	A.P.
1709.	Srisayar	TN
1710.	Suda	Orissa
1711.	Sudi; Halwai, Roniyar, Pansari, Modi, Kasera, Kesarwani, Thathera, Patwa, Sinduriya-Bania, Mahuri-Vaishya, Avadh-Bania, Agrahari-Vaishay)	Bihar

1712.	Sudir, Sudra	Karnataka
1713.	Sudra Das, Dey	Assam
1714.	Sukiyar	Bihar
1715.	Sukli (excluding Solanki Rajputs who claim themselves to be Sukli)	WB
1716.	Sulia	Orissa
1717.	Suna/Swarnakar	Chandi.
1718.	Sunar	Delhi
1719.	Sunar, Zargar, Soni	Haryana
1720.	Sunri, Sundi/Sundhi	Orissa
1721.	Sunuwar (including Koincha/Mukhia)	Sikkim
1722.	Suppalig, Sappaliga	Maharashtra
1723.	Surya Balija (Kalavanthula), Ganika	A.P.
1724.	Sut, Soot	Assam
1725.	Sutar	Maharashtra
1726.	Sutharia (from Sindh)	Maharashtra
1727.	Sutradhar	Tripura, WB
1728.	Sutsali	Karnataka
1729.	Swakulasali	A.P.
1730.	Swakul Sali	Maharashtra
1731.	Swakulsali/Sali	Gujarat
1732.	Swarankar, Sunar, Soni	Raj.
1733.	Swarnkar	WB
1734.	Tachayiri	Karnataka
1735.	Tadavi (Muslim)	MP
1736.	Takankar	Karnataka
1737.	Talpada Koli (where they are not STs)	Gujarat
1738.	Talwar Kanade	Maharashtra
1739.	Tamang	Sikkim, WB
1740.	Tamariya	Bihar
1741.	Tambat	Maharashtra
1742.	Tamboli	Maha., UP

1743.	Tamboli/Tamali	WB
1744.	Tammali	AP
1745.	Tamoli, Tamboli	Bihar
1746.	Tamoli (Tamboli)	Raj.
1747.	Tana	Orissa
1748.	Tandel	Maharashtra
1749.	Tankar	Gujarat
1750.	Tanti	Assam
1751.	Tanti, Tantubaya	WB
1752.	Tanti, Tati	Tripura
1753.	Tanti (Tatwa), Tati, Tatin	Bihar
1754.	Tantripal, Tanti, Tantri	Assam
1755.	Tantubai	Assam
1756.	Tarakan	Pondi.
1757.	Targala	Maharashtra
1758.	Targala, Bhavaiya, Nayak, Bhoiak	Gujarat
1759.	Tarha, Tirwali, Waddar	MP
1760.	Tarkhan	H.P.
1761.	Tassa	Assam
1762.	Tatapux	Pondi.
1763.	Teeli, Teli (Rural only)	J&K
1764.	Telaga, Pamula, Telugu Kachara, Telugu, Telenga (only those members of "Telugu, Telanga,Telenga" who belong to the same caste as Telega, Pamula or Telugu Kachara)	Orissa
1765.	Telenga	Assam, Tripura
1766.	Teli	Assam, Bihar, Goa, Haryana, Manipur, Pnb., Chandi., Raj. WB

1767.	Teli, Nayata, Pindai (Pindara) (all Muslim)	MP
1768.	Teli (Oriya)	Tripura
1769.	Teli, Teli-Lingayat, Teli-Sahu, Teli Rathod, Ganiga	Maharashtra
1770.	Teli (Rathore, Sahu)	MP
1771.	Teli, Samani, Rogangar, Teli-Malik (Muslim), Teli Sahu, Teli Rathore	UP
1772.	Teli, Teli-Malik	Delhi
1773.	Teli, Telli, Kubara/Kubera, Tatkar, Sahu/Sahoo, Bahaldia	Orissa
1774.	Telikula, Jandra	A.P.
1775.	Thacher	Kerala
1776.	Thakarda, Thakore, Patanwadia, Dharala, Baria	Gujarat
1777.	Thakkar (in Ratnagiri District only)	Maharashtra
1778.	Thami	Sikkim, WB
1779.	Thandal Vannan	Pondi.
1780.	Thanu	Orissa
1781.	Tharu	Bihar
1782.	Thatari/Kansari	Orissa
1783.	Thathera, Kansara, Bharawa	Raj.
1784.	Thathara, Thatera, Kasar, Kasera, Tamera, Tambatkar/Tamrakar, Tamer	MP
1785.	Thathera, Tamera	Pnb.
1786.	Thathera or Thater, Tamera	Haryana
1787.	Thathera/Thethera	Chandi.
1788.	Thawin	H.P.
1789.	Theba (Muslim)	Gujarat
1790.	Thelari (in Dhulia, Nasik, Jalgaon and Aurangabad District	Maharashtra
1791.	Thetwar	Maharashtra

1792.	Thiya, Elhura, Thiyyas	Pondi.
1793.	Thiyya	TN
1794.	Thogamalai Koravar or Kepmari (in Tiruchirappalli and Pudukottai dists.)	TN
1795.	Thogata, Thogati or Thogata Veerakshatriya	A.P.
1796.	Thogata Veerakshatriya	TN
1797.	Thogatta Veerakshatriya	Pondi.
1798.	Thogti/Thogati	Maharashtra
1799.	Tholkolan	Kerala
1800.	Tholkollans	Pondi.
1801.	Tholkollar (Kanniyakumari district and of Tirunelveli dist.)	Shencottah taluk TN
1802.	Thollikorvar (Salem district)	TN
1803.	Tholuva Naicker and Vetalakara Naicker	TN
1804.	Tholuva Naicker, Vettalakara Nairko	Pondi.
1805.	Thondaman	TN
1806.	Thondaiman	Pondi.
1807.	Thoraiyan	Pondi.
1808.	Thoria	Maharashtra
1809.	Thoria/Thodia/Thudia/Thuria	Orissa
1810.	Thoriyar, Badaga Thoraiyar of	Nilgiris TN
1811.	Thoti	Orissa
1812.	Thottia Naicken (including Rajakambalam, Gollavar, Sillayar, Thockalavar and Tholuva Naikar)	Pondi.
1813.	Thottian	Kerala
1814.	Thottiya Nicker (including Rajakambalam, Gollavar, Sillavar, Thockalavar and Tholuva Naicker)	TN

1815.	Thottiyar	Pondi.
1816.	Thunnan	Pondi.
1817.	Thurpu Kapus, Casula Kapus	Pondi.
1818.	Tigala (Tigla)	Pondi.
1819.	Tigala, Thigala, Tigler, Vannikula Kshatriya, Vanniya, Vanniyar, Vannia Gounder, Gounder/ Gownder, Padayachi, Kander, Shanbhukula Kshatriya, Agnikula Kshatriya, Dharmaraja Kapu, Kuravan Palli	Karnataka
1820.	Tikulhar	Bihar
1821.	Tilari, Tirali	Karnataka
1822.	Tilvi	Karnataka
1823.	Tiruvalluvar	Orissa
1824.	Tivoro	Orissa
1825.	Tiyar	Bihar
1826.	Toda	Orissa
1827.	Tolikula	Pondi.
1828.	Turha	Bihar, WB
1829.	Turi	Assam
1830.	Turupukapu of Srikakulam & Visakhapatnam Districts who are subject to social customs of divorce & remarriages among their women)	A.P.
1831.	Uppara	Pondi.
1832.	Uppara or Sagara	A.P.
1833.	Uppara, Uppillia and Sagara	TN
1834.	Uppara, Uppar, Uppera, Lingayat Uppara/Sunnagara, Uppiliyan, Beldar, Chunar, Gavandi, Govandi, Gavadi, Goundi Kallu Kutiga Uppara, Melusakkare, Melusakkreyavaru, Namada Uppara, Sunna Uppara, Sunnagara, Padit/	Karnataka

	Padti, Uppaliga, Uppaliga Shetty, Sagar, Sagara, Kerebandiyavaru Govandi, Gavadi, Gopundi, Melusakkare, Lonari, Yekkali, Yakalara	
1835.	Uppukoravar or Settipalli Koravar (in Thanjavur, Pudukottai, Madurai and North Arcot dists.)	TN
1836.	Urali Goundan	Pondi.
1837.	Urali Gounder (throughout the state) and Orudya Gounder, or Oorudaya Gounder (in Madurai, Coimbatore, Periyar, Tiruchirapalli, Pudukottai and Salem dists.)	TN
1838.	Vada Balija, Vadava (Golla or Kondri)	Pondi.
1839.	Vaddar/Vadder, Gadi Vadhar, Jati Vaddar, Mati Vaddar, Pathrvat/Patharod	Maharashtra
1840.	Vadi	Gujarat, Karna.
1841.	Vadra or Vaddara	Pondi.
1842.	Vadukan, Vadagan, Vadugan, Vaduvan	Pondi.
1843.	Vaduvans, Vadugan, Vadukar, Vaduka (Vadukan)	Kerala
1844.	Vaduvarpatti Koravari (in Madurai, Ramanathpuram, Pasumpon Muthuramalingam, Kamarajar, Tirunelveli, Tiruchirappalli and Pudukottai dists.)	TN
1845.	Vaghari, Salat, Salat Vaghri	Maharashtra
1846.	Vahivancha Charan, Gadhvi of Harijan, Vankar and Chamar	Gujarat
1847.	Vaidu	Karna., Maha.
1848.	Vakkaliga	Kerala

1849.	Valaiyar, including Chettinad Valaiyar	TN
1850.	Valakatalavan	Pondi.
1851.	Valand, Nayi (Hindu), Hajam (Muslim), Khalipha (Muslim), Barbar (Hindu)	Gujarat
1852.	Valans	Pondi.
1853.	Vallambar	TN
1854.	Valluvan	Orissa
1855.	Valmiki	TN, Pondi.
1856.	Valmiki, Boya (Boya Bedar, Kirataka Nishadi, Yellappi, Yellapu/Yellapondlu, Pedda Boya),Talayari, Chunduvallu	A.P.
1857.	Vamsha Raj	A.P.
1858.	Vanian (Vanika, Vanika, Vaisya, Vanibha Chetty, Vaniar	Kerala
1859.	Vaniya Chetty, Ayiravar, Nagarathar and Vaniyan)	Kerala
1860.	Vaniyan or Vaniar (Vanika, Vanika-Vaisya,Vaisyachetty, Vanibaacherry, Ayiravar, and Nagarathar)	Pondi.
1861.	Vaniyar	Pondi.
1862.	Vaniyar, Vania Chettiar (including Gandla, Ganika, Talikula and Chekkalar)	TN
1863.	Vanjara (Vanjari)	A.P.
1864.	Vanjari/Wanjara, Vanjar	Maharashtra
1865.	Vankar-Sadhu	Gujarat
1866.	Vannan	Orissa
1867.	Vannan, Vannar	Pondi.
1868.	Vannar (Salavai Thozhilalar) including Agasa, Madivala, Ekali, Rajakula, Veluthadar and Rajaka (except in Kanniyakumari dist. and Shencottah	

	taluk in Tirunelveli dist. where the community is a SC)	TN
1869.	Vannia, Vanniar, Vannikula Kshatriya	A.P.
1870.	Vanniyakula Khatriya including Vanniar or Vanniyar Gounder, Kondar or Vannia Gounder and Vannikandar (other than Vella Vounder belonging to Vanni Vanniyakula Kshatriya Caste)	Pondi.
1871.	Vanniyakula Kshatriya (including Vanniya, Vanniyar, Vannia Gounder, Gounder or Kander, Padayachi, Palli and Agnikula Kshatriya)	TN
1872.	Vansfoda, Vansfodia or Vanza	Gujarat
1873.	Vanza (Darji), Darji/Sai Sutar	Gujarat
1874.	Vanzara and Kangsiwala (Hindu) and Vanzara (Muslim) of Dangs District only	Gujarat
1875.	Vanzara	Pnb.
1876.	Vanzara, Banjara or Vanjara	Haryana
1877.	Varagaveri Koravar (in Tiruchirapalli and Pudukottai dist.)	TN
1878.	Vasudeo	Maharashtra
1879.	Vasudev	Karnataka
1880.	Vasudev, Basudeva, Basudev, Vasudeva, Harvola, Kapdia, Kapdi, Gondhli	MP
1881.	Vathis	Pondi.
1882.	Vayalpad or Nawalpeta Koracha	TN
1883.	Veduvar/Vettaikkarar (throughout the state) and Vedar (except in Kanniya-kumari dist. and Shencottah taluk of Tirunelveli dist. where the community is a SC)	TN
1884.	Veearmushti (Nettikotala)	A.P.

1885.	Veerasaiva (in Kanniyakumari dist and Shenocottah taluk of Tirunelveli dist.)	TN
1886.	Veerasaiva (Yogi & Yogeeswara), Poopandaram/Maalapandaram and Jangam	Kerala
1887.	Veerassiva (Fandaram, Matapathi, Vairagi, Vairavi, Yogiswarar	Pondi.
1888.	Velaan (Velaar)	Kerala
1889.	Velan, Vollan	Pondi.
1890.	Velip	Goa
1891.	Vellala Pillai (Nanjinad Vellala)	Pondi.
1892.	Vellan Chettiar	TN
1893.	Velluthedan	Karnataka
1894.	Veluthedathu Nair (Vilakkithallvan)	Kerala
1895.	Veluthodathu Nair (in Kanniyakumari dist. and Shencottah taluk of Tirunelveli dist.)	TN
1896.	Veluthsdan, Veluthedathu Nair	Pondi.
1897.	Vetta Koravar (in Salem dist.)	TN
1898.	Vettaikaran	Pondi.
1899.	Vetturan	Pondi.
1900.	Vettuva Gounder, Punnan Vettuva Gounder	TN
1901.	Vettuva Navithan	Kerala
1902.	Vettuvan	Orissa, Pondi.
1903.	Vikurup	Pondi.
1904.	Vilakkathala Nairs (Velakkathalavan)	Pondi.
1905.	Village Washermen	J &K
1906.	Vir, Veer, Veeramasti	Karnataka
1907.	Virakadi Veklalar	Pondi.
1908.	Vishavan (in Malabar district referred	

	to in sub-section (2) of section 5 of the State Reorganisation Act, 1956)	Kerala
1909.	Vishwakarma, Akkasale, Alingayat Akkasali, Achari, Viswa Brahman, Davanga Brahman, Kammar, Lingayat Kammara, Ausala, Kammalan, Luhar (Kammari), Kamsal, Lingayat Kammasali, Kamasala, Panchal, Panchala, Skuter, Badagi, Lingayat Badiga, Badiwadli, Soni, Sonar, Pattar, Gejjigar, Silpi	Karnataka
1910.	Vishwakarma including Assari, Chaptegra, Kallassari, Kammala, Karuvan, Kitaran, Kollan, Malayala Kammala, Pandi Kammala, Mossari, Perumkollan, Thattan, Pandithattan, Vilkurup Villasan, Viswabrahamanan or Viswarbrahamanar and Viswakarmala Thachan, Kalthachan, Kamsala, Kanan	Kerala
1911.	Viswabrahmin or Viswakarma (Ausula or Kamsali, Kammari, Kanchari, Vadla or Vadra or Vadrangi and Silpi)	A.P.
1912.	Vokkaliga/Vakkaliga, Sarpa, Vakkaliga, Uppina Kolaga Vokkaliga (rural areas only)	Karnataka
1913.	Vokkaligar (including Vakkaligar Okkaligar, Kappiliyar, Kappilliya, Okkaliya, Gowda Okkaliya Gowda, Okkaliya Gowder	TN
1914.	Wadi	Maharashtra
1915.	Wadhai (Sutar)/Wadai/Bhadai	Maharashtra
1916.	Waghari, Dataniya Waghari, Vedu Waghari, Talpada Waghari, Gamachi Waghari, Godadia Waghari, Chibhadia Waghari, Marada or Marwada Waghari, Wadwa Waghari,	

	Vaghari-Gamicho, Vedu Churalia, Jhakudia (where they not STs)	Gujarat
1917.	Wagher (Hindu & Muslim)	Gujarat
1918.	Wandhara	Gujarat
1919.	Wansfoda	Maharashtra
1920.	Warthi	Maharashtra
1921.	Wynad Chetty (the Nilgiris dist.)	TN
1922.	Yadav, Ahir	Maharashtra
1923.	Yadav (Gwala, Ahir, Ghasi, Gope)	Bihar
1924.	Yadav, Gavli	Daman & Diu
1925.	Yadava (Golla)	A.P.
1926.	Yadava (Konar, Kolaya, Ayar, Mayar, Munyan Eruman)	Pondi.
1927.	Yadava (including Idaiyar, Telugu speaking Idaiyar, known as Vaduga Ayar or Vaduga idaiyar or Golla, Mond Golla and Asthanthra Golla)	TN
1928.	Yadava (Kolaya, Ayar, Mayar, Maniyani and Iruman)	Kerala
1929.	Yandi	Orissa
1930.	Yata	A.P.
1931.	Yavana	TN
1932.	Yekalar, Yaklar, Egilika	Karnataka
1933.	Yeralu	Karnataka
1934.	Yerkula	Maharashtra
1935.	Yerna Golta	Orissa
1936.	Yerukula	Orissa, TN
1937.	Yogeswarar	TN
1938.	Yoggeswaran	Pondi.
1939.	Yogi, Jogi, Jugi Nath	Assam
1940.	Yogi, Jogi, Nath	Tripura
1941.	Yerukula	Pondi.

Index

[A]

Adequately represented, 174

Agrarian castes, 178

Agriculture, 144, 146, 186

Agricultural labourers, 11, 91, 101, 145, 158, 166, 198

Animal husbandary, 118, 157, 183

Appointments, 24, 25

Apportionment, 64

Artisal castes/communities, 113

Artisanal and occupational classes, 74

Artisans, 120,124, 166, 200

Arya Samaj Movement, 188

[B]

Begging, 129, 158

Betal leaves, 154

British policies, 100

[C]

Categorisation, 155

Cattle rearing, 146

Central Asia, 155

Central Government, 31

Chinnappa Reddy, 7

Classification, 28, 64, 65, 166, 176

Cohesion, 196

Commensality, 65

Constituent Assembly, 2

Contradiction, 27

Craftsmen, 125, 182

Cultivation, 122, 146, 162

[D]

Denotified, 182, 200

Discriminate, 23

Dominant Caste, 177, 181, 183

[E]

Economic Criterion, 15

Educationally Backwards, 24, 178, 199
Educational Institutions, 69, 72, 172
Employment, 24, 25, 178, 179
Ethnographic Literature, 76
Equality, 177
Equality of Opportunity, 24
Ex-criminal Tribes, 75, 166

[F]

Female Literacy, 10
Fishermen, 136, 140

[H]

Hereditary Occupations, 128, 130, 170

[I]

Identification, 33, 68, 197
Inadequate, 198
Indigent Classes, 1
Indira Sawhney, 27
Inevitable, 198
Islamic Groups, 75

[J]

Justice Party, 1
Jajmani System, 187

[K]

Kapus, 190
Kunbis, 190

[L]

Landless Labourers, 70, 200
Lingayats, 187, 190
Livelihood, 18, 21, 22

[M]

Mandal Commission, 17, 29, 36, 39, 173
Mandicancy, 129, 158
Marginal Farmers, 144
Menial Occupations, 106
Most Backward, 15, 170
Muslim Communities, 69
Mysore Government, 1

[N]

Nomadic and Semi-Nomadic Tribes, 134, 166, 182, 200
Northern India, 136

[O]

Occupational caste, 199

[P]

Panchayat, 192
Panchayati Raj Institutions, 22
Parliament, 24, 172, 174
Peasantary, 144, 200
Political Mobilization, 178, 182
Political Parties, 193
Political Power, 199
Politicized, 192

Polluting, 128
Preamble of the Constitution, 25
Primary Occupation, 123
Principle of Commonality, 36
Procedural Clarification, 32
Protective discrimination, 175, 193

[S]

Skilled Labourars, 118
Social Hierarchy, 26
Social Justice, 71
Social Taboos, 12
Socially Backward, 26, 199
Socio-economic Advancement, 26
Socio-economic Upliftment, 26
Southern India, 136
Subsidiary Occupations, 104
Supreme Court Judgement, 25

[T]

Tea garden labourers, 75, 87
Temple servants, 158
The Commission, 32
Traditional Artisanal Craft, 32
Traditional Occupation, 29, 107, 119, 122, 124, 125, 158, 169, 182, 192, 198

[U]

Undignified, 128
United Provinces, 2
Untouchable, 1, 33, 78, 85, 142, 176
Upward Mobility, 8, 186

[V]

Vokkaligas, 187, 190

[W]

Weaving castes, 113

[Y]

Yadav, 185, 188, 189
Yadavisation, 189

[Z]

Zamindari Abolition, 189
Zamindari Castes, 189
Zamindari System, 189
Zamindars, 185
Zila Parishad, 192

❑❑❑